The publisher and the University of California Press Foundation gratefully acknowledge the generous support of the Fletcher Jones Foundation Imprint in Humanities.

Zainab's Traffic

ATELIER: ETHNOGRAPHIC INQUIRY IN THE
TWENTY-FIRST CENTURY

Kevin Lewis O'Neill, Series Editor

Zainab's Traffic

MOVING SAINTS, SELVES, AND
OTHERS ACROSS BORDERS

Emrah Yıldız

UNIVERSITY OF CALIFORNIA PRESS

University of California Press
Oakland, California

Library of Congress Cataloging-in-Publication Data

Names: Yıldız, Emrah, 1982– author.
Title: Zainab's traffic : moving saints, selves, and others across borders /
    Emrah Yıldız.
Other titles: Atelier (Oakland, Calif.) ; 16.
Description: Oakland, California : University of California Press, [2024] |
    Series: Atelier : ethnographic inquiry in the twenty-first century ; 16 |
    Includes bibliographical references and index.
Identifiers: LCCN 2023048978 | ISBN 9780520379824 (hardback) |
    ISBN 9780520379831 (paperback) | ISBN 9780520976948 (ebook)
Subjects: LCSH: Shiite shrines—Political aspects—Syria—Damascus. |
    Shiite shrines—Economic aspects—Syria—Damascus. | Muslim pilgrims
    and pilgrimages—Syria—Damascus. | Muslim pilgrims and pilgrimages—
    Syria. | Muslim pilgrims and pilgrimages—Iran. | Muslim pilgrims and
    pilgrimages—Turkey.
Classification: LCC BP194.6.S27 Y53 2024 | DDC 297.3/556—dc23/
    eng/20231228
LC record available at https://lccn.loc.gov/2023048978

33 32 31 30 29 28 27 26 25 24
10 9 8 7 6 5 4 3 2 1

For my mother, Samiye,
and my aunt, Hatice

CONTENTS

ILLUSTRATIONS

MAPS

FIGURES

ACKNOWLEDGMENTS

Writing this book has certainly been a ride. And along that ride, I learned this: one cannot take the journey for its destination. When one remains open to all the encounters that a journey has in store for the traveler, the ride is enriched beyond measure. And if one is lucky, some of those encounters—some fleeting, some long-lasting—become profound experiences, culminating in multiple companionships for the traveler. And one still gets to one's destination, all the more traveled in people as well as places, thanks in no small part to those *hamraha* (road companions).

Among those companions to the writing of this book, my first and deepest thanks go to all the pilgrims, bus drivers and attendants, tour guides, merchants, contraband merchants and consumers, state officials, and journalists who have borne my unsolicited presence across four countries, spanning from Tehran and Tabriz to the east to Damascus and Beirut to the west. I am grateful for their selfless generosity, welcoming me into their journeys, lives, and homes. Without them none of this would have been possible. I hope what follows does some justice to those rich histories of the present they have shared with me. Hania Murtada introduced me to, and facilitated the interviews with, his father Hani Murtada—the senior trustee of the Sayyida Zainab shrine. Pegah Abdollahian, Payam Boroomand, Omid Esmaili Mokaram, Taymaz Manghebati, Marieh Mirzapour, Ali Shirkhodaei, Mona Vala, and Negar Yaghmaian not only proved to be guides to life in Iran but also accompanied and supported me throughout my research forays into multiple state institutions and archival holdings throughout Tehran. They shared their ideas and offered incisive comments about the project as well as countless nights of delicious meals and even more delicious company.

Multiple institutions lent critical support to complete this research, including grants from Die Zeit Stiftung Bucerius Program in Migration Studies, Harvard University's Center for Middle East Studies and Weatherhead Center for International Affairs, and the Wenner-Gren Foundation. The Cora Du Bois Charitable Trust and a Harvard Graduate Society Completion Fellowship afforded me the time and resources necessary to complete the dissertation on which this book is based. The Kevorkian Center for Near Eastern Studies at New York University provided the necessary homebase to finish the task in hand. At Northwestern University, two faculty grants from the Buffett Institute for Global Affairs made possible subsequent archival research in Istanbul and follow-up interviews in Beirut that greatly shaped the sections of the book on the shrine, while a Kaplan Institute for the Humanities Faculty Fellowship afforded me the time to find an accessible and interdisciplinary voice for the book. The Keyman Modern Turkish Studies Program supplied funds to workshop the manuscript with Lara Deeb, Manu Goswami, Minoo Moallem, Andrew Shryock, and Eric Tagliacozzo. Their deep engagement with my work, in the thick of the pandemic, has left its marks on every page of this book. Two visiting fellowships in Germany, at Max Planck Institut für ethnologische Forschung and Forum Transregionale Studien, enabled me to spend a year in Berlin and channel that deep engagement into the book's current form. Significant sections of the first ethnographic interlude and chapter 1 appeared in the *Journal of the Royal Anthropological Institute*, titled "Zainab's Traffic: Spatial Lives of an Islamic Ritual across Southwest Asia" (Yıldız 2023).

The first draft of this book I wrote as a doctoral dissertation at Harvard University. To my committee members, Steve Caton, Afsaneh Najmabadi, the late Mary Steedly, and my advisor Ajantha Subramanian, I would like to express my utmost gratitude for providing me with a bottomless well of wisdom, imagination, and inspiration. While the book has gone through many iterations since that first draft, it still carries traces of their profound engagement with my work. During my time at Harvard, I also had the pleasure of learning from Asad Ali Ahmed, Vincent Brown, Bill Granara, Michael Herzfeld, Cemal Kafadar, Susan Kahn, Smita Lahiri, Gülru Necipoğlu, and Judith Surkis. A special thanks is also due to staff at the Anthropology Department and the Center for Middle Eastern Studies: Susan Farley, Elizabeth Flannigan, Marianne Fritz, and Cris Paul.

One of the most precious gifts of my graduate school years has undoubtedly been the intimate friendships I developed. Among these friends, there are those whom I am lucky to call my intellectual road companions and who continue to sustain my heart, mind, and soul. Thank you: Naor Ben-Yehoyada, Lizzy Cooper-Davis, Seçil Dağtaş, Haydar Darıcı, Will Day, Esra Demir, Ujala Dhaka-Kingten, Namita Dharia, Alireza Doostdar, Maryam Monalisa Gharavi, Vedran Grahovac, Nancy Khalil, Mana Kia, Julie Kleinman, Darryl Li, Jared McCormick, Andrew McDowell, Arafat Mohamad, Chiaki Nishijima, Federico Perez, Sabrina Perić, Mircea Raianu, Ramyar Rossoukh, Ivette Salom, Ben Siegel, Claudio Sopranzetti, Deniz Türker, Anand Vaidya, Julia Yezbick, Dilan Yıldırım, Çağrı Yoltar, and Aslı Zengin.

Since my arrival at Northwestern University in 2016, I have found a supportive and stimulating intellectual community. In that community I have acquired unpayable debts to Ana Aparicio, Adia Benton, Micaela di Leonardo, Brian Edwards, Mark Hauser, Matthew Johnson, Doug Kiel, Robert Launay, Bill Leonard, Hirokazu Miyazaki, Annelise Riles, Cynthia Robin, Shalini Shankar, Mary Weismantel, and Jessica Winegar for their vital mentorship and collegiality. The Anthropology Department as a whole not only extended a warm welcome to a freshly minted anthropologist such as myself but also nurtured me. In the Program for Middle East and North African Studies, I have found stimulating interdisciplinary camaraderie in Rebecca Johnson, Henri Lauzière, Wendy Pearlman, Carl Petry, and Ipek Kocaömer Yosmaoğlu. Members of the Colloquium for Global Iran Studies—Maryam Athari, Foroogh Farhang, Elham Hoominfar, Negar Razavi, Azadeh Safaeian, Sepehr Vakil, Shirin Vossoughi, Ida Yalzadeh, and Hamed Yousefi—gave me a precious community that in critical times carried me back to my work and journey.

There were also times when I doubted if this journey would ever take me to my destination. In those times, Ipek Kocaömer Yosmaoğlu buoyed me with her signature wit and delicious cooking. Malini Sur has been an incredible confidante, who listened patiently and reminded me to trust my instincts along this journey. As the book took its current form, I remained nested in a village of generosity spanning multiple writing groups that provided vital care and incisive commentary. I am grateful to Adia Benton, Ergin Bulut, Umayyah Cable, Başak Can, Seçil Dağtaş, Darcie DeAngelo, Alireza Doostdar, Sarah Fredricks, Ghenwa Hayek, Angie Heo, Hi'ilei Hobart, Darryl Li, Elham Mireshghi, and Nazan Üstündağ. Naor Ben-Yehoyada has been with this project longer, and has worked with me through more reiterations, than anyone else. Thank you for being my most discerning reader and brilliant critic, *jaja*. None of this work would have been possible without the able support of staff at Northwestern, especially Lexy Gore, Nancy Hickey, Kulsum Virmani, William Voltz, and Adam Wagner.

In my journey across the North American academy, I benefited greatly from rich conversations with too many brilliant teachers and colleagues to name here. My gratitude goes to Ervand Abrahamian, Lila Abu-Lughod, Hussein Agrama, Zohra Ahmed, Cemil Aydın, Aslı Bâli, Fadi Bardawil, Amahl Bishara, Simon Coleman, Jatin Dua, Julia Elyachar, Noura Erakat, Sinan Erensü, Tess Farmer, Ilana Feldman, Daniella Gandolfo, Vera Grant, Bassam Haddad, Sami Hermez, Adnan Husain, Aslı Iğsız, Rhoda Kanaaneh, Leili Kashani, J. Kehaulani Kauanui, Laleh Khalili, Mikiya Koyagi, Bruce Masters, Brinkley Messick, Nada Moumtaz, Arzoo Osanloo, Malihe Razazan, Sima Shakhsari, Anu Sharma, Anoush Suni, Eric Tagliacozzo, Khachig Tölölyan, Elizabeth Traube, Gina Athena Ulysse, Leilah Vevaina, and Krishna Winston. A special thanks is due to Michael Gilsenan, who, as an inspiring anthropologist, has mentored me for over a decade with his inimitable wisdom, wit, and brilliance—all of which he continues to carry with the humility of a dervish. Thank you.

I feel extremely fortunate to work with my editors, Kate Marshall and Kevin O'Neill, at the University of California Press's series *Atelier: Ethnography in the Twenty-First Century*. They expressed early enthusiasm and provided unwavering support for this project. Most importantly they encouraged me to write the book I wanted to write. Being a part of the Atelier series introduced me to numerous colleagues whom I feel privileged to call intellectual interlocutors: Alessandro Angelini, Tracie Canada, Erica James, Kathryn Mariner, Kaya Williams, and Laurie Willis, in addition to Darcie DeAngelo. Chad Attenborough deftly assisted me with getting the manuscript into production. Jessica Moll oversaw the production to publication. I am also grateful to the three anonymous reviewers who provided detailed comments that greatly strengthened my arguments. Bill Nelson lent the book a generous hand with his exacting maps. So did David Robertson with the index. At various stages, Allison Brown, Eric Berlin, and Elisabeth Magnus improved the clarity and flow of my prose with their meticulous editing.

I want to dedicate this work to my mother, Samiye Yıldız, and my aunt, Hatice Potak. They have wholeheartedly supported my pursuit of higher education, denied to them under different guises. Thank you for believing in me unconditionally and for reminding me, à la Rumi, that what I wanted also wanted me.

NOTE ON TRANSLITERATION AND TRANSLATION

For transliterations from the Arabic, Azeri, Persian, and Turkish, I use a modified version of the transliteration scheme of the *International Journal of Middle East Studies* (*IJMES*). Place and personal names are rendered in English when they have accepted English spellings, like Parastoo, but are otherwise transliterated as usual. In quotations I have retained other authors' transliterations even when they depart from this system. All translations from the Arabic, Azeri, Persian, and Turkish are my own.

Introduction

780 DAYS BEFORE THE SYRIAN REVOLUTION
1,105 DAYS BEFORE THE PILGRIM ABDUCTIONS
2,572 DAYS BEFORE THE ISIL ATTACK ON THE SHRINE

On January 8, 2009, while reading the daily news from local media in Turkey's Kurdistan, I was astounded by a brief clip from Antep. None of it seemed to make sense. It reported that three days earlier, on January 5, Turkish security forces in Gaziantep had stopped and searched a bus carrying forty-four Iranian pilgrims from Tabriz to the Sayyida Zainab shrine outside Damascus, Syria. During the operation, a joint search team of city police and antiterrorism special forces recovered fifty-seven kilograms of heroin stashed inside the air-conditioning system. The twelve barrels of contraband fuel oil stowed above passengers' suitcases, the report continued, were recovered empty, having already been delivered to their destination in Doğubeyazıt, Turkey, on the border with Iran. Cigarettes tucked in the seats four cartons at a time were destined for the Iranian Bazaar in Gaziantep.

The operation concluded later that day with the simultaneous arrest of five Kurdish men—four with Iranian passports, one with a Turkish one—in multiple regions of southeastern Turkey. They were charged as the suspected traffickers—not only of heroin but also of the oil and cigarettes. Accepting the charges for the oil and cigarettes but denying those for the drugs, they pleaded guilty but requested a reduced sentence in light of their confession. The news piece ended with a picture of Iranian pilgrims, who reportedly claimed that they had nothing to do with the heroin and that the golden amulets hidden in their shoes should be returned because they were for personal and ritual use and did not violate any laws of trade or commerce between Iran and Turkey. A week later, on January 16, 2009, I boarded a plane to Gaziantep to find out more about the route of seemingly religious and deeply commercial mobility.

I probably should have waited longer for the buzz around the bus incident to die down and another cross-border mobility story to take over, but I was anxious to find out how a saint visitation (*ziyarat*) bus had become the vehicle of contraband (*kaçak*) commerce—and one of drugs no less—in a bazaar in Gaziantep that was named after Iranians some seven hundred kilometers away from the closest Iranian territory. It still made no sense.

Prior to walking into the Iranian Bazaar for the first time, I had prepared well. Or so I thought. I had rehearsed my two-minute description of my project countless times. It was crisp, jargon-free, and inviting for a layperson unfamiliar with ethnographic research. I had tried on three outfits before settling on a loosely but classically cut pair of linen pants and a white linen shirt for the occasion. Ruling out sandals as too informal, I had opted for sneakers. And taking to heart the Turkish idiom of eating sweet and talking sweet, I had even picked up a kilogram of walnut baklava to share with the merchants before explaining my research and asking their permission. This final touch, I was sure, would put them at ease.

The reaction to my rehearsed introduction was anything but sweet. Scanning me from head to toe, Metin squinted. "So, let me make sure I understand you right," he said. "You come in here with your white teeth and white sneakers, and white pressed linen pants, and you want to research our black market?" Neither the sneakers nor the outfit was putting anyone at ease. I struggled to respond by reiterating that my research was not exactly on the black market but on the pilgrimage route itself. Metin was not moved by this clarification. "The Turkish or the Iranian state?" he asked. "Which one do you work for, my boy?" I strung my words together, explaining that I was a cultural anthropologist and not a spy. "The Professor will know about that," he said under his breath, then called out for the Professor at the top of his lungs. "We can get this baklava started, though," Metin added with a grin.

He took it off my hands and started playing host to other merchants, briefly chatting with the Professor and pointing in my direction with his chin. The Professor came by a few baklava pieces later—a tall man with broad shoulders, his hands covered in automotive grease. "Hey, save a piece for me, eh?" he protested to those who were buzzing around the box. After an exchange of pleasantries, he paused and prompted me: "Explain to me Weber's theory of charisma." He was dead serious. At this point, the baklava was in ruins like chips among seagulls. Metin was all ears. So was his apprentice.

I gave it my best shot, describing charisma as the authority that comes with the extraordinary leadership skills of a figure who can invoke devotion and commitment in others. "Like Zainab," I said. And because the Professor kept quiet with the intent look of an examiner, I added that while the term had originally referred to religious authority, it is now used in common parlance to refer to other forms of authority, and that—

"Okay, okay, that should suffice for now," the Professor interrupted. He turned to Metin and said, "This boy is no spy. Go easy on him. He has already made a bad life decision by signing up for a PhD." Appreciating his own sense of humor and appropriating a line from *The Simpsons* that registered with me only after the fact, the Professor burst into laughter. Metin gave him a pat on the back and, possibly because of the strange look on my face, walked over to me. Wobbling from left to right on stiff legs and hunching up his shoulders, he pushed mine down and said, "Relax, my boy! Didn't you hear? You passed our security check."

Motioning to Metin, the merchant's apprentice, the Professor exclaimed, "Save the real professor a piece of the baklava, would you?"

Licking his fingers, the apprentice responded, "Too late!" and showed us the empty box.

"You vultures," the Professor yelled. Having regained a bit of my composure, I asked the Professor how he came to acquire his nickname. "I was a master's student of sociology at Mimar Sinan University when I got arrested at the May Day protests," he explained. "Because of my prison sentence, they expelled me from the university and ruled that I could never acquire the teaching license I was working toward. Upon my release, I returned to my hometown, Gaziantep, where I worked odd jobs until my high school friend, a mechanic known here as the Architect [*mimar*], said he could use an extra pair of hands and, more importantly, my brains. So I found myself working in his body shop in what then became the Iranian Bazaar of Antep."

The Professor wrapped up the story of his personal trajectory that had brought him to the bazaar. Metin, the seasoned merchant whom I had approached with my box of baklava, returned with three glasses of tea and joined me and the Professor at the small tables under the fig tree. "One for you, one for the Professor, and one for me," he said and waited for us to taste. I took a sip. It was a fragrant Ceylon tea with generous overtones of bergamot. "Just arrived from Iran. Flavorful, isn't it?" Metin asked rhetorically. "So, Emrah, I am happy to hear you are from the university and not a state functionary or anything, but what is your other gig?" Metin had moved on already. "Are you a journalist? Did you also read that hyperbolic article or what?" Metin took another loud sip from his cup, having fixated on me. A middle-aged man with large almond-shaped eyes and a closely trimmed mustache, he was quick to suggest that he knew the real story behind the case that had brought me to Gaziantep. "And I trust the Professor's judgment, of course," Metin interjected, turning to the Professor, who, until now, had remained quiet.

"Give it a rest, would you?" the Professor finally said, speaking for me. "He is going to write something about this, but like a decade later, and only three hundred people will read it. So you will be vintage, somewhere else in the world. In a language you don't speak. Don't worry, *baba ya*!" The Professor had spoken. And it was harsh.

While Metin was visibly processing this new information, I interjected that I did not have a side gig. And no, I was not a journalist. And yes, I had read the article. And no, the salary wasn't much but steady with benefits. Minus dental and vision of course. "Ah, Amerika!" I joked. The Professor let out a puff, but Metin was not convinced. Coming from a humble background in Istanbul and being an immigrant meant that I found it more than satisfactory to do what I loved and earn a small but steady income, I explained to Metin. I took another sip to catch my breath and bring it back to the new story.

"You're single, and in your late twenties. Become the road you travel. Surely you too will find your *yoldaş* [road companion]. Another tea?" Metin asked rhetorically, as he poured from his small porcelain samovar into the thin-waisted glasses.

The samovar was Russian inspired in its royal rococo aesthetic, handmade in Iran. Metin had most likely picked it up at the Iran equivalent of a garage sale. *Too soon,* I argued with myself. *Don't ask. Just drink your tea.*

"These are matters better taken slowly," Metin said. Into our second glasses of the *kaçak* tea that he was proud of providing ("Everybody in Antep knows my tea"), Metin launched into his account of what had happened on those pilgrim buses. He put it like this: "The numbers of pilgrims were up to thirty buses this season, you know. That means more and more buses were needed to shuttle them back and forth between Iran and Syria. And the numbers of soldiers on the borders? Also increasing. You know, if there is any *kaçak* in the Iranian Bazaar, it is of oil, tea, and tobacco. This was indeed a much larger operation. A one-time thing. Infiltrators. Over the course of my twenty years here in the bazaar, I have heard of maybe two cases like this, and both were the business of large cartels not even connected to the route or the bus companies that carried the pilgrims. The real pity is that we lost our orders of oil and cigarettes. Our batch was in that *ziyarat* bus too. I will tell you what, someone in that operation did not get their cut, and cut the rope on the operation. A mole."

"He watches too many crime series, right?" I asked the Professor. The Professor turned to me. "He does. But in this case he might have a point." Taking another sip, the Professor advised that I had much to learn to appreciate the multiple movements on this route before I could interpret what was going on. The Professor was really a professor. "You know, I am sure they call this type of saint visitation [*ziyarat*] where one travels on cars or buses, with whatever means available, *hajj-i fuqara*'—the pilgrimage of the poor, those of humble means who cannot afford the expenses of a pilgrimage to Mecca. But as they say, this saint visitation and *hajj* are the same thing. Its moniker, the poverty of its pilgrims, is not to be taken literally. If anything, take it as Iranian irony."

I didn't really know what to say, a reaction I was to have several times on that first trip of mine to the Iranian Bazaar. "It is a complicated traffic," I eventually said.

"That's right." The Professor responded. "And this incident that you heard about is not what pilgrimage of the poor is about, at all. You are here for a while, aren't you? Fieldwork and all. Make sure that you cross-check your stories with these imaginative merchants [*tacirler*]! Myself included . . ." The Professor patted my shoulder.

BEIRUT, LEBANON

April 13, 2013

769 DAYS AFTER THE SYRIAN REVOLUTION
444 DAYS AFTER THE PILGRIM ABDUCTIONS
1,023 DAYS BEFORE THE ISIL ATTACK ON THE SHRINE

Syria was burning. And I, along with the Damascene Murtada family that administers the charitable religious endowment, the *waqf*, associated with the Sayyida Zainab shrine, was watching from the capital of Lebanon, Beirut. As the people's revolution was being internationally ignored and transnationally manipulated into an ever-expanding theater of war and humanitarian disaster of colossal proportions, the destination of the *hajj-i fuqara'* route, the Sayyida Zainab shrine, was being dragged deeper and deeper into the "Syrian conflict." I was an hour away from meeting Sayyid Dr. Hani Murtada, most senior guardian and trustee—or as he preferred to retain the original Arabic, *mutawalli*—of the Sayyida Zainab shrine in Beirut. The growing politicization of the Sayyida Zainab shrine, and more specifically the conspiracy theories that the *waqf* and the shrine were proxies of the Iranian state, had concerned Dr. Hani Murtada—so much so that he had moved, along with his immediate family, to Beirut, Lebanon. Over the next two weeks I was to conduct three two-hour interviews with the doctor on the family, the *waqf*, and the pilgrimage route, respectively—a pilgrimage route that was at this point a thing of the past. The shrine was still standing, 1,023 days before the ISIL attack.

The doctor asked me, when I addressed him, to leave out his Sayyid status, marking his direct descent from the Family of the Prophet. "But you can keep using the doctor one!" he added in his signature plays of parallelism and contrast to get a laugh in the most important moment. For him, his earned rather than inherited title was more significant to who he was. After Sunni extremist brigades made two attempts on his life while he was at the Sayyida Zainab shrine, he had relocated his family to Beirut on his wife's insistence. "Not too long, we hope, for a while. We have been Damascenes for over seven generations," the doctor added, smiling. Mahdi Murtada, who was Hani Murtada's nephew and the second *mutawalli* on the *waqf* chain of authority and command, had relocated his family and his engineering company to Dubai. As of April 2013, the day-to-day operations of the shrine (*maqam,* or the "seat" of the saint) were in the hands of the general manager, Mazin, and the chief engineer of operations, Nahid. "We are in touch, of course. They come to Beirut once in a while. In fact, in anticipation of your visit, I asked Nahid to bring a high-quality reproduction of some of our archival holdings," the doctor said, handing me the glossy book.

I wanted to hear Dr. Murtada's take on the future of *ziyarat* to Sayyida Zainab. Having learned my lesson after my clumsy entry into the Iranian Bazaar of Antep just after the story broke about intercepted contraband in the bus, I knew to avoid in my first interview with Dr. Murtada the immediate present of Syria and the increasingly precarious location of the shrine in Syria. "Four hundred and forty-four days ago," I led with a description, "a brigade associated with the Free Syrian Army stopped an Iranian pilgrim bus in Hama and abducted twenty-two male pilgrims, sparing the remaining twenty women on the bus en route to the Sayyida Zainab shrine. As you might remember, Doctor," I continued, "the kidnapping was meant as a warning to the Iranian state not to collaborate with the Assad regime, the brigade declared." I paused. The doctor listened intently. I continued: "In less than two weeks, the Iranian government issued a ban on all road travel to Syria. And yet pilgrim abductions, including an episode in the reverse direction, from Lebanon to Iran, continued. An Islamic Front-aligned brigade called the Northern Storm kidnapped eleven Lebanese pilgrims en route to Qom and Mashhad in Iran at the Reyhanli border crossing between Syria and Turkey." Here I paused and asked my first question: "What do you think is the relationship between *ziyarat,* or more specifically *zuwwar* (pilgrims), and sectarianism now that saint visitors are being turned into bargaining chips in the Syrian conflict?"

"Pilgrim abductions are of course symptomatic of how the Sayyida Zainab shrine outside Damascus is being dragged into the conflict engulfing the region," Dr. Murtada said. "This is unfortunate, of course. That said, what is being spared? Everything is a target in this competition for dominance. This has nothing to do with sectarian difference." The doctor waited for my reaction. When I continued listening, he concluded, "This is the effect, not the cause, of categorical political differences. We have never had such confession-centric politicking in Syria before. So that is new."

Shortly after that first interview, and while the Lebanese pilgrims were still in custody, a previously unknown group named Visitors of Imam Reza retaliated by capturing two Turkish Airlines pilots from the Beirut International Airport to force a diplomatic negotiation. I might not have made it to Damascus on time, but in Beirut I was a bit unfashionably early. A few months after the triple abductions, Qatari diplomats brokered the deal that set the captive pilots free: while the Syrian state released over sixty jailed prisoners, the Northern Storm brigade demanded the release of the pilgrims held hostage on the Syria-Turkey border. The imbrication of militant brigades, pilgrims, and revolutionary guards with the states of Lebanon, Syria, Turkey, Qatar, and Iran is often presented as a horror story of transnational chaos in the Middle East. And as governments and names change, and allegiances shift and coalesce in the region, terrorism and security experts explain away such traffic in state and nonstate actors using the catchall category of sectarianism. Confident declarations about a seamless history of sectarianism in Islam, the Sunni-Shiʻi divide, "dating back millennia," are offered as the internal logic of the region violently working itself out.

It is not only journalists and political experts who resort to such discourse. In scholarly debates as well, one increasingly comes across "sectarianism" as an explanatory paradigm for understanding the Levant in particular and the Middle East more broadly. Dr. Murtada's rhetorical question "What is not attacked?" was the quickest and most thought-provoking primer for those awaiting a book about Iranian saint visitation producing only sectarian difference between two entrenched camps of Hanafi Sunnis and Twelver Shiʻa. This paradigm of "sectarianism," as a sustained line of feminist analysis that extends from Suad Joseph through Lara Deeb to Maya Mikdashi has shown us in the very complex case of modern Lebanon,[1] operates on three assumptions. The first is that people in the Islamic world and the Middle East conceive of religious difference and identity through ahistorical and static categories of sect and recursive intrafaith violence. The second, in this line of thinking, is that Islamic ritual is reiterative rather than generative of doctrinal difference. The third is that transnational mobility inherent to saint visitation across Iran, Turkey, and Syria—sensationalized through the movements of armed and militant groups, revolutionary guards, and pilgrims—renders *traveling while Muslim* suspect in itself. In this schema, Islam is indeed much more than religion; it is instead conceived as an overriding cosmology that structures every part of Muslim life. Ritual, in this cosmology, becomes a manual to religious practice that reproduces a scripturally mandated structure of difference. Precisely because Muslims are assumed to be docile subjects of sectarian faith, their mobility becomes synonymous with the cross-border export of "extremist" ideology and terrorist violence.[2]

This book dispenses with these three assumptions and centers the pilgrimage route in a historical ethnography of *ziyarat* between Iran and Syria via Turkey. It shows that neither sectarian politics nor contraband economics will explain away this complicated cultural biography of saint visitation itself as a transimperial and then transnational grid of connectivity across Southwest Asia. *Zainab's Traffic* illustrates how practices and meanings of pilgrimage are shaped but not determined by scalar processes of spatial production across a shrine, a bazaar, and two borders. Its analysis attends also to how these social institutions in turn are produced, in ways noticed and unnoticed by the pilgrims themselves, by the pilgrimage route. Hence, this book approaches saint visitation as a ritual of mobility. And to study this ritual of mobility, I develop traffic as an analytic to chronicle how these wider processes of spatial production that unfold at variegated scales, from the interpersonal to the interstate, could be better examined with the broader scale of the region in mind. Once we center our analysis of *ziyarat* on its practitioners and their routes, their embedded but mobile roles in this transnational traffic come to the fore. In analyzing pilgrims' micropractices on those routes that traverse that region, we reveal the impossibility of neatly separating the religious from other forms of value and meaning in social life.[3] Neither a political invention of religious tradition nor its commercialized aberration, Zainab's *ziyarat* demands an anthropology of Islam that "re-embeds" Islam back into its dynamic historical and social context of cultural praxis.[4] A saint visitation route provides fertile grounds to do just that while offering an alternative view of Islamic ritual that moves saints, selves, and others across borders.[5]

When the doctor and I finished our first interview, he invited me to Damascus "at the most immediate opportunity."

"I would be delighted," I replied. But we both knew that these formulaic niceties, like the American "Let's do lunch sometime," were ways to say goodbye. The route through Turkey was gone. And the security check for a Turkish passport to Syria for the purpose of research was going to require a bit more than Weber's theory of charisma.

Dr. Murtada is right, I thought to myself. *Political, not theological, deliberation is at the heart of the "Balkanization" of Syria.*

If *ziyarat* was not just about commerce (*ticaret*), as the Professor had cautioned, and not just about politics (*siyasat*), as the doctor had argued, then what else was venerating Zainab about?

TEHRAN, IRAN

October 29, 2014

1,698 DAYS AFTER THE SYRIAN REVOLUTION
1,374 DAYS AFTER THE PILGRIM ABDUCTIONS
460 DAYS BEFORE THE ISIL ATTACK ON THE SHRINE

Shajara! Genealogy, or pedigree in Persian. It was in Tehran in the midst of Moharram processions, and days before 'Ashura, that its radical openness was undeniably revealed to me: venerating Zainab has always been about making kin, making genealogy, and making family. Making the saint a part of one's extended family in enlisting her for saintly intercession was the means to a variety of ends: resilience to endure the pains of life, to find remedies for its maladies, to start and maintain families, and for women, to keep moving despite obstacles, which required a careful navigation of gender, class, and generation in their particular location.

Despite the crippling economic sanctions unleashed by the United States on Iran and its citizens, Moharram proceedings were nonetheless underway in full force in Tehran, even in Meydoone-e Kajj of Tehran's Saadat Abad, along the capital's northern upscale edge and green-turned-purple stronghold—the colors for the election campaigns of Mir Mosavi and Hassan Rohani, respectively. Despite internationally engineered currency devaluations and high inflation, one encountered countless Moharram booths, serving passersby refreshments and vocalizing captivating recitations days away from ʿAshura. The traffic-clogged streets had been converted into venues for open-air concerts. Stunning ritualistic elegies dedicated to Hazrat-i Hossein, Hazrat-i Ali, and others of Ahl al-Bayt continued late into the night.

Many souls, some of them high on a variety of stimulants, from hashish to crystal meth (or *shishe* in Persian), had poured into Tehran's streets to "find themselves" in the figurative and literal ecstasies of commemorative ritual—which also happens to be one of the very few occasions in Iran when public space can be occupied without the scrutiny of the state. It was not these nocturnal revelers who taught me about genealogy, though. It was Hediyeh Khanum.[6] She regretted, "terribly, really terribly," that she had not traveled to Syria when she could. Now not only the shrine dedicated to Hazrat-i Zainab but also the country's historical heritage was within reach of heavy bombardment and rocket fire. Meanwhile, Hediyeh, a housewife in her late forties, sent an elegy Zainab's way. "Here, there, everywhere, we will venerate the 'righteously guided'"—referring to the family of the Prophet, of which Zainab is a member.

Hazrat-i Zainab was a granddaughter of the Prophet, daughter of Imam Ali, and sister of Imam Hussain, who himself was decapitated by the forces of Yazid I, the second Umayyad caliph, in the battle of Karbala in 680 CE in current-day Iraq. Zainab's veneration is intimately tied with her surviving this battle. It is often taken to mark the initial divisions between Shiʿi and Sunni Islam—itself predating the battle fought also over the issue of leadership of the Muslim community after the death of the Prophet Muhammad in 632 CE.[7] In addition to being the messenger and narrator of the Battle of Karbala, Zainab is enlivened by *ziyarat* in this hagiography, as an emblem of

MAP 1. The *hajj-i fuqara'* route (by Bill Nelson).

caring yet assertive, pious yet socially engaged womanhood. Most pilgrims to Sayyida Zainab's shrine look up to the saint as a model to be emulated.[8] "The roads will be built, destroyed, and rebuilt," Hediyeh consoled herself and me. Then she recounted how many pilgrim buses she had observed at the border crossing with Turkey once.

Indeed, the number of Iranian pilgrims had risen steadily from tens of thousands in the mid-1980s to more than 250,000 per year by 2010. This traffic in pilgrims could add up to forty buses a day, particularly around Nowruz, the Persian new year. The pilgrims from Tabriz with whom I traveled in 2010, for instance, traveled around eight hundred miles through Iran, Turkey, and Syria to reach the shrine—approximately the distance between Chicago and New York. During the journey to Damascus and on their way back, pilgrims' visitations within Turkey also included three stops: Veysel Karani's tomb, which contains a piece of Prophet Muhammad's mantle, near the Baykan District of Siirt; Balıklı Göl, an ancient madrasa associated with the story of Abraham and Nimrod, in Şanlıurfa; and the Iranian Bazaar in Gaziantep.

The route might have gone away, but Zainab did not. Hediyeh Khanum, too, was right. Bringing someone into one's most immediate kin, remembering to visit, and undertaking the journey were the point of venerating a saint like Zainab. And if paying a visit was not possible, one could still venerate from a distance, as Hediyeh had to do this Moharram.

Ziyarat was not just about *ticaret* or *siyasat*. It was also about genealogy and kin, as Hediyeh had pointed out. And those who could not pay visits to Zainab were resourceful.

This was still 460 days before the ISIL attack on the shrine.

RITUAL AS REGULATED IMPROVISATION IN THE
ANTHROPOLOGY OF ISLAM

Over the past two decades, Islamic revivalism has become an important object of interdisciplinary analysis. In anthropology and Middle East studies alike, studies of Islamic revival have called into question earlier modernist accounts that projected the secularization of non-Western societies and constructed an Islamic exception to that secular teleology. Against the older modernist binary between secular politics and traditional Islam, this new scholarship sought to make sense of the practices of revivalist Muslims from within the network of concepts on which these Muslims themselves have drawn.[9] This direction of inquiry focused on power, disciplinary practice, and ethical cultivation reiterated through authorizing discourses. In so doing, however, it also shifted attention away from rituals such as pilgrimage, deemed now to be an archaic object of analysis exhausted by symbolic anthropology.[10] Moreover, by shunning the post-9/11 political conditions of religious practices, the anthropology of piety fell hostage to the liberal anti-Muslim trends against which it wrote to begin with.

The chosen objects of analysis in these new anthropologies of Islam are the more individualized as well as more scholastic forms of Islamic piety such as daily prayers (*namaz*) or Qur'anic exegesis meetings (*tafsir*). In analyzing these more individuated projects, this scholarship presents us with Islamic religious practice as a process of ethical cultivation forged in relation to an overarching tradition. By making the tradition itself the principal contextual reference, such work dislocates these practices from the political and socio-economic contexts out of which they arise. It also fails to account for how such practices bring together contested and often very modern discursive traditions within Islam to bear on the material conditions of the present. Most importantly, by assuming that such practices are contained within an Islamic religious tradition, it forecloses an examination of how inextricably religious and other spheres of life are interwoven in the making of religious subjects and meanings.

Within anthropology, Asad's analytical foregrounding of the ethical at the secular limits of the political has been taken to ethnographic task from Egypt to France. While Saba Mahmood famously set it into conversation with liberalism and its assumed feminist subjects in Egypt,[11] Mayanthi Fernando took up the contradictions of French secularism in terms of ethical cultivation—what she names "practices of secularity."[12] In her *Republic Unsettled,* Fernando argued that, like various forms of piety, "secularity too includes a range of ethical, social, physical, and sexual dispositions, hence the need to apprehend the secular via its sensorial, aesthetic, and embodied dispositions and not only its political ones." Samuli Schielke, working with young men who fast but also drink alcohol in Cairo, describes where moral norms or ethical disciplines were transgressed and not simply emulated, and argues that "struggle, ambivalence, incoherence, and failure must also receive attention in the study of everyday religiosity."[13] For Schielke, this call should compel scholars of religion in general and those of Islam in particular to observe that ordinary ethics, which lack the holistic vision captured in the myth of Islamic revivalism, lack the essence of "everyday Islam" and "ordinary piety."

All three of these approaches to Islamic religious practice begin with Asad's key designation of religious practices as ethical cultivation, a designation that disembeds those practices from the political and socioeconomic contexts out of which they arise. The ethical turn and its articulations in studies of ritual fail to account for how rituals bring contested and often rival discursive traditions within Islam to bear on the material conditions of the present. Nor do they account for how these actors' social practices in the spaces they inhabit, build, and venerate produce those material conditions and their communicative context. As a whole, my work contends that studying mobilities of ritual and rituals of mobility can help us break away from both the teleologies of earlier modernist accounts and the discursive scaffolding of the anthropology of contemporary Islam. It is precisely because the contested theological, political, and socioeconomic grounds of *ziyarat* are impossible to ignore that examining the paths of Zainab provides fertile grounds to rethink the dominant paradigms within the anthropology of Islam and offer some correctives to its attendant conception of subject formation.

The critical scholarship associated with the ethical turn in the anthropology of religion has productively deconstructed instrumentalist arguments that explain away practices of piety as corollaries of minoritarian identity politics in the era of the global war on terror, or as mechanisms for coping with political and socioeconomic precarity in the Middle East. As Lara Deeb reminds us, these earlier arguments are rooted partly in an unwillingness to view practices of piety as a form of agency in and of themselves.[14] At the same time, Deeb warns us that in responding to such instrumentalist arguments, it is possible to slip into another sort of reductive analytical framework where piety becomes disembedded from its social complexities and transformed instead into a singular aspect of life unto itself. In this critical and often-replicated slippage, any practice of piety primarily concerned with ethical self-cultivation in line with the teachings of Islam is also assumed to be fully detached from other daily practices of social life, from politics, and, most fundamentally, from complex social environments and relationships.

We can, however, bridge symbolic and discursive studies of religion by considering both the pragmatic conditions of action designated as religious and the metapragmatic constitution of the "authorizing discourse"[15] to achieve wildly diverse ends. Rather than trying to isolate religious practices from their political or economic conditions and reducing them to disciplinary modalities of morality experienced in religious practice, a renewed anthropological focus on pilgrims' action en route to and at sites of religious veneration can help us reintroduce the ways that religious practices and their attendant moral valuations emerge out of a contested social landscape where religious value is but one aspect of action and mobility, and their regulation.[16]

The *hajj-i fuqara'* exemplifies the historicity and dynamism of contemporary Islamic practice. By engaging in theological and diplomatic contestation over their access to Sayyida Zainab's shrine in Syria, Iranian pilgrims have remade routes of mobility, markets, and commerce, as well as the meaning of Shi'i rituals of veneration. These regulated improvisations on the road to Zainab have helped form the region anew, and they have done so by transforming the shrines, bazaars, and borders that they have connected while the pilgrims, traders, border officers, and inhabitants have switched places and occupied multiple modalities of subjectivity, zigzagging spatially across religion, economy, and polity.

TRAFFIC AS METHOD, TRAFFIC AS LOCATION

On January 31, 2016, while the Syrian regime's ambassador to the UN, Ibrahim Jaafari, was meeting with the fractured opposition in Geneva for the first UN-led peace talks in two years, a car bomb detonated in the shrine town of Sayyida Zainab. Military buses, shuttling Syrian state soldiers, Iranian troops, and members of the Fatimiyoun and Zainabiyoun brigades of Afghan and Pakistani fighters, were targeted—leaving twenty-five men, stationed there to protect the shrine after the 2012 abductions, dead.

It was not only a car that the attackers detonated that day in Sayyida Zainab's Koua Sudan District. Those who rushed to the scene to help the wounded were in for two more attacks: two suicide bombers detonated themselves among the helpers and bystanders. There was no need for a public statement claiming responsibility at that point, given that by now the double-wave attack in Syria and Iraq had become the group's signature move to foment fear and factionalism: the Islamic State claimed responsibility nonetheless. The death toll rose to seventy-one, including twenty-nine civilians. That day, at least one hundred more people were wounded.

In Beirut, after the second interview with Dr. Murtada, I had doodled, as if it were a punk band logo, "specters" in my notes. I had doodled all over the neatly divided and otherwise blank page of a moleskine, marked with "take-aways for interview." Specters. Cross-reading the Murtada genealogy in Ottoman state archives and the Murtada family's documents associated with the shrine's endowment (*waqfiyyah*) had given me "specters" of the route. After the attack, the proper metaphor failed me, but "specters" was close. The disassembled places and people once connected were anything but dead. They were alive and kicking. And yet the anthropologist's self-important questions lingered.

How was I to write a road ethnography of an object that was not moving? What if it no longer existed as such anymore?

Only after that ISIL attack did I come to appreciate that the time I had chosen for research, that period of arrested mobility, was not so belated after all; I had not missed my chance in 2000. It was in fact a privileged time to approach the building blocks of a ritual of mobility, as the actors and vehicles sat in a traffic jam but remained hopeful that the roads would sooner or later reopen.

Since my first visit to the Iranian Bazaar in Gaziantep when I stuttered about charisma with the Professor and Metin, I had found not one but many road companions. In the pages to follow, two or three will accompany you through each section.

My paths took me from buses and bus stations to *imamzadeha* (shrines dedicated to the veneration of the descendants of an imam) as well as across bazaars and through border checkpoints. Tracing contacts initially made on buses allowed me to reach former pilgrims to conduct open-ended conversations about *ziyarat* in private homes. And yet, I always came back to the road. I knew I was circling around the sustained fire and human calamity that Syria has become. I conducted about four years of ethnographic and archival research—including a twenty-four-month stretch from June 2010 to December 2013—that spanned Amman, Ankara, Antep, Beirut, Istanbul, Tabriz, Tehran, and many stops in between.

While these paths that I traveled were extremely fruitful, the two bus journeys I undertook as preliminary research in 2009 and 2010 stand out for the crafting of this book. It was on those buses—at their stations, bazaars, and cafeterias—that I had my most profound fieldwork experiences. To cast it in anthropologist Kath Weston's words, in spaces of the bus one seamlessly moved from listening to overhearing, and from overhearing to wondering and subsequently joining in the conversation.[17] At other times it was just as productive to remain quiet. There were stories to be told, and sometimes all that one needed was an attentive ear. On the bus, I met those with wild dreams that they had gone to great lengths to achieve. Others were driven by nightmares just as big—be they medical maladies or the fear of remaining single or being married without children. "It is all in the eye of the beholder." "Zainab always helps when it is time." "Zainab will speak truth to power." These sayings were common to both dreamers and sufferers of nightmares. Yet others were traveling just for the sake of the journey. The journeys they took on buses offered an escape from what one interlocutor, playing on the route's moniker, "pilgrimage of the poor," called Iranians' "poverty of mobility." The play was on the prohibitive costs of undertaking a pilgrimage to Mecca. Those who couldn't afford such costs settled on the saint visitation route to Sayyida Zainab in Syria.

AN ANTHROPOLOGY OF EMERGENCE (AND SUBMERGENCE): SPACE, VALUE, TRAFFIC

Anthropology has often worked with predetermined aggregates, subsequently presenting these aggregates as "social facts" instead of conducting rigorous examinations of the temporally and spatially specific processes and practices out of which they emerge.[18] Contrary to this tendency, this book offers an anthropology of emergence, where distinct realms and scales emerge out of the concrete complexity of social action. The assumption of prefiguration has led anthropologists to configure the "economy" as existing in a disembedded sphere external to the local moral or cultural realms of action under consideration, and to undergo local embeddings.[19] Alternatively, Jane Guyer suggests that instead of tracking "conversions" across spheres of exchange, we should "see not barriers [between spheres] but institutions that facilitate exchanges across value registers."[20] Such a pragmatic approach to social action enables us to overcome the tension between culturally specific "moralities" and the universalizing abstraction "economy" precisely because it takes both "realms" to be shaped and reshaped through people's practices of valuation in concrete social contexts.[21]

Because economy is only one realm of valuation that comes to be perceived as a distinct realm of valuation practice, my research deploys this pragmatic approach to shed light on the mutual emergence of economy with the other two realms of action that anthropologists have tended to treat as essentially distinct: the religious and the political. In addition, following Roitman's emphasis on the importance of circulation in the workings of valuations, I focus on how the tripartite configuration of "value registers"—of the religious, economical, and political—unfolds through value's continuous crossings of terrestrial, conceptual, and temporal borders. What are the values of boarding a bus in Tehran to embark on an eight-hundred-mile journey across Turkey to the Sayyida Zainab shrine outside Damascus, while moving contraband commodities across two international borders? *Zainab's Traffic* posits this central question across the pathways of a *ziyarat* route and probes for possible answers alongside the politically embedded—and spatially generative—encounters of traffic, desire, mobility, valuation, genealogy, and patronage that occur along the way.

Built on extensive ethnographic fieldwork and archival research across Iran, Turkey, Syria, and Lebanon, this book explores the numerous ways that pilgrims, cross-border couriers, bazaar merchants, and the heirs of the shrine encountered doctrinal difference, economic opportunity, and political possibility along the ways of Zainab. In it, I chronicle how the same travelers cultivated techniques of movement across a regional geography increasingly characterized by sectarian violence, economic disintegration, and territorial fragmentation. The book turns these narratives of Islam and the Middle East on their heads by showing how *hajj-i fuqara'* exemplifies the historicity and sociality of ritual practice in Islam. Whether it is through the study of the spatiality and politics of saint veneration in Islam, analysis of cross-border circulation of commodity-currencies amid international sanctions, or examination of pilgrim women's desire for Syrian lingerie alongside their pleas for saintly intercession in marital matters, the project illustrates that the mutually constitutive interarticulation of religious practice, political action, and economic activity relies on both boundaries of difference in value among them and cross-cutting circuits of valuation through them.

Let me briefly clarify how I conceptualize value as an emergent and hence contingent effect conjured up through concrete practices of specific actors on the ground. *Valuation* does not mean the referential act of designating value to specific things: that is, I am not reproducing the theory of value in *The Social Life of Things*.[22] In any given moment, I concede, a realm or "regime" of value looks like a well-bounded segment of the wider reality of transactions, with seemingly established rules of movement and rates of exchange. In that sense, a Melanesian voyager on a *kula* expedition would be comfortable explaining what "realm" each of the items in the canoe belonged to and the ritual procedures through which it would need to be exchanged.[23] Once we run any number of similar *kula*-esque expeditions, however, we may be able to see not only how the *parole* of value differs drastically from its *langue* but also, and more importantly for our purposes, how the relationships between such realms of exchange and valuation and their very definition are creatively put at risk and pragmatically reworked over time.[24]

Valuation in this conceptualization foregrounds the emergent and creative operation through which regimes of value are constituted and come to bear on each other. At any given moment of such a process, these realms of value may seem stable. A semantico-referential analysis à la Saussure may even call the relations within and among these stable forms arbitrary and proceed to show how they constitute discrete symbolic value systems whose operations are independent of context. Once we approach these practices of valuation through a pragmatic lens and study this multirealm constellation in concrete settings, however, we should expect to find the ways in which a hermeneutics of traffic—or what I refer to here as "traffic in value" across the realms of religion, economy, and territory—is at play. In this chess game of mobility, to use the familiar Saussurean analogy,[25] actors on the paths of Zainab creatively uphold, suspend, or even change rules and rates of exchange in a socially conditioned and political instituted traffic. The region's tectonic spatial and political transformations, in this traffic, dictate that the very rules of commensuration and exchangeability, not to mention their tokens of value, are opened up for renegotiation. To put it differently, if practices of exchange cite and reconfigure realms and regimes of value only in the hands of specific actors confronted with particular contexts, then practices of mobility similarly cite, traverse, and reconfigure their geographies. In both cases, people interact with one another through prefigured rules of movement and action. In both cases, people shape the rules while following them. In both cases, they do so while grounding their actions by "citing some anterior discourse but constituting something other than this discourse."[26] This book examines how pilgrims, merchants, and heirs of the shrine make sense of the parameters and contours of the discursive regimes of religion, economics, and polity.

Foregrounding the pragmatic practices of valuation that these actors make along the route of the *hajj-i fuqara'* in its full trajectory, I take a processual approach to the pilgrimage route as it crisscrosses the border landscapes of Iran, Turkey, and Syria. One of my premises is that regimes of value and practices of valuation are located not only culturally but also spatially. By taking space itself as a modality of power,[27] I contest the analytical premises that posit space as reducible either to the contextual backdrop against which concrete social practices unfold or to the reflective and expressive mirror of these practices.[28] Examining space as it relates to processes of valuation at the shrine, the market, and the border, I follow how various social actors negotiate and construct uneven geographies as sites of dynamic relationships between modern states and the people and things that states attempt to contain.

The entanglements of visitation point to a complex relationship between word and deed, the religious and the secular, or, to invoke a very old anthropological dialectic, the sacred and the profane. I present the profanities of piety and visitation and the sacrileges of secularity and valuation as I encountered them along the pathways of Zainab. In so doing, I aim to break out of these binaries by following how pilgrims, merchants, and other border crossers produce, circulate, and consume value not only across the physical borders of Iran, Turkey, and Syria but also across the conceptual boundaries among the religious, the political, and the economic. My approach, which is in part inspired by linguistic pragmatic approaches to cultural analysis[29] that emphasize particular actors' generative practices in social life, repurposes multisited ethnography in a multilingual and multiscalar ethnography.[30] I emphasize the role of translocal networks in conditioning the seemingly bounded social formations of the shrine, the market, and the bazaar on a pilgrimage route. To hone this methodology, I stretch and emulate the productive intimacy of intensive ethnographic research both on the mobile grounds of the route (chapter 1) and at three major junctions along the route—namely, the shrine near Damascus (chapter 2), the Iranian Bazaar in Gaziantep (chapter 3), and Turkey's borders with Syria and Iran (chapter 4).

Zainab's Traffic builds on a growing body of scholarship on Muslim mobilities to chronicle how Sayyida Zainab's route of *ziyarat*—across its shrine, bazaar, and borders—emerges out of the traffic with pilgrims, shrine heirs, and bazaar merchants. What is at stake here is not just the crossing of territorial state borders but also the crossing of conceptual borders between religion, economy and politics, whereby different notions of Islamic authority, economic rationality, and political sovereignty battle for hegemony over subjects, geography, and history.

IN LIEU OF A USER'S MANUAL

Last but not least, some words are in order on the architecture and organization of this book. In addition to this introduction, there are four body chapters, a conclusion, and an epilogue. The first chapter throws us into the traffic of the saint visitation route to Sayyida Zainab. Chapters 2, 3, and 4 are structured around the shrine, the bazaar, and the borders of the route, respectively.

The body chapters and conclusion are each preceded by an ethnographic interlude. The individual placement of these interludes is motivated by three aims: to give the reader a cross section of the actors I encountered along the route; to draw out emically the themes and topics that will be prevalent in the succeeding chapters; and to capture the dynamic and complex subjectivities of the pilgrims I opened with—ones that are not reducible to ethical or political projects alone, precisely because they are irreducible to subjects of religion and religion alone.

If, after reading this book, the reader leaves with a sense of Islam as a religion, and the Middle East as a region, different from what is presented in social analyses of Islam and territory in the region, then I will have achieved my goal. Approaching ritual through the prism of traffic instead of exchange could help us restore that sociality and historicity. Then we can reframe *ziyarat* as a movement across the conceptual borders of religion, economy, and polity—and as such, *ziyarat* is not only ethically but also politically and spatially instituted. One way into that process of political institution is by chronicling the spatial production of its institutions such as shrines, bazaars, and borders; tracing how they connect to one another is the task of traffic as a particularly productive analytic for rituals like saint visitation.

And now, let us get you on the road and onto Zainab's traffic.

Of Ways and Traffic

MATRIARCHS OF A PROPHETIC PATRILINY

WHEN I OPENED MY interview with Fariba Khanum by asking why she had decided to embark on *ziyarat* in Tehran in 2018, she said: "Well, because there is no woman in Islamic history like Hazrat-i Zainab, because there is no figure like her in Ahl al-Bayt, not only on account of her gender but also on account of her generation—that is why I am on the road to Zainab. But then again, there is also no woman like Fatima. You should think a bit more about that, Agha-ye Yildiz." Little did I know that this would be the interview to elucidate the connections among gender, generation, and genealogy for me. Among the more than twenty interviews I had conducted in Tabriz and Tehran following up contacts from the two bus rides I took, Fariba's stood out. In her "early, early sixties," assertive, sharp, and agile with a disarming intelligence, she had been recommended to me by another pilgrim that I had traveled with almost seven years prior.

In response to my first question, Fariba had this to say: "Shariʿati is instructive, I find, in understanding this fundamental genealogical difference before we get to the questions of women and Islam. He says as much in *Fatima Is Fatima* about the Prophetic family. And if you haven't read *Fatima Is Fatima,* you really should." When I looked up from my notes, Fariba was quoting in full. Only after having looked for the reference a month later did I realize that Fariba had started the conversation where ʿAli Shariʿati in *Fatima Is Fatima* had left off.

> And I wanted to begin in this manner with Fatima. I got stuck. I wished to say, Fatima is the daughter of the great Khadijeh. I sensed that this is not Fatima. I wished to say, Fatima is the daughter of Mohammad. I sensed that this is not Fatima. I wished to say, Fatima is the wife of Ali. I sensed that this is not Fatima. I wished to say, Fatima is the mother of Hasan and Hussein. I

sensed that this is not Fatima. I wished to say, Fatima is the mother of Zainab. I still sensed that this is not Fatima.

Shortly after listening to the audio recording of our interview and finding the reference, I felt inadequacy and anxiety wash over me for not having caught where Fariba had set the tone, that brilliant hidden reference. A bit taken aback by that incredibly astute entry into the interview, and despite the real risk of showing that I didn't know my Shari'ati very well, I hear myself in the recording barely managing to slip in a "Please say more." Fariba, unfazed by my obliviousness, goes on: "Zainab is important to me, and many other women, precisely because Zainab is unique in the Prophetic family. And Zainab's *uniqueness* one should see *as a relation to* other members of the family."

She continued, "You should think about all these names and all these women, the social relationships in the family of the Prophet, if you really want to understand why Zainab's saint visitation is profound and radical." I am indebted to how expansively Fariba thinks about genealogy across gender as well as across class and generation, with regard to social relations and the web-like connections across spatial and temporal borders, aggregating into a traffic—of spatial, historical, and conceptual movement assembled around the figure of Sayyida/Hazrat-i Zainab.

. . .

In "The Traffic in Women," Gayle Rubin explores the role of women across various cultures and times as objects of marital exchange.[1] To broaden the scope of analysis framed as a bilateral exchange, Rubin replaces the term *exchange* with *traffic.* To Rubin, the concept of exchange in the study of this ritual of mobility switched the process for the product of the ritual at hand. Rubin notes that the exchange of women in marriage, given and received reciprocally, is only notational; thus she views heterosexual marriage as akin to theft and integral to patriarchy in the broader traffic of the "sex-gender system." I build on Rubin's intervention here in that, choosing exchange as what Simon Coleman calls "the analytical trope" for *rituals of mobility,* be they marriage or saint visitation and other forms of pilgrimages, cloaks a complex web of political negotiations in the social praxis of subjects like pilgrims.[2] Traffic as an analytic recovers and centers those multiple negotiations in the anthropological study of ritual. It is particularly the *extrareligious* sociality, spatiality, and temporality of ritual that such an orientation brings back into anthropological analysis of Islamic and Islamicate ritual. Here I return to Rubin's "The Traffic in Women"—and especially its call for analyses that "demonstrate how marriage systems intersect with large-scale political processes like state-making."[3] Only such a political economic approach, according to Rubin, could show women being subjects of valuation as much as objects of value. The trope of "exchange of women" à la Lévi-Strauss Rubin considers too limiting an approach to marriage that moves entire extended family units and kinship regimes and constitutes sex-gender systems. It is in this broader political economy of sex that Rubin sees marriage as a socially emergent ritual. Rubin then returns to the question that various schools of thought, from Marxian political economy to Lacanian psychoanalysis, have contended with— namely, what is a woman? Repurposing a Marx quote on enslavement of black people, Rubin writes: "What is a domesticated woman? A female of the species. The one explanation is as good as the other. A woman is a woman." Rubin goes on: "She only becomes a domestic, a wife, a chattel, a playboy bunny, a prostitute, or a human dictaphone in certain relations. Torn from these relationships, she is no more the helpmate of man than gold in itself is money."[4] Here I don't ask, "What is an Iranian woman?" Rather, my questions of exploration are "What or who are the saint visitors, and what kind of a traffic has this pilgrimage route built?"

. . .

I listened to my interview with Fariba Khanum again, extracting it from a hard disk in my closet in 2022. How I wished I could sit down with Fariba Khanum again and say: "Zainab is the daughter of the great Fatima. I sensed that this is not Zainab. I wished to say, Zainab is the granddaughter of Khadijeh. I sensed that this is not Zainab. I wished to say, Zainab is the aunt of Ruqayyah. I sensed that this is not Zainab. I wished to say. Zainab is the mother of Um Kulthum. And I still sensed that this is not Zainab." How I wished I could tell her that I now understood the silliness of my question as to why women wanted to visit Zainab—she had decisively showed that women are in the Prophetic lineage. They are the matriarchs of a prophetic patriliny. And not only Zainab, but particularly Zainab, has been fundamental to its perpetuation across time and space.

"This is slow work, Agha-ye Yıldız. Have patience with yourself to learn, do you see?" Fariba Khanum would have said something along those lines and smiled, as she always did, looking directly into one's eyes.

I flashed back to the last time I had seen her with that look, accompanied by that generous smile. "Why don't you start with all the issues of *Rah-i Zainab* magazine in the National Library that you can get your hands on and go from there?" she had inquired. "I think there you will find an important base, not the only one but one important one among many that is part of all the different paths that take one to Zainab . . ." She paused to see if I was following. I nodded. "That is a great suggestion. I look forward to following up on it, Fariba Khanum." Fariba gave me a deadline in return: "And if it is helpful, we can have another chat about where you go from there in about two months' time?"

"It would be very helpful, if I could trouble you!" rolled out of my mouth in excitement! I tried to check myself with "Thank you for taking the time, Fariba Khanum." Fariba laughed.

"Very well then, Emrah *jaan*. This is very exciting!" She meant it too. Fariba had an unmatched generosity. "Some more cinnamon tea?" she then asked. Rhetorically. She knew I was a bit *bitaroof*—without courtesy.

ONE

Zainab's Traffic

SPATIAL LIVES OF AN ISLAMIC RITUAL
ACROSS SOUTHWEST ASIA

BEFORE SYRIA WAS SHATTERED by the current conflict, tour buses of Iranian pilgrims heading to the Sayyida Zainab shrine near Damascus would stop in Gaziantep at the Iranian Bazaar. Once the buses parked, the distinct smells of Iranian rice and stew (*khoresh*) from the pilgrims' mobile stoves would reach the bazaar a block away.[1] Merchants then knew to expect pilgrims' arrival within twenty minutes at the bazaar, where they would shop for appliances, lingerie, and textiles. On one such day in 2011, I sat in Metin's store with Mona, a Tehrani woman in her late thirties and a film editor for a state broadcaster. I was acting as an apprentice and teaching Metin's sixteen-year-old son—when business was slow—how to read and write Persian.

Metin's store carried small appliances, but when Mona entered she was discussing with her friend how and where to find a corset of Syrian design for a newlywed friend. Metin, a seasoned merchant in the bazaar, pointed Mona and her friend to the Ataturk Arcade across the street, telling them to ask for Osman and Yaşar. As was often the case during my apprenticeship and interviews at the bazaar, Iranian pilgrims were surprised to hear a merchant speaking Persian in Gaziantep. Metin and I had discussed this very point that afternoon, so I realized he was going to bring Mona into the debate over the religious virtues of a route of *ziyarat* (saint visitation, minor pilgrimage to the tomb of a holy person) if its travelers were so enmeshed in trade. Metin asserted, "The [Hanafi] doctrine has it, *hajj* remains the singular pilgrimage in Islam."[2] When he attempted to brush aside *ziyarat*'s religious value because women buy things en route, Mona replied: "Why do you want my belief [*iman*] to account for lingerie? Does Christianity account for women's use of undergarments? Or men's use of underwear, for that matter? You buy your Zamzam [water] and prayer beads.[3] Another one buys pans and lingerie. To me, if there are bazaars around *ziyarat,* it means *ziyarat* is alive and well. Antep merchants are alive and well. Everyone makes what they want to make of *ziyarat* in their spiritual world [*donya-ye ma'navi*]."

Mona, like many pilgrim women, saw no ethical incongruity between embarking on the visiting Zainab and buying lingerie. In fact, there was even congruence. If what compelled some of these Iranian women to go on *ziyarat* involved seeking saintly intercession to achieve marital happiness and sexual satisfaction—themes prevalent in my follow-up interviews in Tabriz, Tehran, and Khoy, Iran, between 2012 and 2018—then it would be understandable to summon other material means of working toward that goal as well—say, Syrian lingerie for a wedding night or anniversary. Rather than viewing religious modesty as contrary to the consumption of lingerie, Iranian pilgrims like Mona considered the mixing of sacred and profane along the route as the socially generative engine behind religious rituals like *ziyarat.*[4] To put it differently, *ziyarat*'s possibility of bringing ritual to bear on the pilgrims' immediate material needs and desires was precisely what attracted so many Iranians to the paths of Zainab and helped generate the route's religious value.[5]

In addition to my apprenticeship at the Gaziantep bazaar, in June 2010 and again in August 2011, I embarked twice on the eight-hundred-mile journey—commonly known in Persian, alongside visitation sites within Iran like Jamkaran, as a *hajj-i fuqara'* (pilgrimage of the poor). This particular *hajj-i fuqara'* begins in Iran, where pilgrims board chartered or regular-line buses across the country, then pass through Turkey before reaching their main destination outside Damascus—the shrine devoted to Sayyida Zainab—often coupling the veneration of the saint with a visit to the mosque dedicated to Sayyida Ruqayya in Damascus proper or a side trip to Beirut, Lebanon.[6] On the bus, I observed the practice of *ziyarat* as a generative sphere of political and socioeconomic negotiation, or what Pierre Bourdieu has called "regulated improvisation," rather than the disciplinary reiteration of a discursive tradition.[7]

Instead of relying on the trope of exchange—giving and receiving reciprocally in a bilateral transaction, as with the offerings of a pilgrim for the blessings of the saint, this chapter develops traffic as a more suitable trope of analysis for the anthropological study of rituals of mobility like *ziyarat.* By *traffic,* I refer here to (1) vehicles, people, goods, and ideas physically moving across space and time; and (2) messages transmitted through a social communicative idiom, say that of religion. With its focus on social actors and vehicles, traffic as analytic helps us think across the mobility/immobility divide more precisely in terms of the varied "force, speed, rhythm, route, experience and friction" of mobility.[8] Taking these lessons learned from exacting studies of mobility and extending them into the anthropological study of rituals like saint visitation helps fine-tune traffic into an analytic and a method for multisited, multitemporal, multilingual, and "multiscalar" ethnography.[9] Such an ethnography of a moving object like saint visitation in turn reintroduces into the anthropology of Islam a conceptualization of ritual that is, like traffic, spatially and materially improvised across contingent divides of gender, class, and genealogy.

My argument is that the ways of Zainab could be productively understood as a triple traffic: (1) a traffic over space, as one traverses Iran, Turkey and Syria; (2) a traffic across time, mobilizing different pasts in framing Zainab's *ziyarat*; and (3) a categorical traffic in value, deeply conditioned by the first two, and in pilgrims' regulated improvisations, traversing the conceptual borders of religion, economy, and polity. My contention is that such a spatial approach produces a dynamic and social conception of ritual, whereby ritual can be understood as generative rather than merely reiterative of religious traditions.

Here I build on a long genealogy of feminist anthropological scholarship on Islamic rituals, including saint visitation, that has productively deployed gender as an analytical category and show how Islamic ritual engenders religious dispositions differently for biological men and women; however, rather than reiterate that line of argument in how Islamic ritual mobilizes gendered selves differently, I follow Mona's lead in her exchange with Metin and focus on the flip side of this relationship—how women's gendered selves mobilize an Islamic ritual differently (from cis-gendered men) to lay claim to transnational mobility in a time and place characterized by many as gripped by a "poverty of mobility."

VEHICLES OF TRAFFIC: SOCIALITY OF RITUAL AT THE JUNCTIONS OF THE MIDDLE EAST

After the tour guide announced over the microphone my pending presence on the bus for research and asked the twelve passengers for their permission, I boarded in Tehran to begin the journey to the Sayyida Zainab shrine in mid-July 2011. The first few hours were spent explaining myself to some pilgrims who were content to be interviewed by me to alleviate the trip's monotony. By the time we pulled out of Tabriz, the bus was almost full with thirty-six passengers. About two-thirds were women, mostly in groups of three or more. Just ten hours into the journey, the foods that had been prepared for the road were starting to make rounds. I was caught in the middle of a conversation among five women of the same extended family, as one offered me a *kuku sabzi* (Persian frittata).

I conducted the first such interview with the Razavi family members, including the newlywed Nargis. Nargis had undergone three months of testing with various invasive biopsies and had undertaken numerous trips to local *imamzadeh* (tombs of persons with Prophetic lineage) in Tehran and to a *du'anevis* (prayer writer) in Qazvin specializing in fertility. She had come close to convincing her mother-in-law, Maryam Khanum, that she was not responsible for this "drought" (*buhran*)—as Maryam Khanum described her son's four years of marriage without a child. Maryam Khanum asked Nargis to do one last thing to settle the account once and for all: a *ziyarat* to Syria to venerate Sayyida Zainab and ask Sayyida Ruqayya for help in conceiving. So Nargis wanted to collect the saint's *baraka* (blessings).

Nargis's story, the first to be shared with me on the bus, exemplifies the possibilities of making *ziyarat* one's own. *Ziyarat* might initially seem like an amalgam of contradictory practices because of its assemblage of actors, goods, and physical spaces. From the vantage point of its traffic, however, its contradictory practices can be seen as diverse tactics for bridging the gap between script and social action in religious practice. This is not to say that Nargis and others on the buses could imbue their journey with any value they liked or make a plea to the saint for any wish at all; rather, it is in the pilgrims and their concrete practices, and not in jurisprudential debate about *ziyarat,* that we can identify, spatially and temporally, how that bridging works. The bus was the primary vehicle for pilgrims' improvisational acts to effect that bridging across shrines, bazaars, and borders in saint visitation.

With sweets making the rounds, the conversation got lighter, and topics shifted from the personal to the journey itself, particularly the figure that the shrine venerates: Hazrat-i Zainab. While pilgrims from different walks of life in Iran explained to me how Hazrat-i Zainab was a source of inspiration (*ilham*) for all Muslims, few could explain why most Sunnis venerated her less frequently, if at all. The regionally contested genealogy of the very figure that the shrine venerates was not pertinent to the pilgrims; instead, they repeatedly explained the popularization of the route in relation to the Cultural Revolution. For instance, Maryam Khanum recounted how one of the most-read women's magazines of Iran, like *Banuvan* (Women),[10] had been shut down in 1979, then relaunched in 1981 as *Rah-i Zainab* (Path of Zainab). Self-described as the venue for an unapologetically Islamic and anti-imperialist stance for the empowerment of women, *Rah-i Zainab* was one of the many forms through which the figure of Zainab was imbued with new revolutionary rigor shortly after the Islamic Revolution in the heat of the Iran-Iraq War. This emblematization of Zainab helped motivate many Iranians to venerate her in person in Syria. In other words, *Path of Zainab* refers both to the discursive path of the magazine following Zainab as an emblem of Islamic and revolutionary womanhood and to her literal physical travel from Karbala to Damascus. The magazine featured many serialized articles, often translated from Arabic, that reworked the Karbala narrative for the revolutionary circumstances of Iran and heralded Zainab as a skilled orator speaking truth to power in the face of the injustice inflicted on Imam Hussein and his kin. Further, and perhaps most importantly, they highlighted Zainab's role in protecting the surviving members of the Ahl al-Bayt genealogy and ensuring the perpetuation of the imamate as an institution.[11]

As Maryam Khanum's best friend and travel companion, Negar Khanum, attested, murals, posters, and other artworks during the Cultural Revolution featured Zainab, rendering her a pervasive public figure. She added, "The female morality police officers were called Khahar-i Zainab [Zainab's sisters]." In etching Zainab into the Iranian social landscape during the Cultural Revolution, no one has done more work than the painter Nasser Palangi, according to Maryam and Negar. Remembering how they first took an interest in attending Islamist feminist student group meetings and making their way into the streets, Maryam Khanum remarked that they or someone they knew always carried a poster of Sayyida Zainab—sketched for the journal by Palangi.[12]

When I visited Maryam Khanum at her house in Tehran, she shared her collection of newspaper clippings, political protest banners, and posters from those days. The poster that featured Zainab carrying ammunition to the war front, she said, still gives her the chills. "It was tough days, and seeing a strong woman figure we already knew from the Karbala narrative indeed touched people, when it often felt as if Iranians were all alone against all odds," she recounted. Zainab's story often legitimized the participation of young women in the revolution.[13] Moreover, political figures in the new revolutionary order actively promoted Iranian women's emulation of Zainab by undertaking visitation to her shrine near Damascus in publications like *Rah-i*

FIGURE 1. Article titled "Zainab, the Hero of Karbala," with a Nasser Palangi stencil, *Rah-i Zainab* magazine, 1984.

Zainab. The freshly appointed Supreme Leader Imam Khomeini himself, in one such article, detailed the virtues of women visiting Zainab and drawing inspiration from that visitation to emulate her.

Although such emblematization contributed to Zainab's popularity in Iran, it was the state's direct funding of visitation that broke ground in terms of pilgrimage numbers: the Bonyad-e Shadeed, the Martyrs' Foundation's voucher program. According to the older of the two trustee heirs of the Sayyida Zainab shrine *waqf*, Sayyid Dr. Hani Murtada, it was in no small part thanks to this program that from 1984 onwards the number of Iranians visiting Sayyida Zainab got a boost: around one thousand Iranian pilgrims, primarily widows of war, embarking on the paths of Zainab each week.[14] While the emblematization of Zainab and state-level encouragement of her visitation particularly during and after the Iran-Iraq War was unprecedented, the discussion of *ziyarat* and women's sexuality was already prevalent in Iranian literature and scholarship on the ritual of explorations and encounters. In Sadegh Hedayat's short story "Alaviyeh Khanum" (1943), for example, the protagonist's sexual encounters with a bus driver in Mashhad are often mobilized as windows into the superficial nature of her piety, suggestive of how the public performance of devotion and religiosity assumed in *ziyarat* is just an excuse for existential wanderlust and repressed desire.[15] 'Ali Shari'ati's *Fatima Is Fatima* (1971), on the other hand, portrays women undertaking *ziyarat* in Iran in stark contrast to oversexualized women of Iran's secular middle class. Despite the differences between the two narratives, both assume that *ziyarat* and sex are mutually exclusive. But if Mona's statement or Nargis's sought-after remedy serve as any indication, Iranian women did not see *ziyarat* and sexuality as mutually exclusive realms of social action. Sexuality and religion most explicitly intersected around questions of marriage as a social institution. Pilgrims of Sayyida Zainab almost always approach the saint with wishes (*hajat*) pertaining to this social institution and their role in it, whether they are hoping to find a suitable husband, save a rocky marriage, or conceive a baby.

THE DESTINATION OR THE JOURNEY?

Throughout my research, I encountered as many reasons for undertaking *ziyarat* as the number of pilgrims themselves. That said, finding a remedy (*shifa*) to a lingering malady, or *dard,* through saintly intercession often lay at the heart of pilgrims' commitment to taking the journey, however they might have defined that *dard*.[16] For example, when I asked Nafiseh—a twenty-eight-year-old teacher from Tabriz seeking Hazrat-i Zainab's help in conceiving a child—what *ziyarat* meant to her, she explained, "*Ziyarat* has to do with paying a visit. To your elders and ancestors. Cherishing someone. I pay visits to family and friends as well as saints. And I enjoy traveling to receive the answers to my questions, hopes, and wishes from elders. Considering a saint as part of your own pedigree underpins the wishes, as if they are those of a child directed to a paternal figure, one that is not God." Nafiseh elaborated further, "If God finds that my wish is not virtuous, in that it doesn't have a good outcome, then it will not be granted. When God finds my wish to be virtuous, he will make sure it will be obtained." Switching from Persian to Azeri, as if to impress upon me, the "Istanbuli" anthropologist, the logic of saintly intercession and its felicity as a reflection of God, Nafiseh said: "I should then not be discontent with any malady [dard]. If it is God that gives me the malady, God too will show me the way to its remedy [darman]." As Nafiseh made clear, seeking saintly intercession was not simply an opportunistic co-option of religious discourse for material ends that confused the mediating saint for the singular object of worship in Islam, God. Though pilgrims might very well go on ziyarat motivated by a concrete wish, the fulfillment of that wish was understood to depend on whether God found it to be virtuous and timely—and hence squarely an internal good of the same religious practice. The broader process of visitation indeed was framed as a way of connecting with God via the assistance of the saint, rather than worshipping the saint herself, as some literalist interpretations within Salafi schools of jurisprudence had constructed and condemned saint visitation in Islam. To Nafiseh, it was the ultimate faith in God's supreme power of judgment that the process of seeking saintly intercession affirmed.

Throughout these visitation trips, pilgrims anticipated their encounter with the saint and prepared for it. On the bus, they reviewed ziyarat guides, which contain guidelines for proper conduct in the shrine (maqam in Arabic) and precise supplications to be recited for each wish, which they memorized. In one such supplication, Sayyida Zainab speaks directly to the Prophet about the injustices perpetuated in Karbala.

When, following the circulation of sweets, Nargis's sister-in-law, Fereshteh, announced that she would be reciting her supplications, the group dropped the conversation about the exchange rate between the Iranian rial and Turkish lira amid sanctions imposed on Iran and began a collective recitation of all the supplications in a guidebook she had picked up in Tabriz. The shift in the pilgrims' mood with the start of the recitation of rowzah texts, or less frequently ta'ziyeh excerpts, was palpable.[17] For pilgrims, the suspension of their excitement over the journey and its shopping opportunities, in these rather brief episodes of religious practice, not only gave solemn recognition to the hardships that Zainab had to endure but also drew similarities to the difficulties that they would face if their wishes were not granted. Some in the group would gently drum on their chests and shout the name of the saint whenever it was mentioned. As Kabir Tambar has argued in the case of Alevi ritual practices in Turkey—listening to sermons, wailing, weeping, and praising—the rituals produce rather than simply externalize, generate rather than reiterate, an embodied appreciation for the saint.[18] In other words, they do not simply repeat an already-formed religious conviction about virtue; they provide the conditions of possibility for such religious convictions to emerge from the improvised practice itself. It is precisely through suspending or improvising with the proper conduct of *ziyarat*—as outlined in guidebooks, collected through hearsay, or emulated in collective practices—that the Iranian pilgrims find their connection to God via the saint. Most pilgrims I interviewed positioned the shrine as a gate (*bab/dar*) or threshold (*astaneh*) that allowed them to forge, with the saint's assistance, their connection to God.

From the very moment one walks into the shrine, as Fereshteh recounted in a follow-up interview, "a sense of serenity and peace takes over [one's] body." Passing the entry, some women and men touch or kiss the door to show respect, collect the blessings from the saint, and become closer to God.[19] Others recount the moment pilgrims take turns touching the *zarih*, the gold-covered brass that encapsulates the saint's tomb, and chant supplications over it. Some kiss the *zarih*, pressing their faces against the brasswork. Still others, who have written their wishes on paper money, throw them into the tomb, hoping their voluntary donation, *sadaqa,* will return to them in the form of saintly blessings, *baraka.*

Outside the shrine, most pilgrims continue their Bourdieusian "regulated improvisations." In the courtyard, some listen to recordings of *ta'ziyeh* recitations or pay one of the people who will recite the desired sections of the Qur'an for a small fee.[20] Beyond the courtyard, groups of pilgrims eat and drink tea. Some women with portable propane ovens make *halva*—the dessert typically distributed to fulfill vows or venerate those who have passed during times of mourning.

While theological and political debates about the motives of pilgrims and the virtues of *ziyarat* continue unabated, for the pilgrims themselves, finding a remedy for their malady through saintly intercession is paramount. Farideh, a thirty-two-year-old textile worker from Tehran, was on her second *ziyarat* when we met in the summer of 2011. Three years after her first visit, she was returning to thank Sayyida Zainab for helping her find an appropriate suitor.

To give thanks, she had arranged for the sacrifice of a lamb in the shrine town and donated the skin to a Shiʿi seminary there and the meat to locals—primarily Iraqi and Palestinian refugees at the time. After paying a visit to Zainab, on this second trip Farideh wanted to visit Hazrat-i Ruqayya in the mosque dedicated to her in Damascus, known as an efficacious site for couples hoping to conceive. She explained: "For the past three years, we have tried everything. The past year I spent shuttling from one doctor's office to another," Farideh paused, and confided, "I even prepared special aphrodisiacs following a few homeopathy recipes that I copied from another friend. Thinking that there was some sort of curse on our marriage, my husband and I even got a *duʿanevis* [a prayer writer] famed for his ability to undo curses that might affect fertility of either or both partners." Farideh elaborated on their multipronged plan for becoming parents: "After the doctors and occult specialists all failed in finding a remedy [*darman*] for my malady [*dard*], I set out for Damascus again. It was, after all, Sayyida Zainab who had found the time appropriate for me to get married and to someone I chose. This time I hope that Sayyida Ruqayya will help us complete our family."

While the visitors of Zainab undertook the intersubjective and religious work of mitigating the problems they were facing through saintly intercession, their spatial movements generated a larger traffic that brought them into charged encounters not only with the saint but also with bazaar merchants and border officers. In this landscape of *extrareligious* traffic, Iranian pilgrims' patterns of veneration and visitation reflect an awareness of their political embeddedness within larger structures of state authority, a recognition of the creative gap between the scripture and the practice of religion, and a sense of their agency in bridging that gap in social action. With the traffic in Zainab, we observe both creatively improvised invocations of Islamic traditions of pilgrimage and visitation and claims to transnational mobility that belie a sharp distinction between religion and other realms of social life in an Iran characterized by diminished possibilities for mobility.

"POVERTY OF MOBILITY"

When I arrived at the bazaar in Gaziantep built to serve pilgrims en route to Damascus, I introduced myself to a group of merchants there as an anthropologist studying the *hajj-i fuqara'* route. The most seasoned among them, Metin, ushered me into his store full of toasters, blenders, electric tea brewers, and other commodities popular with the Iranian pilgrims. He said he would happily help with my research in Gaziantep on one condition. "Let us get something straight," Metin said. Pointing to the sugar cube next to his thin-waisted glass, he asked me, "Do you know where these come from? Damascus. On the same buses ... The ones that carry your so-called poor pilgrims [*fukara hacilar*]. They have money for *Tefal* pans, they look for Paşabahçe glassware. Who are the *fukara*? They or we?" After these rhetorical questions, Metin concluded, "There are no *pilgrims milgrims* [*hacı macı*] in those buses. I do not interfere in anyone's belief, but there is one *hajj* in Islam—and that is to Mecca. These people are visitors [*zuwwar*]. They are what we call in Turkish 'tourists of belief' [*inanç turisti*]. They are undertaking saint visitation [*ziyarat*]. As they themselves say, it is both visitation and trade: *ham ziyarat ham tijarat*. I might benefit from their travels as a merchant, and I am no imam, but I know that since the time of Abdelhamid II, since Ottoman times, the Iranian state has supported *ziyarat* to expand its territory. [Back then] they were in Iraq. Now they are onto Syria."

Metin knew all too well that these Iranian "tourists of belief" might not feel the need to evaluate the visitation of Sayyida Zainab against the yardstick of *hajj* to Mecca. If such a hierarchy must be asserted, he also knew, some other *zuwwar* might agree with him. Yet the prevalence of Metin's views among the merchants, and the sectarianizing undertones of those views, show how this contestation does more than assert Sunni ritual minimalism as an index of sophistication and purity over the Shiʿi. Metin also makes claims about the historicity of Iranian *ziyarat* to Syria as a function of interstate territorial rivalry, reframing the contemporary practice of Iranian veneration of Sayyida Zainab as a reiteration of Iranian "missionizing" in Hamidian Iraq. While he charts a regionally networked geography of *ziyarat*, he populates that geography's routes with commodities that move along pilgrims. The mutual imbrication of contraband goods that travel along pilgrims in the same buses, in Metin's setup, calls into question the religious value of *ziyarat*.

The pilgrims, however, begged to differ: they asserted that they were deprived not of money but of movement. That is why, as mentioned earlier, my interlocutor Mona reframed the terms of the debate over the religious value of *ziyarat* in her exchange with Metin as a historical and geographical traffic. Upon our second meeting in Tehran, Mona shared the experiences of her aunt, Nour Khanum, in the Sayyida Zainab shrine as another example of spatial restrictions on Iranian pilgrims. When Nour Khanum wanted to perform her daily prayers (*namaz*), guards redirected her to a separate prayer room adjacent to the zone that hosted the saint's tomb. Mona's aunt resisted and continued her *namaz,* arguing that it was a common Shiʿi practice. The guards retorted that they were Shiʿi too and that she was not the first *ajam* (Iranian) pilgrim to enter. Nour Khanum reiterated that a Shiʿi should not stop another Shiʿi from praying anywhere. In protest, she went with the other women to hold their *namaz* next to the burial place of Dr. ʿAli Shariʿati, a towering intellectual of the revolutionary period in Iran, who had himself written extensively on *ziyarat* and on Hazrat-i Zainab, and who was by his wish buried in the shrine's cemetery. "From the grounds of Karbala to those of Samarra, to Sayyida Zainab and Sayyida Ruqayya, it makes no difference," Mona concluded. "The fear of the righteous Iranians is what we encounter. The Sunnis, the Shiʿa, and even Christians, everyone comes to visit, but they ban our practice of *namaz* in the presence of Zainab. That is unjust. We, Iranians, we are *fuqare-ye harakat* [deprived of mobility]."

It is possible to frame the link that pilgrims themselves are drawing between restrictions on Shiʿi ritual and restrictions on Iranian mobility as one that builds up a Turnerian (Shiʿi) *communitas* through the practice of saint veneration.[21] This framing presents the Iranian pilgrims on their way to Sayyida Zainab as people who are deprived of the *hajj* to Mecca—as Metin has done, for instance. Here I want to take Nour Khanum's play on the moniker for the visitation of Hazrat-i Zainab seriously and think about the connections between the restrictions placed on Iranians' mobility in conjunction with *ziyarat* and the historical and spatial production of these routes. Particularly the post-1979 restrictions, including a singularly sustained and intensified regime of sanctions placed on the country's entire population by targeting its national currency,[22] are as much a part of the *ziyarat* geographies described here as the manuals for conduct in the presence of Hazrat-i Zainab. I find such an interpretive turn away from the Karbala paradigm productive in that it centers our analysis on not only among whom but also against whom Shiʿi *communitas* comes to be defined and how those definitions inevitably implicate those who have restricted Iranians' mobility on political grounds. This interarticulation of religion with politics and economics in turn supports my broader argument about the inseparability of religion from other forms of value and meaning in pilgrimage as ritual traffic—a ritual of temporal as well as spatial movement shuttled in buses between Iran and Syria via Turkey, and since 2019 via Iraq.

Throughout my observations along the road to Hazrat-i Zainab, I came to conceive of the practice of *ziyarat* as a generative sphere of political and socio-economic improvisation—though there are regulations and limits on such improvisation. Here the interplay between the internal and external goods of a tradition à la MacIntyre[23]—and specifically the possibilities of moving across the putatively separate realms of economy, polity, and religion itself—are the constitutive elements of *ziyarat* as a widely observed religious practice.

The *extrareligious* sociality of ritual practice—the iceberg and not its tip— begs for a reconceptualization of religious ritual at the center of anthropological analysis. If we, as anthropologists, no longer symbolically or ethically overdetermine pilgrims' exchanging supplications for the blessings of the saint to explain away saint visitation, then we must develop the necessary analytical tools to engage with the multiplicity of actions that take place both before and after that ritual exchange.[24] The *ritual traffic* generated by pilgrims from Iran (as well as by bazaar merchants from Gaziantep and shrine heirs hailing from Damascus) offers us a productive analytic to examine *ziyarat* as an Islamic ritual. When we approach ritual through the trope of traffic rather than exchange, ritual emerges as a socially negotiated and historically grounded practice that thrives on, rather than exposes, conversion across internal and external goods of religion, and across the analytically supposed realms of religion, economy, and polity.

The stories I recount here that speak to the gendered and gendering mobilizations of saintly intercession are irreducible to opportunistic co-options of religious discourse for material ends that, as the scripturalist jurisprudential scholars would maintain, confuse the mediating saint for the object of worship. While visitors of Hazrat-i Zainab are motivated to go on *ziyarat* by a concrete wish, the fulfillment of that wish depends on whether God finds it to be virtuous and timely.

In Iranian pilgrims' mobility across Iraq and the Levant, we observe these creatively improvised invocations of visitations in forging gendered connections to a female saint, requesting resolve in the face of the very gendered (im)possibilities of mobility that the majority of Iranian pilgrims face *as women*. Questions of marriage prospects, fertility, and sex life—in other words, the sexing of family, community and genealogy, kin and kindred— come to the fore in these creative improvisations. Minoo Moallem convincingly showed how the emblematization of Zainab as revolutionary womanhood shortly after the 1979 Revolution in Iran unexpectedly offered considerable space to women who otherwise would have been denied the opportunity to participate in political mobilization.[25] On a regional scale and with a pilgrimage route to venerate the same figure, Zainab's *ziyarat* had similarly unintended spatial consequences on a regional scale. And it is those spatial lives of Zainab's visitation that I hope to have captured here with the analytical trope of traffic in this chapter. The politically disembedded ethical subject premised in the anthropology of piety misses the complex spatial and discursive traffic that the route has generated, and how pilgrims cultivate themselves not only ethically but also *socially and politically* in that traffic.[26] In stark contrast to inward-looking subjects invested exclusively in ethical cultivation, pilgrims on the paths of Zainab chart out a far less static, more dialogical relationship between political, religious, and economic realms of social life.

If, as Gayle Rubin maintains, a woman "only becomes a domestic, a wife, a chattel, a playboy bunny, a prostitute, or a human dictaphone in certain relations," and "torn from these relationships, she is no more the helpmate of man than gold in itself is money," traffic repurposed for the study of Islamic ritual gives us new analytical purchase on the precise junctions of those relations. Ritual traffic, as opposed to ritual exchange, shows that the movement across those subject positions is central to the spatial life of saint visitation and its attendant process of subjectivation for Iranian visitors traveling the paths of Zainab. In Zainab's traffic the visitors become and unbecome mothers, wives, war widows, playboy bunnies, or feminist genealogists. Torn from these relations, themselves forged by spatial, temporal, and categorical movements, they are no more ethically overdetermined Muslims than crypto in itself is money.

Parastoo's Pathways and
Observant Participation

PARASTOO AND I SAT across the aisle from each other on my first bus ride from Arjantin Square in Tehran to Sayyida Zainab outside Damascus. She was my curious neighbor. I was a novice student of *ziyarat*, and she was, as it turned out, a seasoned observer of academics, an anthropologist of the anthropologists. She was a terrifying interviewee who had already observed the observer and was keen to participate in the ethnographic encounter. I tried to begin, as I was self-taught in ethnographic methods, with a broad and open-ended prompt: "Why are you on the road to Zainab, Khanum-e Parastoo?" Parastoo registered the question and paused. An answer formed in her eyes, but another thought seemed to intervene. She looked up with a mischievous smile in her expressive eyebrows and counterquestioned: "Agha-ye Setare, in these interviews that you speak of, are the interviewees also allowed to pose questions?" At the time, Parastoo's playful Persianization of my name and her use of the *agha* honorific in tones of innocent curiosity cloaked for me what was coming my way.

"Of course, you are free to ask any questions about the research, the institutions, the funding, you name it," I responded.

"Can I start with mine, then?" she asked. That one turned out to be rhetorical. "Agha-ye Setare, do you have a boyfriend or husband? Are you in love?" I was stunned. Parastoo, on the other hand, didn't skip a beat. That was not her point, but merely a transition to talking about her answer to my question. "I can see you are not, but you once were, weren't you? Think about it, why not ask Zainab for her help? I for one want a love marriage and not a business contract like what my older sister got. She is sitting down there." Parastoo motioned toward the front of the bus diagonal to me and sighed. She recovered quickly from another racing thought and returned to my question. "That is why I am on the road to Hazrat-i Zainab." Then came her question: "And you? What are you on the road for, Agha-ye Sitare, if not for love?"

Parastoo was curious—genuinely so. I was shocked to the core. Only eight hours into the journey, here I was, an older gay man talking to a younger straight woman about being in love, on a pilgrimage bus somewhere around the lake of Van, having recently crossed into Turkey from Iran. For a split second I thought maybe this was a good time to just get off the bus. Parastoo's glimmering eyes were still lingering on me for a sensible answer to a very legitimate question. "Hmm," I mustered. "I hadn't had such a specific wish in mind. Some help in writing about this *ziyarat* route from Iran to Syria via Turkey would be good," I added. Parastoo was not moved.

Nor did she appreciate such a generic answer when she had just poured her heart out. She had the speed and snark of a jaded twenty-three-year-old who was too smart for her own good. Over the course of our journey to the shrine, I was to find out multiple times that she was perfectly capable of entertaining herself in conversation. "You know, at least you will see all the beautiful *ayna-kari* [mirror-work] and the murals in the shrine, don't you think? You would like that, wouldn't you?"[1] Parastoo grinned at the keenness of her insinuation. "You must have been to other shrines in Iran, though, right?" Parastoo had just as strong convictions about architecture as about love: "I think that is one of the most beautiful elements of Persian architecture. *Ayna-kari* that reflects and refracts light emanating from chandeliers, turning ceilings and columns into streams of infinitude and openness. Wouldn't you agree?" Parastoo looked up, smiling. "Agha-ye Setare, without conversation and company [*sohbat-o-mohabbat*] the road won't get shorter!" As I would find out soon enough, she was right on both accounts.

Parastoo would describe her experience to me in Tehran in a follow-up interview three years later. "I realize that sounds perhaps superstitious [*kho-rafati*] to your ears, but there is no other way to describe it. When we parked I knew . . . Like I felt the heat, not in my hand, but inside my body, close to my heart and belly, when I touched that intricate brasswork around the saint's resting place. That is why," Parastoo continued, "I thought that my wish for true love in marriage was suitable and timely, and that the saint found it suitable. Look at me now with Umid!" She was right on both accounts again. "Once it becomes safe again to travel," Parastoo daydreamed, "I want to take Umid to Sayyida Zainab too. After all, she has blessed me with this love and this marriage, and she is part of this family. On his ever-postponed holiday from the oil company he works for in Bandar Abbas, of course. Next opportunity we get, I think we will go on the road to Zainab again."

Parastoo continued, "I still remember that heat of the brass, whether it was from Zainab or from the hands of others who have reached out to her and touched the brass cage too, or more likely a mixture of both, I did not know. And I did not care. For me at that moment, there was such a comforting heat from being in the saint's presence and touching the cage that I burst into tears. An older Iranian woman standing behind me touched my shoulder gently and looked into my eyes smilingly. I tried to smile back. To help my catharsis, she went on to rub my back gently like my grandmother used to do. She said with a Shirazi accent, 'Now, don't forget to make a wish and throw some money in the cage.' I nodded and did as she said.

"Zainab gave me hope [*umid*]." Parastoo smiled, playing off of Umid's name in Persian.

TWO

Crafting Patronage

GENEALOGY AS TRAFFIC ACROSS GENERATIONS

"THAT PARKING LOT . . ." Doctor Hani Murtada paused. "Let us say it has a complicated story." Parastoo would have been delighted to hear that, I thought.

The parking lot was complicated not just in its history but in its sheer foot traffic as well. The anthropologist in me had assumed that the passengers, having finally reached their destination, would simply collect their suitcases, check into their hotels, and get some rest before visiting the shrine. But Parastoo, the anthropologist of anthropologists, smirked at me as she watched the bus attendant, Ali, try to tell me, in three different indirect ways, that he wouldn't be pulling the bags out until after pilgrims had completed their "first visits." Those first visits were happening "right now," he added with a shy smile. Parastoo, translated for me across the *taarof* (courtesy) divide: "He is saying you should go, make your *abdast* [ablutions], and visit the shrine to pay your respects with some supplications, or a few *rak'ah namaz* [cycles of prayer]!"

Confused, I protested. "But, he's not saying that at all!"

"It would be rude for him to tell you directly what this time slot is for, given that he is talking to an educated man, an anthropologist at that!" Parastoo hit back. I never had to be reminded what Iranian *taarof* was like, when my desires for directness were met with more indirectness because I was asking people to lose face.

Ali, with his almond-shaped eyes, looked up and blinked. A small laugh escaped his lips. His cheeks and ears quickly turned red.

"Very well, let us pay our first visit, then," I said. "Let me first find where I can refresh my *abdast*." Parastoo looked at me with some pity in her eyes. Then she spoke. "We will first need to get through the line." I turned my head to see the growing line of pilgrims, men and women, who looked as if they were getting ready to insert themselves into a very full subway car during rush hour. But this car would be sorting them into separate lines before they could enter the shrine's inner chamber under the golden dome.

I was thinking it, and of course, Parastoo already had it. "Isn't it funny that we are all squeezed in anticipation, like really close to one another, only to be sorted by gender?" I nodded and smiled. "I am actually pretty sure Hazrat-i Zainab would have disapproved!" Parastoo uttered. I smiled again but avoided any proclamations of my own. We were already thirty minutes into the wait in the mixed-gender crowd, and Parastoo was too bored and restless to entertain such a response. "Aghe-ye Sitare," she said—and it was that elevating intonation that announced an uncomfortable question just around the corner. Disarmingly, Parastoo asked it—"You know your *namaz* [daily prayers], right?"

"Yes, I know my *namaz*, Parastoo Khanum." I responded. And I thought my response was controlled, but she responded, "Okay, okay. I was just asking, you know. You had also said you understood *taarof.* And we saw how that turned out."

Emrah, you are not going to win this one, I thought to myself.

The line had moved about two meters. We were still between the parking lot and the shrine.

"Emrah, are you here?" The doctor asked. I came back to our interview from my memory of that interaction in the parking lot. "You seem preoccupied today, I must say." The doctor waited for an explanation, it seemed. "You are right, please accept my apologies," I responded. "So what I was saying about the parking lot—" The doctor redirected my wandering attention and explained.

The number of pilgrim buses had considerably burdened the infrastructure of Rawiya, a small village just outside Damascus that is home to the Sayyida Zainab shrine. With the transportation of Iranian pilgrims firmly in the hands of Damascene businessman Saib Nahhas and his company *TransTour,* the potential alleviation of this burden presented the shrine with a lucrative opportunity for generating more revenue. Through his connections to the Ba'th Party, Nahhas had made his fortune by imposing an effective monopoly over Iranian visitors' travel to Syria between the late 1980s and early 2000s. By 2005, travel firms working out of Iran had not only broken into Iran's transnational *ziyarat* market, they had taken it over. Nahhas refocused *TransTour*'s energies and routes from Lebanon and Jordan, getting more involved in the inevitable spatial transformation of the shrine town than ever before. Dr. Murtada had made a business agreement with Nahhas for the construction of a hotel and parking lot on *waqf* property, in which Nahhas had agreed, albeit unenthusiastically, to receive 15 percent of all revenue from the parking lot and half from the hotel in exchange for financing their construction.

The doctor continued with "[his] side of the story." It took three years for the doctor's accounting team to realize that Nahhas had found a way to receive 25 percent of the parking lot revenue: he had manipulated the in- and outflows of construction-related expenditures between the *waqf* and his company to make up the difference by tax evasion. When his accounting tricks became apparent to a state inspector, Nahhas paid off state functionaries tasked with the investigation so that the "misunderstanding" could be addressed privately. To add insult to injury, the doctor continued, Nahhas had managed to assume partial use rights to the land on which the hotel and parking lot were built. The doctor expressed fury when he recalled the Nahhas episode: "We should have known better, of course, but now everybody knows that Nahhas is an indecent, dishonest, and corrupt man. He is known as a thief in Damascus now—one who is overzealous enough to steal from a *waqf*! That is why the second parking lot is particularly important to us. And that is why this one we built on our own with our funds!" The second parking lot, next to the southern wing of the shrine complex, was completed after four months of construction in 2009. Right before the Syrian uprising turned into a full-fledged regional conflict, revenues from the lot and the informal booths that cater to its users generated around 2 million Syrian pounds (around $80,000 USD) a year up until 2012, when the Syrian pound under sanctions started its downward spiral.[1] Following the business deal with Nahhas that went south, the *waqf* was faced with loss of revenue as a result of dwindling visitors as well as landed property—both crucial to the sustenance of the religious charitable trust associated with the shrine.

Hani and Mahdi Murtada wanted to form an alliance with a Kuwaiti construction company to revive the stalled plans for the construction of two hotels. Because they wanted to reach out to "other segments of visitors," as Dr. Murtada put it, their proposal included a five-star establishment practically next to the shrine, overlooking its courtyard. A three-star hotel was allotted land behind the cemetery. However, the increasing political instability in Syria as well as the Kuwaiti company's shifting demands in the final phases of negotiating (including 30 percent of all profits, as opposed to the

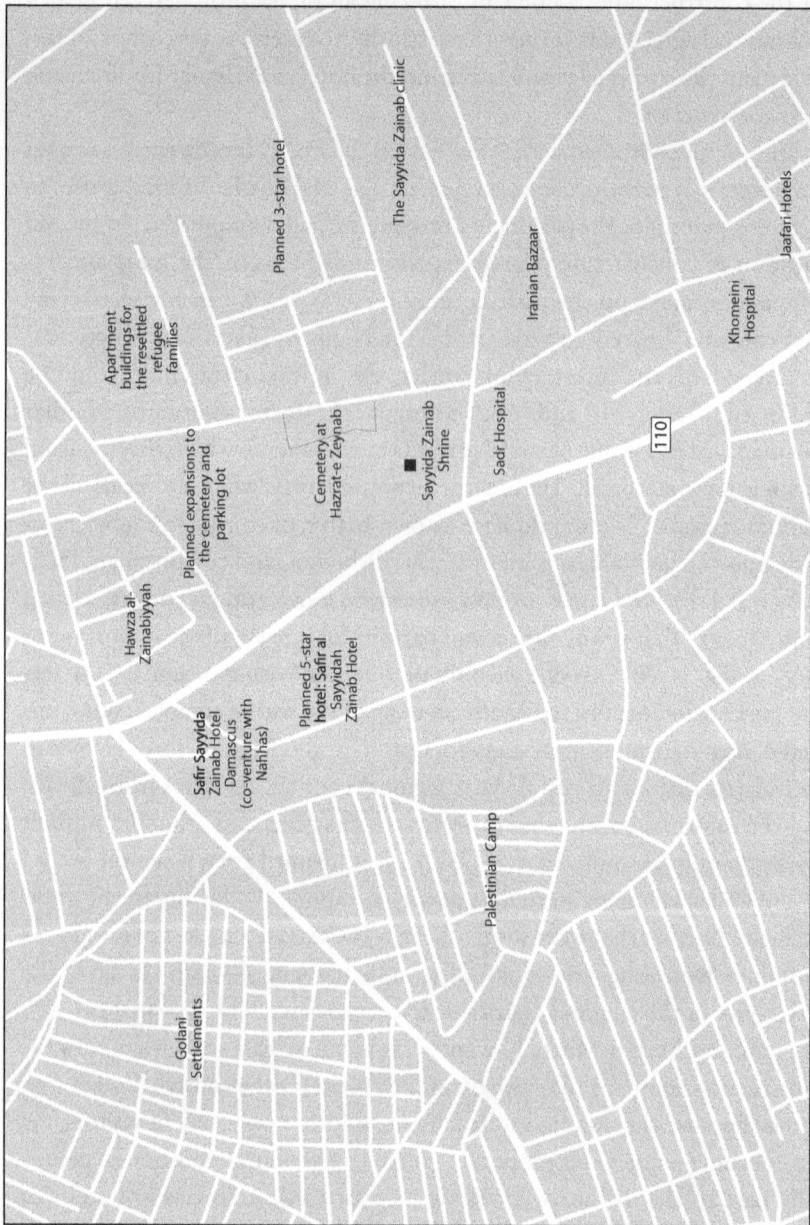

MAP 2. The Sayyida Zainab shrine in Sitt Zainab (by Bill Nelson).

original 15 percent) rendered the construction impossible. "Business. It is always complicated," the doctor explained and looked up. I nodded and kept quiet. What would Parastoo have thought of this complicated story? I could picture her pointing out how uncomplicated it all "actually" was. She would have, most likely after a sweeping monologue on how everything boils down to money, seamlessly segued into brighter, shinier subjects like the "warm" brasswork encasing Zainab's resting place, known as the cage (*qafas*), or the dome of a thousand mirrors.

The energy inside that dome, for a self-professing agnostic like myself, was jaw-dropping. I felt the heat burning in the bodies that revolved around the tomb. Some ran the tips of their fingers across the brasswork encasing Hazrat-i Zainab. Some, sitting cross-legged on the carpet, read to themselves from little supplication booklets.

The light refracted into millions of beams in the perfectly circular dome. The refractions themselves were the effect of the mirror inlays that filled the room with amplification—the Iranian art form known as *ayna-kari,* "mirrorwork." Whether it was the effect of the place itself, which some of the visitors took to be miraculous, or the effect of the architectural design, the heat and the light instantly transported me to a place of wonder. Maybe *wonder* was just a secular name for the religious miracle, but by the time I completed my first circumambulation inside the shrine, I was ecstatic.

Parastoo and I had followed the gender-segregated paths as we entered the main hall, so when we caught up with each other again I quickly shared my first impression: "The only element missing in there is the soil." With a small smile and a dimple in her cheek, Parastoo responded, "How about the tomb? Don't you think death, even the figure of a saint, represents the soil? That soil we all return to?" That energy had given me a brain fog. And with her usual incisiveness, Parastoo shone her light through that fog, generating a crystal-clear refraction—a refraction only the dome of a thousand mirrors could match.

The doctor, in a separate interview devoted to the shrine's expansion, had provided snapshots of the brasswork cage and the dome of a thousand mirrors. "It was a donation from a Pakistani businessman," the doctor shared matter-of-factly. The famed Iranian merchant of steel and iron Abu Qasim Hamadani had financed the intricate glasswork that coats the ceiling and tops the columns that hold the dome above the *qafas.* When the initial plans for construction were being revised in 1978 following preliminary approval from the Syrian state, Reza Pahlavi, then the shah of Persia, had pledged $3 million to finance the tiling of the shrine's facade. Shortly after the Iranian

FIGURE 2. Initial architectural sketch for the hotel and parking lot in the back, in *Al-Mawsem: A Quarterly Illustrated Magazine of Archaeology and Tradition,* edited and self-published by Mohammad Saeed Al-Touraihi, 1997.

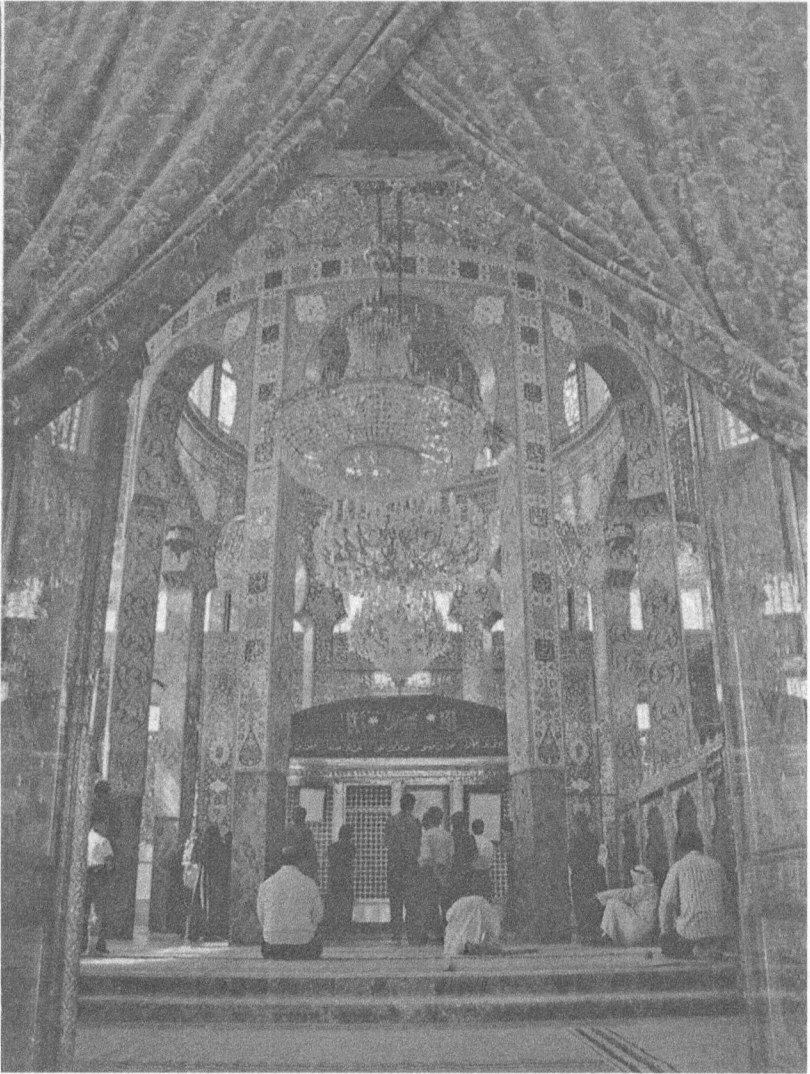

FIGURE 3. The saint's tomb and its *qafas* (cage) in the Sayyida Zainab shrine (photo by author, 2011).

Revolution, however, the incoming government reversed that decision, and the only funding ever to be pledged to the *waqf* by the Iranian state never reached the Sayyida Zainab shrine.

In conjunction with these movements of donations and capital, spatial construction, and architectural and aesthetic transformation, the organization of political power around the shrine shifted from prophetic patriliny toward patronage relations with donors and businessmen. In what follows, I chronicle how the Murtadas choreographed the transnational career of the Sayyida Zainab shrine. We will see how, in the process, they transformed their patrimony into landed property tied to the only administratively independent *waqf dhurri* (private or family religious endowment) of Syria. The shrine of Sayyida Zainab and the town built around it sit precariously at the intersection of patriliny, patrimony, and patronage.

Let us begin by tracing the transnational career of the *waqf dhurri,* the private (family) religious charitable trust, associated with the shrine. In drawing out the *waqf*'s involvement in a portfolio of real estate development and service industry projects, ranging from a clinic to a cemetery, I show how the Murtada family negotiated notions of patrimony and patriliny into a regime of patronage by forging co-ventures and an economy of donations to fund the shrine's spatial transformation. Then I turn to the broader spatial and demographic transformation of Rawiya to contextualize the transformation of the shrine town, which remained a village well into the 1960s but then grew rapidly into a bustling shrine town by the late '90s.

THE TRANSNATIONAL CAREER OF A *WAQF DHURRI*: MERCHANTS' DONATIONS FROM WEST AFRICA TO SOUTH ASIA (1950–2016)

"First came the Lebanese, particularly merchants who made their fortunes in western Africa. We're talking the 1950s through the mid-'60s." The doctor paused for a second and then continued. "Then the Iraqis took over, from the late '60s into the mid-'70s, when their economic conditions were excellent. It was only after the 1979 Revolution that they got overtaken by Iranians. And unlike the Lebanese or the Iraqis, who primarily wanted to donate to the shrine, the Iranians set up their own seminaries and channeled all donations to those institutions." The doctor wanted to bring up a "a conventional misconception" that many, including some scholars of Sayyida Zainab, held concerning the relationship between the Iranian state and the Sayyida Zainab shrine: "It is absolutely wrong, therefore, to say that expansion of the shrine was funded by the Iranian state. We accepted donations from individual Iranians, mostly wealthy merchants, but never from the state itself. It was the donations and our own assets that made construction of the shrine possible."

FIGURE 4. The shrine circa 1975, in *Al-Mawsem: A Quarterly Illustrated Magazine of Archaeology and Tradition,* edited and self-published by Mohammad Saeed Al-Touraihi, 1997.

FIGURE 5. The shrine circa the early 2000s, in *Al-Mawsem: A Quarterly Illustrated Magazine of Archeology and Tradition,* edited and self-published by Mohammad Saeed Al-Touraihi, 1997.

Given the misconception of the shrine as the primary site that lends legitimacy to an Iranian incursion into the country and the broader Levant, Dr. Murtada's emphasis on individual donations as the primary source of funding for construction merits a closer look. The impressive golden dome (see figure 5) illustrates the disjuncture between the conspiracy theories around the finances

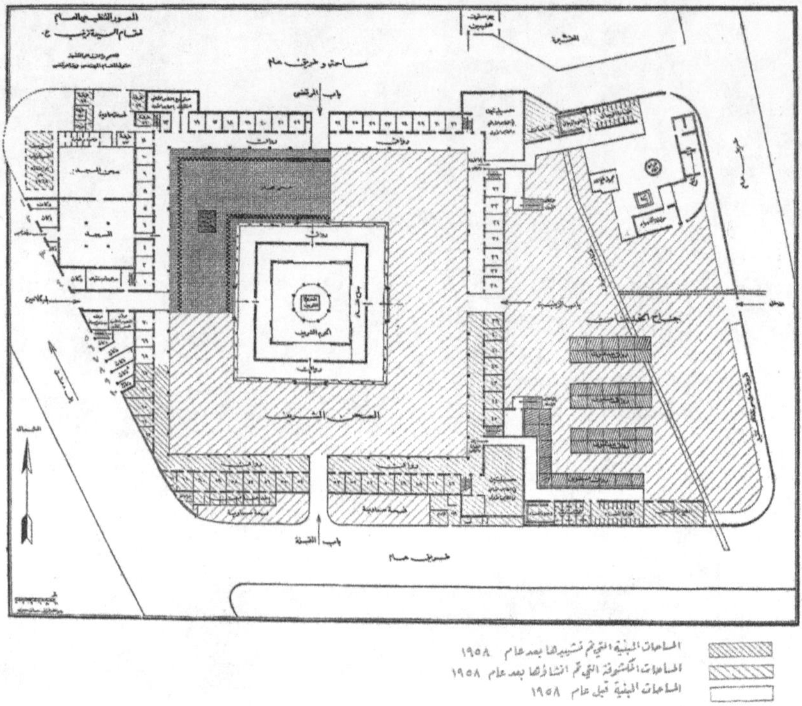

الصور الثلاثي للحرم الشام
قسم العينة الرئيسية - ٤

المساحات المبنية التي تم تشييدها بعد عام ١٩٥٨
المساحات المكشوفة التي تم انشاؤها بعد عام ١٩٥٨
المساحات المبنية قبل عام ١٩٥٨

FIGURE 6. Expansion plans circa 1993, in *Al-Mawsem: A Quarterly Illustrated Magazine of Archaeology and Tradition,* edited and self-published by Mohammad Saeed Al-Touraihi, 1997.

of the shrine and the actual finances. Although the inscription on the dome states that it is "a gift from the people of Iran to Syria," this statement has been falsely cited to argue that the Iranian state has financed and hence controlled the shrine since the early '80s.[2] Contrary to this popular and scholarly misconception, it was an Iranian Swiss businessman based in Zurich who donated the dome. As Dr. Murtada recounted, "He sent in his own construction crew and materials from Switzerland, and it took altogether two years, 1980 to 1982, to complete the project. He had only one condition: he wanted to stay anonymous, and to this day we have honored that request."

The shrine's library, which features custom-made bookshelves adorned with intricate mother-of-pearl inlays as well as hand-crafted chandeliers and table lamps, was the gift of a Shi'i Lebanese textile and ivory merchant originally from Bourj el Barajneh in what is now considered Greater Beirut who had amassed his fortune in Senegal. He also financed the construction of the marble hallway on the northern wing of the shrine. He, too, wanted to remain unnamed for his contributions. The northern wing was funded through a $5 million donation from Bassam al-Ghadir, a Shi'i Saudi Arabian businessman.

Aside from the $3 million from Reza Pahlavi that never materialized for the tiling of the shrine's facade, according to Hani Murtada, the only other state-level funding that the supervising committee considered was a $2 million donation from the Pakistani government to finance expansion of the southern wing. But under the current circumstances that make construction impossible, those funds were never received either.

"A close friend and business partner of [the famed Iranian merchant of steel and iron] Hamadani," as Dr. Murtada described him, who also decided to stay anonymous, funded the construction of the shrine's minarets in 1982, increasing their height from twenty-four to fifty-four meters. Another Saudi Arabian national, "an architect himself," Dr. Murtada added, funded the new entrance to the shrine, which was completed in 2008. Although all construction inside the shrine was completed by 1988, construction outside continued well into the 2000s. Even though a few small plaques tucked away do acknowledge the donors, material evidence of the merchants' donations remains shielded from view. Most pilgrims who visit the shrine, in other words, do not experience the *maqam* as partially constructed by donations, and even the pilgrims who do mark only the construction of the past three decades as donated.[3]

Yet both that anonymity and certain aesthetic choices that the supervising committee has made—such as the glasswork ceilings, the tile facade, and the shape of the golden dome—further fuel what the doctor has termed the "misconception" of the shrine's relationship to the Iranian regime, reducing the shrine to a satellite and base of operations for the regime. "How could a *maqam* be a self-governing *waqf* and an Iranian satellite at the same time?" the doctor asked rhetorically.

In stark contrast to *sayyid* genealogy, which is perpetually reiterated as honorific in daily speech, and those undertaking business co-ventures in Syria, who are publicly celebrated, many businessmen who donate to the shrine remain anonymous, pointing to a different regime of patronage that adopts an inclusiveness different from the categorical exclusivity of Prophetic genealogies. In the absence of a self-named actor behind the donation (what the doctor described as the "standard" anonymity of *zakat*),[4] the people watching what was being built with those donations supplied their own: the Iranian state.

FIGURE 7. Construction of the minarets, 1981–82, in *Al-Mawsem: A Quarterly Illustrated Magazine of Archaeology and Tradition,* edited and self-published by Mohammad Saeed Al-Touraihi, 1997.

With the number of pilgrims growing and the construction projects around the shrine increasing, the doctor claimed, the Murtada family members, as the *mutawalli* of the *waqf,* were "required to play an active role in managing and ensuring the shrine's sustainability." The increasing numbers of students and scholars in Shiʿa seminaries and the rising numbers of Iranian pilgrims raised the question of sustaining the shrine, according to Hani

Murtada. Implementing architectural expansion plans through merchants' donations was how the doctor told me this sustainability could be achieved. Those construction projects around the shrine, forged in the name of sustainability, turned out to be the main engines of the spatial transformation of Rawiya. In other words, the institution-building efforts of the Murtada family reshaped Rawiya into Sitt (lit. "Lady") Zainab—as the shrine town is now locally known. The Murtadas were no strangers to maintaining a diverse business portfolio and keeping their position as central actors in the transnational and transimperial career of the Sayyida Zainab shrine.

From a clinic to a cemetery, the Murtada family has framed patrimonial holdings in terms of landed property ready for real estate development. While the overwhelming majority of construction projects that culminated in the shrine's contemporary shape were financed through donations from individual donors, the supervising committee also had plans for projects that would be financed through joint redevelopment ventures on the endowed lands. After the committee relocated more than two hundred refugee families to the apartments it built behind the shrine, the shrine recovered about 20 percent of the property that had been settled by those fleeing the Golan Heights. Three lots of this land formerly settled by refugees were cleared and slated for further expansion and construction. The first one, next to the cemetery, was reserved for new burial sites in what was already the largest Shiʻi cemetery in Syria. The second lot, on the southern side of the shrine, was converted to a parking lot to prevent congestion around the shrine and provide space for pilgrim buses to load and unload. The third and largest lot, across the street from the shrine, was slated for the construction of two hotels for pilgrims that would also generate revenue for the shrine. Compared to the makeshift hotels and hostels that Iranian pilgrims frequented—such as the Shirazi hostels, where some seminary students also lived—the hotels that the *waqf* built and planned to build were more luxurious, with modern amenities like internet and air-conditioning. These hotels, furthermore, were just one segment in the broad business portfolio that the Murtada family was building.

Shortly after Hani Murtada returned from Canada to Syria to take over guardianship of the shrine, he started practicing medicine in Damascus. Parallel to his professional activities, the doctor was also involved in charitable organizations and initiatives that brought affordable and accessible health care and medicine to all Syrians. It "logically followed," the doctor recounted, that one of the many charity organizations that catered to social needs of the locals in and near the shrine town would be a clinic run by the *waqf*, where Dr. Murtada did not practice medicine but rather oversaw staffing and operations. The clinic received approximately half of the 5 million Syrian pounds that the *waqf* allocated to public charity (*khayriyyah*) in its annual budget. It provided a range of specialized services from childbirth and pediatric care to general medicine and dentistry at a cost higher than the Syrian state hospitals but cheaper than the Iranian and Iraqi hospitals. When I saw the clinic in 2010, it was frequented mainly by Syrians and Iraqis, while the Palestinian Golan Heights refugees obtained services from the UN and Red Cross.

Opening in 1982, the shrine cemetery gained traction primarily among Iranian and Lebanese nationals when Dr. ʿAli Shariʿati was buried there in 1977 in accordance with the wishes expressed in his will. Following his burial, Iranian as well as Lebanese Shiʿa flocked to the cemetery, with the numbers of burials increasing from 35–50 per year in 1982 to 150–200 in 2010. Not unlike the Karbala burial grounds in Iraq,[5] as Hani Murtada recounted while providing me with these numbers, the cemetery became popular among a transregional population of *sayyid* Shiʿa seeking to be buried near revered figures and those with Prophetic genealogy, a kinship connection to the Prophet's family (Ahl al-Bayt). Because the initially allotted burial spaces filled up by 2000, Dr. Murtada proposed to expand the cemetery another fifteen thousand square meters.

Although the land around the cemetery had originally belonged to the *waqf* of the shrine, and the *waqf* had paid out of its own funds to relocate the refugees settled there by the Syrian government, the Murtada family was forced to buy back ten thousand square meters of land from private owners and the state in order to find a location for permanent settlement of these refugees. According to Hani Murtada, Syrian state officials questioned the necessity of such an expansion for the cemetery, arguing that there was a nondenominational cemetery located just eight kilometers outside Rawiya and used by Sunni and Shiʿi Syrians alike. The officials stressed further that this cemetery had enough space to accommodate hundreds of burials a year. Only after the expansion was cast in terms of "burial tourism" for Lebanese and Iranian nationals who acted on the Twelver Shiʿi belief in the value placed on securing burial grounds in close proximity to Ahl al-Bayt members, and figures like Dr. ʿAli Shariʿati, did state officials concede. As demand for a lot in the cemetery increased, so did its property value. By 2010 the cemetery division of the shrine's *waqf* was charging $2,000 USD for an individual burial plot, and $10,000 USD for a family one, culminating in an annual revenue of $250,000 USD.

Randi Deguilhem observes that a shift occurs in the historical career of every privately designated *waqf*. Such a private or family charitable trust increasingly moves away from paying substantial portions of its revenues to the designated beneficiaries named in the *waqf*'s foundational charter and toward paying for more publicly engaged projects. In the case of Sayyida Zainab shrine's *waqf dhurri,* following her argument, that transformation is not explained by the internal logic of *waqf* as a peculiar cultural and religious institution of Islam. As the only *waqf dhurri* in Syria that is not fully governed by the Wizarat al-Awqaf, the government ministry in charge of administering religious charitable endowments, the Sayyida Zainab shrine's *waqf dhurri* enjoyed a flexibility of economic operations that opened up lucrative, if limited, possibilities through tax-exempt real estate assets—often prime landed properties slated for "redevelopment." In fact, the exceptional status of the Sayyida Zainab shrine and the Murtada patrimony was partially what attracted so much fury from the second prime minister of the newly independent Syria.

Given that in relation to other nonprofit and foundation-like corporations theorized in the political economy scholarship, a *waqf*, or Islamic charitable trust or endowment, can be understood, as Nada Moumtaz puts it, as holding God's property in perpetuity.[6] Properties intended for this purpose by the *waqif,* the founder, must thus remain outside of profit-driven endeavors, such as the real estate market, and be used instead for the "public benefit." With the rise of finance capitalism and intensification of privatization of land, as Moumtaz points out, the institution of *waqf* transformed alongside landed property when the latter became a "financial asset and real estate wealth that needed to be grown to benefit the nation's economy."[7]

It was not in other words, the Sayyida Zainab shrine alone that came under state scrutiny. At the heart of the push for reform was the institution of the *waqf* (pl., *awqaf*) itself.[8] As part of the massive restructuring of state institutions in Syria following independence,[9] the newly established state called for the cancellation of all self-governance capabilities of *awqaf,* rendering the trusts functionaries under the newly established state institution called Wizarat al-Awqaf (Ministry of Religious Endowments). An exception was made for the Sayyida Zainab *waqf* on the grounds that the Murtada family had continuously guarded the shrine for more than seven centuries,[10] often relying on family assets to maintain it as a distinct family *waqf,* or *waqf dhurri.* Yet that exception came with a qualification. A new supervising committee was to be established with two of the five members appointed by the state. The Murtadas who served as *mutawalli*, Dr. Hani Murtada and Sayyid Mahdi in addition to the latter's son Riza Murtada, and the chief engineer, Nahid, were the other members of that board of trustees.

The Sayyida Zainab shrine remains to this day the only *waqf dhurri* in Syria that is not fully governed by the Wizarat al-Awqaf and instead remains in the hands of the Murtada family. In fact, with minimal interference from the state-appointed members, the committee first drafted a new construction plan to expand the shrine as early as 1950. The patrimonial assets of the *waqf* were then slated for real estate development in collaboration with Syrian and international businesses before the Iranian pilgrims could flock to Rawiya.

THE MURTADAS: DAMASCENE HEIRS OF THE SAYYIDA ZAINAB SHRINE (1896–2016)

The first record[11] of the Sayyida Zainab shrine in the Ottoman state archives comes from an 1896 document concerning a certain Mustafa Emin Effendi's request for a salary from the Ottoman capital for having taken care of a small shrine over the previous decade. He is recorded as a Christian merchant originally from Aleppo who, following a miraculous encounter with Sayyida Zainab while on a visit to Damascus, took a Muslim name and relocated to the village of Rawiya, where he started caring for the shrine. After a decade of voluntary work, Mustafa Emin Effendi, whose attempts at securing a state salary for taking care of the shrine had gone unanswered by the Ottoman state officials, asked to be placed on the state payroll. When I asked Hani Murtada if this name and story rang a bell for him, he first patiently listened to the letter's contents. Then, without skipping a beat, he told me to "put a big question mark" next to this document.

He took a sip of his tea.

"The only noteworthy historical anecdote" he could share from the Ottoman era had to do with forged last names that inflated the numbers of Murtadas in Syria, particularly around Damascus. The relationship between the Murtada family and the Istanbul-appointed *wali* (governor) of Damascus was in such excellent condition, according to the doctor, that the *wali* excused the male members of the family from compulsory conscription into the Ottoman army. This gesture had unintended consequences. "It was known at the time that those who went did not come back," explained Dr. Murtada. "Given that people knew that the Murtada last name could get them out of military service, over the course of just a few months the family name, which had been confined to a single lineage in Damascus, proliferated into ten new ones with our last name. All of a sudden, everyone was a Murtada." Was the first Murtada that the Ottoman state chronicled in association with the shrine, Mustafa Emin Effendi of Aleppo, indeed one of those "invented" Murtadas? At the doctor's request, I put a second big question mark next to this document. The doctor turned to the *waqfiyya* documents again. The Photoshop-enhanced rendition of the shrine's charter coupled with a *sayyid* genealogy dating back 750 years was prefaced by a shorter, more unusual, genealogy composed as a series of eighteen leaves attached end to end. He handed me the glossy book.

The doctor explained that the edited volume, printed in the Netherlands, contained reproductions of the family's documents that pertained to their trustee status, or *waqfiyya* documents.[12] It was also sold at the shrine's souvenir shop. In preparation for our interviews, Murtada had presented me with a copy. Its reproductions included documents pertaining to the 750-year-long genealogy of the Murtada family as *mutawalli* of the Sayyida Zainab shrine—what he called, in short, the *maqam*. In the long list of projects that Murtada had designed and completed around the shrine, the souvenir shop and the glossy genealogy of the family that it contained were just the most obvious. He instructed me to turn to the leafy genealogy, which featured a complete pedigree of all those who had biological ties to the Murtada family and who had over the centuries cared for the shrine.

Each leaf bore the name of a male member of the Murtada family. The seriality of the composition was interrupted only at one place—on the leaf bearing the name of Sayyid 'Abbas. The transfer of guardianship of the shrine seemed to have passed from father to son over twelve generations of Murtada men before Sayyid 'Abbas. At the leaf etched with 'Abbas's name, the sequence forked, creating what seemed like two branches of Murtadas from which the succeeding *mutawalli* candidates of the shrines were drawn. The document that opened the Murtada *waqfiyya* archive was also striking in its visualization of patrilineal kinship. Thanks to other genealogical maps I had encountered in the archives, I was familiar with the use of trees, whereby a branch indicates a generation; a genealogy of leaves, however, was a first.

When I inquired about this difference, or deviation, from standard genealogical representation, Dr. Murtada pointed out that this was not a complete

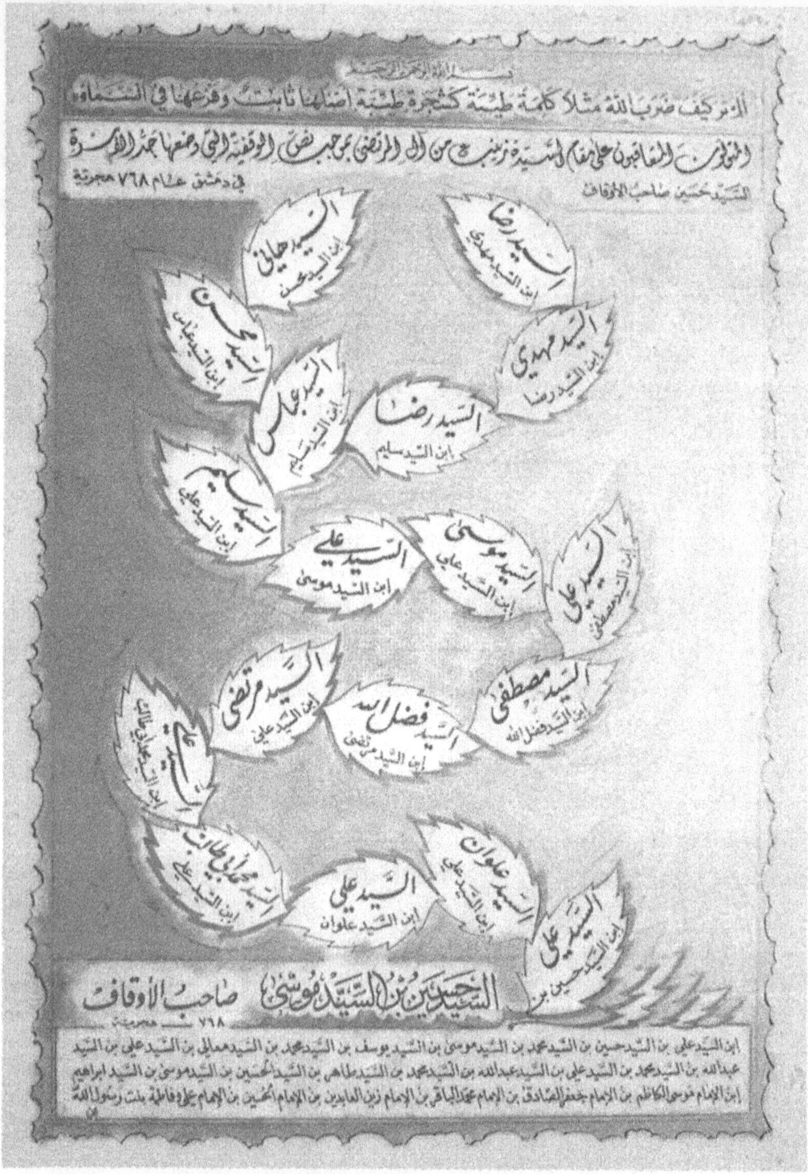

FIGURE 8. The leaf genealogy of the Murtadas in *Al-Mawsem: A Quarterly Illustrated Magazine of Archaeology and Tradition,* edited and self-published by Mohammad Saeed Al-Touraihi, 1997.

family genealogy of the Murtada men going back fifteen generations but rather only of those who had cared for the shrine. To mark that particular difference, and to present it as a genealogy of guardianship, the calligrapher himself had opted for the leaves, the doctor explained. To my eyes, the sinuous form made the split look like yet another curve that the sequence of leaves had taken over the course of the Murtada family's long genealogy—the calligrapher's crafty way, it seemed to me, of disguising the fork, or the splitting of guardianship between two "wings of the Murtada family," as the doctor would explain.

It was not a subject that the doctor wanted to dwell on at the time of my interviews with him. Setting the seeming linearity of the leaf genealogy aside, the doctor moved our discussion to the place of Sayyida Zainab in Iranian practices of tracing Prophetic descent and how Zainab's genealogy provides the Shi'a with another branch of Prophetic descent to draw *sayyid* genealogies of their own.

According to the doctor, the shrine had been under the guardianship of his family for the past "750 years, at least," dating back to Mamluk times. Running through the many state stamps archived as *waqfiyya* documents in the volume on the shrine, Dr. Murtada pointed out that the number of international visitors remained meager well into the 1950s, when advances in transportation technology and road infrastructure opened up the possibility of mobility for others to pay a visit. Until the 1960s, the pilgrims and visitors to the site came primarily from the immediate environs of Damascus and Lebanon.

"But in this long history," Dr. Murtada clarified, "it was really my great-grandfather, Sayyid Musa Murtada, who in 1836 changed the course of the shrine, and established the *waqf dhurri* for the shrine relying on his own possessions. And he had the vision to protect the shrine through generations to come." According to the more selective genealogy of guardians that Dr. Murtada shared, however, his great-grandfather would have been Sayyid Salim, not Musa—who was Salim's grandfather.[13] When I double-checked the name with the doctor, he quickly asserted that Sayyid Salim was alternatively known as Sayyid Musa—by his grandfather's name. This explanation obscured rather than revealed the process of succession from Sayyid Salim onward.

One of my very few findings from the Ottoman archives on the shrine was the dates around the same time as this succession. The Ottoman document filed under Şura-yı Devlet[14] holdings chronicled the conclusion of an inheritance case from 1910 that determined how the guardianship of the Sayyida Zainab shrine would be split. Mentioning Sayyida Zainab together with a much smaller shrine dedicated to the Prophet Noah in the Baqaa Valley of modern-day Lebanon under the guardianship of the Murtada family, the court declared that guardianship should be organized after Rida Murtada's death between his sons Sayyid ʿAbbas and Sayyid Rida as sons of the same father but different mothers.

There was no mention of which party, the brother or son of Rida Murtada, had brought the other to the court and through what courts the case had traveled the hierarchy of the Ottoman judicial system. The document simply records the settlement: all property-related rights pertaining to the charitable holdings of the *waqf* were divided in two equal parts: one half would go to the surviving brother of Sayyid Rida, Sayyid ʿAbbas. The other half, the court ruled, would be further divided among the three sons of the deceased: Sayyids Mahdi, Sabil, and Muhammad. The de facto guardian of the shrine, as far as its day-to-day operations and maintenance were concerned, was named as Sayyid ʿAbbas. The sons of the deceased would maintain half of the negligible income generated through donations, but they either relinquished any claim to the management of the shrine or wanted the revenue without being involved in its day-to-day operations. The winner of the settlement seemed to be Sayyid ʿAbbas—Dr. Hani Murtada's grandfather.

According to the doctor's timeline, Sayyid ʿAbbas oversaw the shrine on his own between 1910 and 1945, while the eldest son from the "other side" (*taraf*) of the family, Mahdi Murtada, found himself mired in Syrian politics. Aligned with the national resistance against the French Mandate, "he spent his life either in prison or as a fugitive on the run." He died two years before Sayyid ʿAbbas, in 1945. Mahdi's brother Sabil was from Sayyid Rida's second marriage, which was conducted in the Beqaa Valley and seen by the family as illegitimate, but Muhammad, the third son, the doctor continued, was not found to be pious enough and hence was deemed unfit to serve as a guardian of the shrine. Following the deaths of Sayyids ʿAbbas and Mahdi, the Murtada family faced a dilemma of succession. When the doctor described the burden of succession as falling on his father, it often felt as if he was referring to himself. In that respect, this very patrilineal bond, between father and son, formed around the pilgrimage of a matriarch and as such underpins my suggestion that it might be productive to approach saint visitation as a ritual of mobility that helps, in hands of social actors like the doctor, or Parastoo, rebuild the shrine at its center of veneration. Under the material conditions of *ziyarat* to Zainab, genealogy itself becomes a traffic across generations that itself only "differentially includes" to build a fiction of linearity and continuity as a proxy for authority.

In 1947 Muhsin Murtada—'Abbas's son and Dr. Hani Murtada's father—was invited to serve as the next *mutawalli*. An engineer by profession, Muhsin had trained in France and then Canada, where he lived at the time he was summoned, not unlike his father, to take over the guardianship of the shrine.

Just months after Muhsin Murtada moved back to Syria, the Sayyida Zainab shrine faced a major challenge: the second prime minister of the Syrian Republic, Khalid al-'Azm, single-handedly revoked the shrine's *waqf* status. His rationale was that if Sayyida Zainab, as the granddaughter of Prophet Muhammad and the daughter of Imam 'Ali, was a figure to be venerated by all Syrians regardless of doctrinal differences, and not only the Iraqi and Syrian Shi'a, then the shrine should be administered under the authority of the Syrian state, not a Shi'i family. And that was when, "for the first time in the history of the shrine," as Hani Murtada put it, the Murtada family reached out to the Iranian ambassador in Syria to intervene. They were told by the Iranian cultural attaché in the consulate that the Iranian ambassador in Damascus was simply following the orders of his colleague in Beirut. The family involved the Iranian ambassador in Lebanon to solicit an Iranian intervention with the new prime minister in Syria to ensure the self-sustenance of the shrine in Syria. "The Iranians in Beirut lent their support to us then," continued Hani Murtada. Thanks to these diplomatic efforts intervening on the behalf of the Murtada family and their control of the Sayyida Zainab shrine and its charitable trust, Prime Minister al-'Azm withdrew his proposal to "nationalize" the shrine.

Muhsin Murtada enlisted the technical expertise of his well-known engineering company in Damascus to revive these initial plans for expansion. In order to raise the funds for construction, he also secured the place of two affluent Shi'i merchants from Damascus and Baghdad. Although the initial attempts of the well-known Iraqi merchant Hazim Bahbahani seemed promising, his deteriorating health stalled the fundraising and construction efforts for the next decade. Mahdi's son, Rida, who was only eighteen when his father passed away, was summoned from France to assume his role on the committee in 1958. Trained as a civil engineer and an architect in Switzerland and France, Rida, five years later, finalized the architectural plans for the shrine's expansion and took over Muhsin Murtada's role as head of the supervising committee. When Muhsin's health improved in 1966, he came back to serve on the committee until 1975.

Hani Murtada recounted this period of transition: "1975, that is when I was summoned from Canada to assume my responsibilities. It was my second year of medical residency in Montreal. I had an older brother who lived and worked in France. But the family picked me, and all I could do was to honor this request and come back to Damascus." The doctor paused. When the doctor assumed his responsibilities, he knew that the expansion plans had to wait, as Syria has been moving from one regime to another. "And the numbers of Iraqis, including the wealthy merchants whom we had approached to raise the funds, were nowhere to be found toward the end of the Ba'thist regime in Iraq and the takeover by Saddam Hussein."

Even though the initial plans for construction on *waqf* property were reapproved in 1971, the permit to build was not issued until 1985. While for the Murtadas, plans for expanding the shrine were almost a priority, they also worked at maintaining the landed assets of the *waqf*, as 50 percent of all those immovable assets were resettled by refugees fleeing the Golan Heights in 1967. Almost 75 percent of those landed assets linked with the shrine continue to provide homes for those refugees. Subsequently, the initial plans had to be revised. That also meant seeking a new permit to build, taking the Murtadas back to the approval process all over again. The "approval process," although conceived positively—as if approval would be the logical result—in Syria was a moniker for an extremely lengthy process that in fact promised that approval would not be given at first. This bureaucratic traffic with the Syrian state in part motivated the ongoing planning of expansions to the grounds of the shrine, redressing the interior and exterior of the shrine and opening the patrimonial lands of the shrine *waqf* to tourism-related joint ventures with private enterprise. Moreover, in order to take back some of the resettled land from the Golan Heights refugees now calling Rawiya home, the supervising committee built apartments behind the shrine that it then donated to those families living in the most immediate environs of the shrine. This new housing made the planned relocation less contestable, but it also used up all the funds that the supervising committee had initially raised from Iraqi merchants in acquiring land and completing construction.

SITT ZAINAB'S SPATIAL TRANSFORMATION (1985–2016)

In 1985, just three years after Dr. Hani Murtada returned to Syria, he was invited by the Hafiz al-Asad regime to teach at the University of Damascus. After another decade on the university's faculty, he was appointed as the dean of the Faculty of Medicine. His success in leading the university impressed the regime so much that Bashar al-Asad appointed him minister of higher education, making him the first person outside the Ba'th Party and the first Shi'i Syrian to be given such a role in the 'Alawite-dominated state under the al-Asad dynasty. Hani Murtada's ministerial career proved to be rather short-lived, though; because he consistently ran up against the educational committee of the party on policy decisions, he stepped down as the minister after only two years in office.

In 2003, following Rida Murtada's retirement, his seat on the committee was passed on to his eldest son, Mahdi, who, like his father, was an engineer. It was Mahdi who instituted an engineering and construction division for the shrine, while Dr. Hani Murtada focused on the general structure of command, which included the establishment of an accounting and donations division, a legal team of three lawyers, and a general manager (Nahid) to attend to daily operations. The shrine's *waqf* employed altogether 120 staff members in three divisions before the Syrian revolution turned into a full-fledged civil war, and the majority of the construction initially planned in the 1950s was completed by 2002. The period between 2002 and the start of the Syrian conflict could be described as the shrine's golden age, as the number of visitors broke a million a year for the first time shortly after the 2002 renovations. Despite this expanding staff support, however, Dr. Hani Murtada and Mahdi Murtada continued to lead the supervising committee meetings every Monday from 9 a.m. until noon. They also made sure to attend Friday prayers and the subsequent luncheon for esteemed guests at the shrine every Friday. But those days had long since passed: "Now I am in Beirut, and Mahdi is in Dubai. Nahid still reports to me every week, and Mahdi and I are in constant correspondence. We are still planning an expansion for the southern wing, but that will have to wait for now . . . The Murtadas and the shrine have survived many twists and turns of history. We will endure through this episode too, I hope."

From the challenges posed by local state actors such as the Syrian prime minister al-'Azm to transnational ones such as the Sunni extremist brigades targeting the grounds more recently, the Murtadas have skillfully mobilized not only the transnational networks of their own family but also myriad other transnational actors, including donors, pilgrims, ambassadors, and cultural attachés. As they have continued to act as guardians of the Sayyida Zainab shrine, they have constantly negotiated and reinforced the patrimony of the shrine that the Murtada patriliny bestowed upon them. In the next section we turn to how this genealogical regime, and the network of patronage that the Murtada family members have orchestrated through it, have done more than expand the shrine architecturally. More fundamentally, through their expansive projects patrimonial lands associated with the *waqf dhurri* have been redefined as landed property.

For Dr. Murtada, this retooling of prophetic patriliny into a broader regime of patronage was also a genealogical act to steer the *waqf* of the shrine to sustainability. And his playing down of his *sayyid* status and therefore Prophetic lineage that had seemed like false modesty at the time was indeed analytically revelatory: to understand *ziyarat,* among other things as an act of genealogy-making, as Fariba had already shown us, approaching genealogy itself as a traffic across generations requires supplementing patrilineal claims with a broader analytic view—one that studies the linearity, exclusivity, and continuity of genealogy as *claims to* prophetic patriliny rather than neutral descriptions of its empirical reality.

The apparent discontinuities between pilgrims' projects of kin-making in undertaking *ziyarat* on the one hand and the Murtadas' fulfillment of their family's responsibilities to the site and its *waqf* in tandem produced Hazrat-i Zainab's genealogy itself. And this co-production of genealogy can help us approach genealogy itself as a nonlinear, differentially inclusive, and often discontinuous traffic across generations. Spaces that such genealogy-making projects have produced and inhabited, like the shrine, serve as fertile archives for studying those projects up close. This complicated scene in which pilgrims, clerics, and students as well as the Murtadas undertake multiple levels of patronage negotiations requires us to approach genealogy with more expansive analytical frames than those that tend to confine kinship to patriliny and men spreading out across pristine oceans. Here, I instead present genealogy as the premise of a spatial movement of that patrilineal network around a matriarch who sustained that patriliny at a time of great distress. The Sayyida Zainab shrine is similarly sustained by the genealogy-making practices of pilgrims like Parastoo. Yet the very spatial transformation of the shrine remains predicated on a patriarchal regime of patronage. Such seeming contradictions, as well as discontinuities, are not resolved but are worked through in processes of genealogy-making. With a matriarchal figure at its center, the multiple notions of genealogy at work in the *ziyarat* of Zainab show how prophetic patriliny itself changes once it is cast against and rethought through the regimes of patronage necessary to sustain the spatial transformation of the saint's shrine and its associated *waqf.*

With the growing architectural and institutional formalization of the *waqf*, which employed around 120 people right before the Syrian conflict, the expenses involved also grew exponentially. This large staff, Dr. Murtada recounted, "cost around 50 million Syrian pounds a year." The doctor continued, "Another 5 million went to the fifty members of the Murtada family that collected salaries from the *waqf*, as stipulated in Musa Murtada's foundational charter. The physical upkeep of the shrine and utilities for a million visitors annually meant a cumulative bill of 10 million Syrian pounds a year. The *mutawalli* saw that the shrine faced ever-growing expenses, paid out of an ever-shrinking endowment. Although the accounting division projected every year that 10 million Syrian pounds would be added to the endowment, the *waqf* ran a budget deficit each year because of unforeseen expenditures. The only time their budget broke even was the year that the second parking lot came into operation. Hani Murtada put it bluntly: "Mahdi and I thought the hotels, combined with the cemetery and the parking lot, could finally ensure the shrine's financial sustainability without jeopardizing the landed property of the *waqf*. The October [2013] rocket attacks that destroyed the entrance of the shrine cost us 6 million [Syrian] pounds to fix. How did we fund it? We went back to the Saudi Arabian donor who had financed its original construction but came back empty-handed. That meant selling the last pieces of land that the *waqf* owned in Damascus. These construction projects were not meant to make money for our own good, you see? For that you need to see how the Iranian clerics and their seminaries work. To this day they [the Iranians] have not grasped that Sitt Zainab is not Qom or Mashhad, and Syria is not Iran."

The latest unexpected expense that the doctor was at pains to address was the damage that the brigade had caused the shrine. The double-wave attacks of ISIL had ripped and rippled not only through the most unsuspecting crowds but also through places of worship. The extreme violence and destruction had inscribed themselves into the physical geography and political ecology. The cracked tiles—some half-fallen, some shattered into thousands of pieces—still hung from the mortar at the base of the minaret.

Under these circumstances, the doctor reckoned, a patron would have to be found. How else would the *waqf* be able to fund the renovation of the lower third of the minaret and the retiling of its facade? And that was only half of the problem. The tiles were funded through donations that came from Iran, and the tile-makers of Damascus, while known for their excellent purples, had no match for the turquoise of the artists and craftspeople in Iran.

For the renovated sections not to stand out, the new tiles would have to match the turquoise of the old ones. "But one should always rebuild after destruction and rebuild more beautifully, so the destruction becomes a blessing in disguise." Perhaps going back to the same donor, an Iranian living in diaspora, the doctor exclaimed, could solve all these problems!

As Dr. Murtada recounted in Beirut, soon after the establishment of the Shirazis in the shrine town, the number of seminaries proliferated in Sitt Zainab. Hani Murtada estimated their number in the twenties, including at least one that accepted only women students. In this context, around the same time that the numbers of Iranian pilgrims started surging, from approximately 1985 onwards, enrolling as a seminary student in Sitt Zainab became a convenient way for many to secure residence in Syria. Some of those "displaced from Iraq," as the doctor often described them, could stay in Syria as permanent residents thanks to the permits secured through their studies in these seminaries. Like Hassan Shirazi, most of these clerics who founded the seminaries were refugees themselves, following Saddam Hussein's seizure of power in Iraq, albeit for different reasons. The first seminary (*hawza ʿilmiyah,* pl. *hawzat*) in Rawiya was the Hawza Zainabiyya, established in 1973 in the vicinity of the Sayyida Zaynab shrine. Its founder, Sayyid Hasan Shirazi (1934–80), was an Iraqi cleric from Karbala, where his father was renowned as the founder and leading scholar in an important seminary. As Laurence Louër chronicles in *Transnational Shia Politics,* Hassan Shirazi and his brother, Muhammad Shirazi, attained the status of *marajiʿ al-taqlid*[15] (sources of emulation) through their learned trajectory in theology *and* their patrilineal pedigree—which included several important Shiʿi scholars and claimed to reach back to the Prophet Muhammad.[16] Not unlike other clerics and leaders of seminaries in Iraq, the Shirazis were politically active *sayyids.* Those political activities would lead to Hassan Shirazi's exile from Iraq in the early 1970s, after which he found refuge in Damascus. It did not take long before he turned his new refuge into grounds for recruitment. Assembling other seminary students and teachers in exile in the vicinity of the shrine, Hassan Shirazi founded the Hawza Zainabiyya. After the new institution stabilized, however, Shirazi relocated to Beirut and traveled only on occasion to lecture in Syria.

The seminaries' "donation" economy—the collection of *khums* and *zakat* from visitors in places of veneration and pilgrimage—allowed "the students [to] live like kings," as the doctor put it rather hyperbolically.[17] In fact, everyone, including the state officials involved in issuing residency permits (*iqama*), was happy with this economy, because in order to keep residency permits flowing in the direction of the seminaries, at least part of that donation economy in Sayyida Zainab had to "fill coffers" in Syria's state institutions like the Ministry of Religious Endowments. At the same time, the donation economy generated tensions over the political question of national origins and the status of refugees in Syria, and more broadly over regimes of patronage and the role of bribery in state development. The tensions were also about religious differences and the way the "traditions" of various clerics displaced from Iraq and Iran were reterritorialized and rearticulated on Syrian soil, where only 2 percent of the population identifies as Shiʿi. In "Following Sayyida Zaynab: Twelver Shiʿism in Contemporary Syria," Edith Szanto writes:

> Every contemporary Shiʿi *mujtahid* [a follower of any *marjaʿ al-taqlid*] begins his *fiqh* manual, which is the proof of his claim to the *marjaʿiyya*, explaining why it is necessary that Shiʿism, as long as they are not capable of *ijtihad* themselves, must follow a *mujtahid* and *marājiʿ al-taqlīd*.... The most important *marājiʿ al-taqlīd* in Sayyida Zaynab are ayatollahs ʿAli Khamenei, Sadiq Shirazi, and Muhammad Husain Fadhlallah.[18]

Iraqi and Iranian clerics and religious scholars continued to move to the town of Sitt Zainab, whether as a result of forced displacement or by choice, and as their numbers grew, so did the number of religious schools and Shiʿi institutions of learning, such as the *hawzat* and *husayniyyat*—meaning "seminaries" and "congregation halls" respectively. By enlisting the visiting pilgrims to donate to the seminaries and schools in exchange for collecting the blessings of the Sayyida Zainab, the clerics tapped into a considerable source of income that otherwise might have made its way to the shrine. What worried the Murtada family, however, was less their economic loss and more the theological contestation. The doctor relayed the family's general stance bluntly: "Sadr, Khomeini, Fadlallah—they were all the same to us, really. We always stay away from merchants [*tujjar*] of belief—the ones who make a business out of religion and on top of it all are political figures." The doctor paused and gauged my reaction. He knew at this point that I could not maintain a poker face in conversation. Seeing that I was intrigued by his skillful opening of a can of worms, the doctor continued. "As my great-great-grandfather, Musa Murtada, stated in his will, Sayyida Zainab was the granddaughter of our Prophet, and as such this shrine does not belong to this or that sect, and we cannot endorse this or that cleric. Every Muslim respects, loves, and venerates Sayyida Zainab. That is why we ask our Iranian visitors in particular to avoid self-flagellation and not to hang Khomeini and Khamenei posters around the shrine." The doctor caught his breath. "There is no room for extreme and divisive practices in a Sunni-majority country such as Syria. Every place has its own rules and customs. These practices I already mentioned, and caliph condemnation, are not among those we endorse as proper customs [*'adat*] and belief [*iman*]."

Every group, as far as they were able, aimed to exert their influence on the landscape of Sitt Zainab. Distinct clerical orientations, themselves products of complex histories and presents in Iran, Iraq, Lebanon, and increasingly Afghanistan and Pakistan, founded their own religious schools and dorms for a variety of students in the seminary system, and also hostels, hospitals, and clinics that catered to local residents, including Palestinian refugees displaced from Golan Heights and more recent waves of Iraqi refugees, the clerics themselves among them. The Sadr Hospital, built in 1993, and the Khomeini Hospital, built in 2002, were spatial testimonies to the fact that the Sayyida Zainab shrine and its town had emerged as the new grounds on which Shi'i figures of prominence battled for hegemony by providing services to local populations who were miles away from their original centers of influence—be they Qom or Mashhad in Iran or Najaf and Karbala in Iraq. Maybe, after all, the doctor did not give "the Iranians" credit where credit was due. Maybe they knew exactly how Sayyida Zainab was not Qom or Mashhad. And maybe they knew all the better how to make use of that difference. The transformation of Rawiya into the shrine town of Sayyida Zainab was shaped not only by contestation over pilgrims' donations. In the day-to-day interactions, too, the ritualistic differences between the Shi'a of Iran and those of Syria produced many cases of heated exchanges in chapter 1. Iranian pilgrims demanded to pray within the main hall of the shrine, and the family's refusal led to the construction of a mosque next to the shrine with *waqf* funds and later, nonetheless, to gender-segregating the traffic of pilgrims in and out of the shrine. Because the mosque employed a Sunni Hanafi imam to lead the Friday sermons, most Iranians instead chose to pray in a different space of worship.

In citing the urgency to address such a need for a space of worship, another mosque was constructed through a collaborative effort of Iranian state officials and some staff members of the Khomeini seminary in town. Built in the shrine's immediate vicinity, the mosque had a visibly Persianate aesthetic and was staffed by Iranian *muezzins*. The doctor thought that the new mosque meant an end to the Iranian pilgrims' demands to pray in the shrine's main room. He was wrong. The demands kept pouring in, while Sitt Zainab's two additional mosques filled only on religious festivals. But it was not only religious holidays, like the Persian New Year, that kept the *ziyarat* traffic in Sayyida Zainab alive; along with those pilgrim numbers, the town was, by the early 2000s, home to just as many seminary students. Because Sayyida Zainab was a relatively new location compared to historical centers of Shiʿi religious learning in Iraq and Iran like Karbala or Qom, Sit Zainab, the town's underdeveloped landscape, made it possible for displaced clerics to move their institutions—some of which were banned in Iran or Iraq—to Syria. Such relocation further increased the numbers of pilgrims visiting the shrine.

For the Murtada family, the exponential growth in traffic around the shrine came at a price. First, they lost most of their donation revenue from the *qafas* to those religious seminary students and staff members who made a business out of asking pilgrims for donations on the streets. "Even more valuable items brought specifically for the shrine," such as carpets or brasswork, were claimed as donations by the religious schools and hospitals. In the context of increasing competition over donations—which Dr. Murtada associated with the plethora of religious schools and seminaries that solicited donors on the streets—the shrine found itself "forced to find different ways" of raising the necessary funds to balance the books. With other social institutions such as the Khomeini Hospital, the seminaries, and the "Iranian mosque" claiming most of the Iranians' donations, those different ways had to be something other than donations, Dr. Murtada reckoned. He hoped that instead of tapping into their ever-diminishing endowment and landed property assets, the shrine's trustees could build a diversified portfolio for the *waqf* that would finally render it financially self-sustaining.

The contestation over daily prayer in the main hall characterized perfectly for the doctor "Iranian attempts to interfere with governance of the shrine." Although an unofficial policy of gender segregation already existed in the way pilgrims made use of the shrine, it was rather hard, particularly when the traffic in the main hall was heavy, to maintain those rules of separation. To remedy this situation, and citing cases of harassment by male visitors, Iranian women asked that the hallways of the shrine be divided into two gender-segregated loops. The board of trustees conferred and agreed to implement the change.

Dr. Murtada recounted that in early 2003, when he was serving as minister of higher education and al-Asad asked his opinion on the soaring numbers of Iranian visitors, he had responded: "We should look at [*ziyarat*] as religious tourism. One million people every year. If each spends about one thousand US dollars: one billion dollars. And we know from the merchants on the market that the numbers are no different for the Iranians than for the Lebanese or the Iraqis." The doctor was not frugal with his numbers and shared them with me to substantiate his point: "How much they actually spend ranges from five to ten thousand US dollars. In other words, the revenue generated by visitors of Sayyida Zainab alone is larger than that of oil production in Syria! In our plans for building a parking lot and two hotels, and so forth, we were working with a projected capacity to accommodate around two million annually. That was the plan for 2020." The doctor sighed and with a little nod to his left and then his right repeated a few sentences, what sounded like a short supplication, under his breath. "Well, plans … " The doctor commenced again. "The Iranians had their seminaries and the donation wheels running well. We wanted to secure the financial stability of the shrine without relying on endowment possessions in the form of real estate. After the first set of attacks, in order to cover the associated expenses, we had to sell land in Damascus. This is all because the shrine had not become financially self-sustaining even in the heyday of the pilgrimage. But the seminaries and the *husayniyyat,* the clerics, they were another story altogether."

CONCLUSION

With the number of pilgrims at one million and projected to surpass two million prior to the Syrian conflict, the very material effects of Zainab's visitation on Syria's economy were palpable. Yet the growing share of religious seminaries and their patrons in the economy that had developed around Sayyida Zainab's visitation drew donations away from the shrine. As it was observed from the outside, however, the expansion of the shrine to help its *waqf* attain financial stability separate from donations only reinforced conspiracy theories about the covert relationship between the shrine and the Iranian state. One theory went so far as to suggest that the whole *ziyarat* route was an invention of the Iranian state, a religiously cloaked way to connect with Shiʿi Arabs of Lebanon and compromise the ever-elusive pan-Arab unity. Although the account varied from one actor to the next, the Murtada family and their oldest *muta* were the ones who choreographed the transnational career of the Sayyida Zainab shrine. Such choreographies often involved careful interweaving of patrimony, patronage, and property in refiguring both the shrine dedicated to venerating Sayyida Zainab, and the family tasked with that shrine's perpetuation. In the transnational career of the

Sayyida Zainab shrine, the interpenetration of patrimony and property through regimes of patronage transformed the landed assets of a *waqf dhurri* into a highly diversified portfolio of landed property.

The regional dynamics that put Sayyida Zainab on the map of Shiʿi visitation animated the genealogy, iconography, and history of the saint and the shrine in significant but selective ways. The selective constructions of genealogy[19] in fact made it possible to reimagine *ziyarat* not only as an increasingly sectarianized religious practice but also as the grounds to rethink genealogy and patronage in the context of saint veneration.

Engseng Ho's use of genealogy is illustrative here. In *The Graves of Tarim* (2006), the patrilineal pedigree serves as the generative and enduring thread of a transregional landscape of mobility and diasporic identity. Tracing Southeast Asia's Indian Ocean connections back to Tarim of southern Yemen, Ho presents this patriliny as the elementary unit of kinship for the Hadrami diaspora, whereby claims to Prophetic descent instantiate genealogy as theory and practice in the making of a cosmopolitan and regionally connected diaspora inseminated into existence by traveling men. Here instead I tracked them to show how patrimony often turns into landed property ready for real estate development. That transformation of patrimony into property in the transnational career of the Sayyida Zainab shrine contradictorily remains unknown to most pilgrims—whose aggregative force has transformed the operations of the *waqf* associated with the shrine. In contrast to the graves of Tarim that Ho studied, where a shrine with known originators and destroyers set men into motion outward from Hadramout, the centripetal force and expansive spatial transformation of Sayyida Zainab's shrine pulled many pilgrims like Parastoo as well as businesspeople like Nahhas into a regime of patronage that provincialized Prophetic genealogy itself.

Zainab's traffic charted instead, for Parastoo or Hani Murtada, discontinuous, improvised, and less-than-linear ways of making kin with Zainab. In continuous response to the shifting demands of various pilgrim populations, the guardians of the shrine shaped the physical space of the site, approaching different donors to secure financial support as one source became untenable and another opened up. Members of various generations also suspended their own personal careers in order to serve the continuity of the shrine. Such improvisatory compromises as these, between personal and religious needs, have arisen around this pilgrimage over decades, if not centuries.

Banu's Pathways and Familial (De)Attachments

"IT IS NOT LIKE we have too much time on our hands, you know. Every three weeks he comes home from Abadan, and he's exhausted! And I'm exhausted! What has that to do with Hazrat-i Zainab?" Banu finally exploded. About five minutes prior to this explosion, which led to some tears as well, Parastoo had introduced me to her older sister, Banu, and their mother, Marieh Khanum. Before I could introduce myself and ask if they would like to talk about their *ziyarat* experience, Parastoo had told Banu and Marieh Khanum, "His questions are vague and open-ended. He just wants to know why you are going to Hazrat-i Zainab really and what meanings the journey has for you." That mischievous smile appeared again on Parastoo's face, and Banu knew what was coming her way from experience. The two sisters could not have been more different in temperament. Parastoo began, "So, Banu *joon*, why don't we set aside here for a second the important role model that Zainab represents to you, which is probably true for every woman on this bus. Why don't you tell Agha-ye Setare why you really went on the *ziyarat*." Extremely proper but visibly enraged, Banu turned around in her seat and addressed me: "My apologies for my little sister, Aghe-ye Setare. I guess she got the tail end of the stick in her manners. Don't you think, Mama?" Banu said, turning to Marieh Khanum. And there I saw the motherly original of Parastoo's smiling eyebrows.

"Well, it has been three years since your marriage, and, God willing, only one thing is missing—the fruit of your union with Payam!"

Marieh Khanum, as Parastoo had explained to me, had arranged Banu's wedding with Payam—the son of a business associate of Parastoo's father. And now she was trying to arrange a child for the marriage. Banu, an up-and-coming doctor with career ambitions of her own, and Payam, a junior material engineer in the oil industry, had sounded to Marieh Khanum like a match made in heaven. After much negotiation and multiple dates with Payam, Banu found herself surprisingly agreeing with her mother. Both upwardly mobile, thanks to their education, Banu and Payam had much in common in their trajectory in Iran. Yet after the honeymoon months were over, it slowly sank in that Payam and Banu were not seeing each other for more than a few days during his monthly visits to Tehran. Time was indeed limited for baby-making, as Banu had told her mother. Now, as Banu's mother, relentlessly focused on becoming a grandmother, joined in coalition with her little sister, the enthusiastic future auntie, to bring up the subject yet again, Banu once again tried to deflect: "Under these circumstances, my job, Payam's job . . . We are fortunate that we get to see each other and keep our relationship going, let alone think of adding another member to our family. Each of us is slated for a big step in our careers, and hopefully if Payam gets promoted, he can move to the headquarters in Tehran, and I'll finish up my residency. That would be a much better time for a baby."

"No need to wait that long. Maybe his baby will hasten Payam's promotion at work, you know," Marieh Khanum suggested. And for that too Marieh Khanum, with Parastoo's cooperation, had a plan. A particularly racy line of lingerie, commonly known in the region as Syrian lingerie, was on offer to make the best use of the very limited time Banu and Payam had for intimacy. Banu, rolling her eyes, sighed. Turning to me, she asked rhetorically, "Do you see what I have to put up with?"

Undeterred, Parastoo interjected, "Google says we are nearing Gaziantep. Time is of the essence before we reach the bazaar. Remember what Nafiseh told us: the inventory is larger in Damascus, but the prices are better in Gaziantep." Knowing how long it might take to decide, Parastoo paused, pulled out her phone, and held the screen in front of Banu's face. Before Banu could say anything, Parastoo continued: "Here is a little catalog."

"What the heck is this?" Banu responded, shocked by what she was seeing.

"Well, this model has a remote control, and the speaker sewn into the bra plays *Rude Boy* by Rihanna."

"I am not gonna turn into a stripper for my husband, that is just wrong on so many levels," Banu protested. Turning to her mom, Banu said, "You cannot possibly expect me to objectify myself like that!"

"That is not objectification—that is imagination. It is still you who decides when you are going to give Payam the remote," Parastoo responded. "He might think he's in control; but it's really you who is controlling everything!" Banu ignored Parastoo's comeback.

Swiping left on her phone, Parastoo pressed on. "Okay, okay, you are really more of a dancer anyway. How about a Nescafe thong? They are apparently edible!" At that point I thought the rage in Banu's eyes was going to cut right through Parastoo like a laser.

"That's it! I am not discussing my bedroom with you! Enough. Don't you have any shame?" Banu protested.

"Oh, lighten up a bit, *azizam*. Let your imagination run wild a bit."

Realizing that she was not going to win this one, Banu tried to fold her mother into the conversation. "Do you see what a monster you have raised?"

Marieh Khanum, undisturbed by Banu's attack, fired back with a Persian saying: "Garlic says to the onion, 'You stink!' You raised her with me, honey."

Parastoo let out a loud chuckle and said, "Well, let me just send you the catalog. You still have an hour and a half to decide which ones you might like." Noticing that I was taking my leave on that note, Parastoo asked, "Agha-ye Sitare, you can help us haggle in Turkish, right?"

Not wanting to become another pawn in Parastoo's plan, I replied, "If Banu would like me there, I'd be happy to help haggle in Gaziantep." I excused myself and made my way to the back of the bus.

THREE

Arrested Mobilities and Fugitive
Markets beneath a Fig Tree

HOLDING ONTO THE LAST drag from his dying cigarette, Metin scanned me up and down. I was on my fifth cup of *kaçak* tea. Whether it was the validation I felt after passing the bazaar security check or the sheer caffeine, I had finally worked up the courage to ask how his side business in contraband cigarettes was going. Metin, his two apprentices in the shop—Yavuz and the elder of his two sons, İsmail—and I were sitting together on teetering *iskemleler* (wooden-framed stools), sipping our tea outside Metin's shop. Other merchants had congregated under the fig tree in front of his shop on that particularly hot day, and everyone seemed to have found comfort in inhaling the flavor of cardamom and intrigue, watching one of the bazaar's most seasoned *tüccar* (merchants) teach an outsider about business. Most people who had congregated were *tüccar* or *çırak* (apprentices) themselves from the shops along Türkmen Street. There were also a few *seyyar satıcı* (mobile sellers) who worked the informal booths along the sidewalks. Given that it was three o'clock with no Iranian buses or customers in sight, the gathering seemed content to have a momentary distraction from the all-too-familiar heat of Gaziantep, watching as Metin tested my knowledge of the commodities in his store that he had been teaching me over the previous week.

Each time Metin recounted the trajectories of sugar from Syria and tobacco from Iran, his story would end with a twist. But every time it started the same, commenting on how he had gotten caught up in the *ziyarat* route through a marriage.[1] Metin warmed up: "The same buses carried women hungry for marital (or other) intimacies, and men thirsty for beer or seaside festivities in the Mediterranean backwaters of Adana and Antalya, who leave Iran as pilgrims and switch buses in Antep to visit the Turkish coast as tourists!" As if he did not want me to forget, Metin elaborated, "They carry sugar for your tea from Tabriz, and your tea for that thin-waisted glass from ... as far as Afghanistan and Sri Lanka. They carry oil for my car from Aleppo. Cigarettes from Urumiyeh." Slowly reaching for the overflowing ashtray, Metin stubbed out his already-finished Bahman cigarette. Produced in Iran, Bahmans were brought over in the same buses that shuttled pilgrims and were particularly popular among the Gaziantep clientele. They had all the flavor of Turkish tobacco but none of the state-imposed tariffs to ruin that flavor.

Metin almost always opted to have his cigarettes transferred from Urumiyeh, although the most secure and frequently used route for contraband tobacco ran through Urfa and Van to the Iran border. That route was coordinated by a set of Turkish, Kurdish, and Iranian middlemen, and the cigarettes on the route often accumulated multiple informal "taxes" throughout their journey to Antep. Metin sought to avoid "replacing one tax—that of the state—with another—that of the middlemen." Two options were therefore to work with either pilgrimage bus drivers or his acquaintances in Iran. Metin also had a third option—a network partially assembled and structured through his complicated family ties. It was this option, itself born out of the paths of the *hajj-i fuqara'*, that Metin chose. It involved fewer intermediaries. This method had served him well for some twenty years, and he spoke of it with confidence, often joking about the mutually constitutive relationship between his family and his business, all thanks to the *hajj-i fuqara'* route.

Like Hani Murtada, Metin acknowledged the benefits of the Iranian pilgrimage route, which had provided him with a second family and a decent livelihood in commerce in particular, and had made the Iranian Bazaar in Antep a major hub for a variety of business in general. And like Dr. Murtada, he held strong opinions about Iranian travelers on the ways of Zainab. Whenever an Iranian pilgrim came into his store with a specific brand request, then left without buying anything because he did not carry those brands, Metin would launch into a monologue about his Iranian customers and their "pilgrimage of the poor." Metin held similarly strong opinions about his profession itself: commerce—*ticaret* in Turkish (*tijarat* in Persian, a shared Arabic cognate). The municipal government had publicized a plan, under a broader project of "urban renewal," to formalize the Iranian bazaars. It also came with preferred offers to those merchants working in informal stores and trading in contraband commodities. The first part of the multipronged plan to formalize the Iranian Bazaar included the construction of an arcade called the Atatürk Pasajı. Metin quickly dismissed the Pasajı as a speculative project that ran counter to the nature of bazaar business.[2] He began, "I am more

FIGURE 9. Huzur Zuccaciye (Serenity Glassware), in the Iranian Bazaar in Antep, 2014 (photo by author).

conservative in my business decisions. It sounds like some merchants in the bazaar are too bored with their situation! Mark my words; they're looking for trouble . . . There is absolutely no need to come under the purview of those vultures in the bank with payments." Metin was wary of banks, of trusting an institution that would dispense as it pleased with his hard-earned money.

Metin continued, "Our livelihood is hanging on a cotton thread after all. If a bomb goes off somewhere in Karbala, we know that means more pilgrims in Antep, but if one goes off somewhere along this route, in Syria, for instance, we all know then the Karbala merchants are cheering. It is all interconnected, as your friends would probably say." He concluded, "If the traffic is so unpredictable, holding onto only one kind of merchandise is too risky. Why add more risk to this already risky business by going into debt? I'd rather keep my many trades afloat and just focus on my kitchen appliances and glassware merchandise for the Iranians, and the sugar, tea, and tobacco for the locals."

Some of these revealing monologues were meant as advice for his apprentice, Yavuz, some as direct lectures for me, if I was present. If the Professor was not present to take the edge off Metin's analysis, these lectures were quite something. İsmail, his son, was all too familiar with such speeches. When one such monologue presented itself, the sons and the apprentice often found some excuse to leave the vicinity as soon as Metin's discussion of religion, economics, or politics showed the first signs of devolving into a soapbox speech. If Metin noticed that Yavuz was trailing after İsmail, Yavuz would immediately be summoned back and reprimanded for not paying attention to the bazaar university's most seasoned professor.

While most young merchants of the bazaar, such as Osman and Yaşar, disagreed with Metin about the risks and costs of moving to the Atatürk Arcade, virtually everyone followed his mantra of keeping a diverse business portfolio that belied a sharp distinction between formal and informal business. His was a "hybrid" model, as he put it: a formal shop catering to the Iranian pilgrims as well as informal booths and carts to reach the Antep locals. Indeed, it was the combination of these seemingly contradictory business practices, formal and informal—on record and off the record—that ensured the vitality of the bazaar and determined its merchants' success. And it was that combination, which relied on and exploited the distinctions drawn between risk and debt, that ensured Metin's ability to stay afloat in the murky business of contraband.

Neither Metin nor any other merchant I met in the bazaar thought of contraband sugar, tea, or tobacco as smuggled goods. By the end of 2013, when the Syrian conflict was thought to have reached its climax, İsmail put it bluntly: "People, including state agents, are smuggling tanks, rockets, and soldiers across the border. That is not called 'smuggling,' but what *we* do *is*Moving sugar and tea should be considered *vergisiz ticaret* [duty-free trade/commerce]."

Indeed, the definition of contraband commerce as duty-free trade might have been one of the very few things all merchants in the bazaar could agree on: there was in fact little deliberation about the morality of contraband commerce, let alone consideration of its legality. Moreover, local customers and bazaar merchants alike highlighted not only the economic necessity of contraband commerce in the face of contradictory regional economic policies and tax regimes in Turkey but also the Antep locals' demand for *kaçak* tea and tobacco as a matter of taste that distinguished the southeast of the country, including but not limited to Turkey's Kurdistan. In other words, the domestic products were deemed not only too expensive because of heavy taxes but also lacking in strong taste and rich flavor. As Ali, an Antep local in his forties and one of Metin's most dedicated customers, put it, "It is the Rize[3] tea that tastes foreign to us, not the Ceylon from Iran, Sri Lanka!"

Approached from the intersection of Türkmen Street and İnönü Avenue, a major artery with bustling traffic in the heart of city, the shops, makeshift booths, and parked carts of Gaziantep's Iranian Bazaar looked like the props of a set. As Mona put it, the bazaar was "like a passageway to postpilgrimage consumption." It was hard not to agree with this description when I first set foot in the bazaar. Iranians like Mona, but also Parastoo, Banu, Fariba, and others on their way to Sayyida Zainab, had given the bazaar its name; they also gave it its market value of $75 million USD, according to the estimates of municipal government officials. The bazaar named after the Iranian people and goods that circulated through its passageways was a motley assemblage amid two- and three-star hotels (described by the same official as "nests of prostitution" [fuhuş yuvaları]) and mechanic shops that specialized in expanding gas tanks and building secret compartments into vehicles' existent architecture. Cartons upon cartons of cigarettes traveled into Turkey in compartments carved from seat cushions, and just as much as contraband tea in the wheel wells of long-haul passenger buses. Taxis in particular filled their expanded gas tanks with fuel oil that was priced in Syria at one-tenth the price in Turkey. And the houses that supported sex work and automotive body work had most recently become home to Syrian refugees.

It was this motley assemblage that welcomed Iranian pilgrims into the center of historical Antep. Huge window displays, overflowing with electronic Turkish coffee machines and handcrafted silk and cashmere scarves, filled one column of Mona's passageway into the bazaar. The other column was composed of contraband goods: self-packaged nylon bags of sugar and tea, cartons of cigarettes, and fire-red lingerie sets (with little Christmas lights sewn into the tips of the bra) exquisitely displayed on top of mobile *tezgahlar* (carts). These wooden displays on three wheels were the mobile stores for their vendors.

The Iranian Bazaar's development was deeply embedded in the transformations of Antep. It was, however, also a direct result of the remarkable growth of the pilgrimage route. Many Gaziantep locals also frequented the carts to see the contraband inventory of the week. The Iranian pilgrims' goods of choice tended to be kitchen appliances, pots and pans, glassware, and, more recently, Syrian lingerie. According to some of the bazaar's seasoned merchants, large business deals—those in which as many as four trucks' worth of stainless-steel kitchen appliances, blankets, and other textiles were traded at once—took place only in Gaziantep and nowhere else in Turkey. Gaziantep, as a function of its proximity to the Turkey-Syria border, was also a hub where contraband goods such as cigarettes, sugar, and tea exchanged hands rather quickly from courier to merchant and then to consumers.

The pilgrimage buses themselves were vehicles of this motley mobility, and doubly so in the Iranian Bazaar: they shuttled customers to the bazaar's formal stores that catered to "Iranian tourists," and also shuttled commodities into contraband carts for the Antep locals.

The rhythms of the bazaar, synchronized to the engines and wheels of Iranian buses, punctuated an otherwise sleepy corner of the city center of Antep. As you might recall from chapter 1, the smell of Iranian rice infusing the air from makeshift cookers was the bazaar merchants' signal that a pilgrim bus had arrived. The Iranian pilgrims might have given the bazaar its name and set the pace of the place, but a variety of other actors animated the Iranian Bazaar of Antep: the *mimarlar,* or "architects," at the mechanic shop expanded standard gas tanks to carry more than double their capacity of *kaçak* oil from Syria. The men and women who worked as informal mobile vendors of a great variety of things ranging from sugar and tobacco to jewelry and embroidery haggled with locals over bulk prices. And Antep merchants continued to cater to the pilgrims, whom they saw as shopping in a place free of economic sanctions.

The pilgrimage route not only diffused the aroma of saffron rice but also breathed new economic life into Antep's Iranian Bazaar; however, by the time I started my long-term fieldwork there in 2012, as the Syrian conflict intensified, that smell was nowhere to be found. Following the abduction of Iranian pilgrims outside Hama in 2012, the *ziyarat* route through Turkey ceased to exist. Without that usual traffic of buses that I had experienced in 2010 and 2011, merchants of the bazaar spent most of their time drinking tea and being in debt and short of money. Metin, though, never spoke about being short of money. His story, at least financially speaking, was one of success. I first met him, a sixty-year-old merchant, in the bazaar in June of 2010, back when he owned a profitable little shop selling glassware, kitchen appliances, and pots and pans to Iranian pilgrims. Across the sidewalk from his store, he had employed a mobile seller, Yavuz, to work as his apprentice. Yavuz, a nineteen-year-old recent high school graduate, was to learn Persian and the "business" inside the store, when he wasn't busy with the *tezgah,* the mobile cart that displayed the inventory of the week, such as guaranteed contraband tea and cigarettes that, like Turkey-produced Kents, had been smuggled back into the country from Iran.

When I met Osman and Yaşar, they were in a heated conversation with Metin. Metin, who had told me that all of his downtime conversation and gossip was about his neighbors in the bazaar, ushered me into the conversation and introduced me. The two brothers had just brokered a wholesale shipment of Syrian lingerie from Souq al-Hamidiyyeh in Damascus, where the Iranian pilgrims were known to shop before embarking on the bus journey back home. Osman and Yaşar had devised a plan to lure some of those Iranian pilgrims to the Iranian Bazaar in Antep. Their store featured an already impressive women's undergarment selection from Istanbul. Making the next big move, Osman and Yaşar had taken out a hefty bank loan to move their store from the fringes of the Iranian Bazaar to its center—the newly constructed Atatürk Pasajı, or Atatürk Arcade. The arcade was modeled after the Gulistan Mall in Tehran—that city's first full-fledged mall—and was financed by the metropolitan municipal government of Gaziantep through a mortgage program to formalize the informal stores of the bazaar. These transformations in the bazaar made Metin resentful. They most likely reminded him of how he had not changed a thing in his business for the past ten years, in stark contrast to Osman and Yaşar's takeover and expansion of their father's fabric shop.

The story of Metin's relationship to the pilgrimage route, however, went beyond business, and he was worried about more than the competition that the arcade would bring. He worried about the future prospects of his only daughter, Narmin. Twenty-five years ago, Metin had met an Iranian pilgrim woman, named Nazanin, who was passing through Gaziantep on her way to Sayyida Zainab after her husband had been martyred in the Iran-Iraq War. She was among the first Iranians selected to visit Sayyida Zainab on the voucher program that Bunyad-e Shaheed had funded, sending—according to Nazanin—"around two thousand Iranian nationals every week to Syria." Metin and Nazanin "fell in love at first sight," according to Metin, and kept in touch after Nazanin's first trip to Sayyida Zainab. On her second trip, six years later, Nazanin and Metin slept together. That night would turn into a second marriage for the thirty-five-year-old Metin. By the time of the marriage, Nazanin was already four months pregnant with Narmin, and Metin had a wife and two children in Gaziantep. When Metin and I met, he and his two sons in Gaziantep were supporting two families, including the one formed on the paths of Zainab with Nazanin. His daughter, Narmin, who lived in Urumiyeh with her mother, in a way embodied the constitutive linkage between the route and kinship. Metin and Narmin's half brothers were busy seeking a suitor for Narmin. She herself dreamed of studying at a university in Turkey. Because taking trips to meet suitors that she would ultimately reject gave her a chance to travel, she did not mind the back-and-forth. She was preparing for Turkey's entrance exams for foreign nationals so that she could study fine arts at Mimar Sinan University. Because their Islamic marriage was recognized only in Iran and Metin remained married, in Turkish civil code, to his wife in Antep, Narmin had only Iranian citizenship. The buses that took Narmin to Gaziantep for occasional visits also shuttled Metin to Urumiyeh, where he secured Iranian cigarettes for delivery to Gaziantep and spent time with his Iranian family.

KAÇAK LEAKING THROUGH FORMALITY, *TICARET* LEAKING THROUGH *ZIYARAT*

Electricity and petroleum stolen from grids of distribution. Livestock, tea, and tobacco traded as contraband goods across borders. An apartment built without permits. A defendant who flees trial. In these seemingly disparate situations, the goods tapped and the actors named are described with the qualifier *kaçak* in modern Turkey. Conventionally translated into English as the equivalent of "smuggled," the semantic domain of *kaçak* in Turkish (loaned into Kurdish as *qaçax* and Persian as قاچاق) is more capacious than "smuggled" signifies. A nominalized form of the verb *kaçmak*—to flee, seek refuge—*kaçak* helps us recover the act of breaching a formal contract in order to seek refuge as a constitutive vector in the interlinked formations of bureaucracy and the economy. Taking *kaçak*'s semantic domain as a field of theorization, I tease it out of its entanglement with *ziyarat* buses to track the many forms the term takes in the hands of bazaar merchants maneuvering under historically specific material conditions.

Conceived as "fugitives" of breached contracts, the spatial lives of *kaçak* goods and people chart out a more expansive and dynamic set of relations between economics, politics, and in our case religion than conventional framings of economic informality allow. Unlike terms such as *illegal, illicit,* or *informal,* the term *kaçak* is not negatively defined against ever-shifting formations of the legal, the licit, and the formal in economy and politics. As a function of this positive difference, *kaçak* already exceeds conventional analytics of informality that an exclusive focus on economic imaginations, its devices, and their attendant operations and operators could account for. Precisely because *kaçak* is positively derived from the act of fleeing, and because that flight to seek refuge is itself equally a political act, we are provided with a window into how the concept of *kaçak* is a boundary-crossing and hence boundary-producing concept that leaks between the formal and the informal, the licit and the illicit, the legal and the illegal. This leakage, or fugitivity, which is part of *kaçak's* semantic domain in Turkish, renders contraband commerce's entanglements with *ziyarat,* encapsulated in the expression *ham ziyarat ham tijarat* (both pilgrimage and trade), such fertile grounds to recast the study of religious ritual in the context of its political economy and ecology.

Below I center my analysis on the careers of many *kaçak* goods moving between Iran, Turkey, and Syria. Some of these goods were shuttled in the pilgrims' buses; some had distinct cross-border circuits within which the buses played a relatively small role. There was another connection to the pilgrimage route and the Iranian Bazaar. While the formal shops primarily catered to the Iranian pilgrims, the same merchants maintained, across the sidewalk from their stores, informal carts that carried a variety of *kaçak* goods. The merchants who moved them show that entanglements of formal and informal economic practice are the engine of, rather than an obstacle to, the functioning of national economies. With such a focus on dynamic movements of fugitive commodities at play in and out of Iranian pilgrim buses, examining informality as a relatively recent and primarily urban effect of neoliberal capitalism in the Global South provides little analytic utility.[4] More specifically, this chapter provincializes the urban and neoliberal optics prevalent in the anthropology of informality[5] by cross-reading recent scholarship on laborers of contraband trade with that on the state and market.[6] Such an approach attuned to the interlinked formations of states and markets beyond their borders necessitates a retooling of the recent scholarship on economization, politization, and network creation[7] for a study of "state effects"[8] in *kaçak's* relationship to bureaucracy, particularly when it is moonlighting in the pilgrimage buses. Conceiving *bureaucratization* as an incomplete process is itself fundamental to the production of socioeconomic and politically fugitive acts and actors—like Metin and his tobacco and tea designated as *kaçak.* It is at this juncture and on a route of *ziyarat* as "religious tourism" that merchants like Osman, Yaşar, and Metin simultaneously make *kaçak* a part of *ziyarat* and informality a part of a state-sponsored formalization scheme. Osman and Yaşar's use of mixed methods—namely, of formal and informal economic action—is quite literally what the Atatürk Arcade gives rise to, while aiming to formalize otherwise informal activity. In the interim, the Iranian pilgrims are lured to shop en route, taking potential business away from the Souk Hamidiyyeh in Damascus, Syria.

"GUARANTEED CONTRABAND"

Two weeks into my apprenticeship at the bazaar, I asked Metin if I could take a picture of the large sack of tea in his store. He paused, looked at the ceiling, then let his eyes find mine. With a dismissive hand gesture of approval, he responded, "Shoot, shoot!" He then asked dismissively, "Of all things in the store, you picked this?" To him, *kaçak* was utterly uninteresting: as far as tea consumption in Antep was concerned, it was not the exception but the norm.

It would take me another month to grasp the pervasiveness, if not outright dominance, of *kaçak* tea among locals in Gaziantep. After I had realized this fact, it ceased to seem extraordinary when shop displays would advertise new shipments of *kaçak* tea, "guaranteeing" the *kaçak* status of the merchandise. But to show how I got there, I will ask you to follow along for a while with the commodity, the tea itself, and contextualize it in its transregionally networked and historically sedimented circulation. The photo I took in Metin's shop of the assorted brands is a good place to start. The brand Mahmood Tea, highly sought after, not only in Antep but throughout Turkey, was distributed by the Dubai-based tea division of the Altunkaya Group—active in numerous sectors of food production throughout the Middle East. The Altunkaya Group was headquartered in Gaziantep. The brand Alokozay, seen in the photo, was produced by a company based out of Kabul, Afghanistan. The Altunkaya Group happened to be the brand's official distributor. Finally, the brand Layalina was produced and distributed by Zein Brothers and Company based out of Aleppo. I came across Layalina as the brand most frequently shuttled back on the pilgrimage buses returning from Syria to Iran via Gaziantep.

All three brands claimed to source their teas from Sri Lanka. Brands like these make up the approximately 80,000 tons of contraband tea that makes its way to the markets of Turkey, which—I think it worth repeating—is the fifth-largest producer of tea in the world. In production, Turkey trails behind China, India, Kenya, and Sri Lanka—countries that are commonly referred to as the "Big Four of Tea" and that together account for 75 percent of global production. Turkey's Black Sea region, and particularly the provinces of Rize

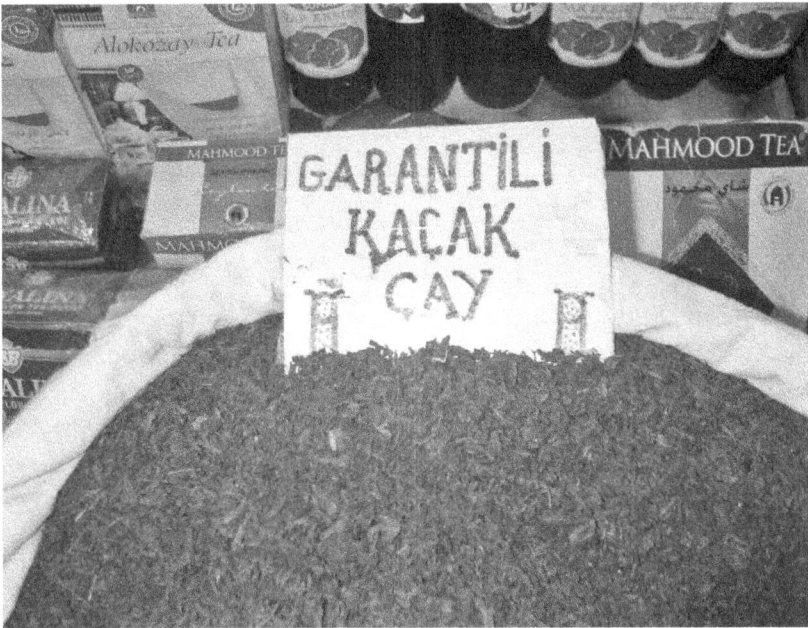

FIGURE 10. Guaranteed contraband tea, in the Iranian Bazaar in Antep, 2014 (photo by author).

and Ordu, account for the country's 215,000-ton annual output. Rize Province alone puts out 62.5 percent of the annual produce.[9] Thanks to the 145 percent customs tariffs collected on tea to protect this regionally concentrated economy, between the years 2006 and 2016 only around 4,000 to 5,000 tons of tea per annum were imported.[10] According to the Rize Chamber of Commerce chairman, Nevzat Paliç, "The biggest threat to the domestic production of tea is not international competition. It is rather the unhealthy *kaçak* tea entering into the country from [our southern borders of Syria and Iraq]. Its immediate banning would not only prevent the outflow of precious foreign currency. That ban would also help increase the value of our domestic product."

The tobacco market was no different, according to Metin. Turkey's religiously inflected health campaign that effectively recommoditized tobacco and alcohol products through heavy tariffs aimed at protecting domestic producers of tea and tobacco effectively made these two commodities some of the most popular contraband goods in circulation in the country. While the Erdoğan administration received praise from the World Health Organization in 2012 for running the most successful antismoking campaign in the world, based on the officially reported 15 percent decline in domestic consumption of tobacco products,[11] the merchants begged to differ. As Metin pointed out, domestic consumption had not declined so drastically; it had simply gone "off the record." Invoking the state's own language, Metin argued that more people had turned to contraband tobacco and alcohol. The Kent cigarettes produced in Turkey for the British American Tobacco Company and slated for export to Iran made their way back to the domestic market in Turkey as *kaçak* cigarettes. Graphic images of cancerous lungs and the usual warnings about the detrimental effects of tobacco consumption in Persian marked the cigarettes as Iranian products. Yet a quick glance at the Persian printing on them revealed that they had been produced and packaged in Tire near Izmir, Turkey, to be imported to Iran.

The case of Kents was one of Metin's favorite examples to drive home the point that contraband in general was the effect of states and their unfair economic policies, which disregarded domestic demands and tastes. He put it as follows: "Imagine a product that is domestically produced both for export and for consumption within Turkey. And now imagine that there is a sevenfold price difference between the very same products that are exported and those consumed within the country. Let me get more specific and ask you a question. With all the costs associated with bringing those Kents back to Turkey, what would you do if the price of one pack of Kents from Iran were still one-fourth of the domestically sanctioned price?"

Everyone who had congregated under the fig tree outside of Metin's shop, even those who often disagreed with his take on the bazaar or the next steps in its transformation, nodded vigorously in agreement. But İsmail and I knew that the final twist to his diatribe was yet to come. Metin always saved the best for last. Turning his head slightly in the direction of Osman and Yaşar but avoiding direct eye contact with them, Metin finally came to the point he really wanted to make. As İsmail was stepping out to light his cigarette, Metin put it bluntly: "And let me just say this for all our younger merchants—going into debt to have a store in this new mall or arcade, or whatever, is akin to buying the domestic Kents, when the Iranian Kents are perfectly fine. The only difference is that it is your own state ripping you off for the same thing in the case of Kents, and the banks in the case of the new mall. That is not how the counters of the bazaar turn!"

Teasing out the contradictions of the Turkish economy and its policy of heavily taxing tobacco, Metin sketched out how Turkish citizens had found ways to negotiate those contradictions. In that sketch, there was an implicit inversion of market logics. For Metin, the transnational circuit of Kent cigarettes exemplified how state policies produced contradictions; the trading of contraband in the bazaar not only offered a material way out of the financial burden of those policies but also underwrote an alternative, if not inverted, moral economy that underpinned the very logic of the bazaar and its merchants' actions. The younger generations of "organic entrepreneurs," as Osman and Yaşar referred to themselves, however, wanted to exploit the distinction drawn between market and bazaar economics themselves. Let us now turn to their trials and tribulations as they attempted to formalize their business in *kaçak* merchandise by setting up shop in the Atatürk Arcade.

Following the goods and people that move in and out of the Iranian Bazaar allows us to consider the variety of rationales at work in the production of social institutions, encapsulated in the social-life-of-X schema, which has been a sustained line of inquiry in anthropology.[12] As briefly described in the Introduction, the study of *kula*, the Melanesian system of circuits of exchange and its ecologies of circulation, was influential both for its powerful "provincializing" of maximalist rationality[13] and for its key insight that the circulation of goods, people, and ideas helps make sociocultural worlds, including those made in the name of the economy[14] and bureaucracy.[15] Here I synthesize these economic and political anthropological strands in the sociality of the bazaar in Gaziantep. Such a synthesis shows how *kaçak* goods, people, and ideas on the move continue to configure new modes of citizenship and negotiate their "differential inclusion" in regimes of market and territorial integrity alike. And yet, from Metin's two families that straddle Iran and Turkey to the goods that piggyback on the pilgrim buses, circuits of goods and people thrive on crisscrossing those territories not despite but because of the very modern state borders that demarcate Iran, Turkey, and Syria.

THE MANY CAREERS OF CONTRABAND IN TURKEY'S BAZAARS: A *FERYATNAME* OVER *KAÇAK,* 1932

On December 17, 1932, just short of a decade after the founding of the Republic of Turkey and a bit more than twelve years after the establishment of the French Mandate in Syria, the Turkish daily *Cumhuriyet* ran on its front page a letter of lamentation, known as a *feryatname* in Ottoman Turkish. Written by a textile merchant from Mardin, a small border town three hundred kilometers west of Gaziantep, the letter directly addressed the editor in chief. It made such a strong impression on the editorial team that the renowned journalist and public intellectual Yunus Nadi devoted his front-page editorial to this "citizen's lament." Nadi prefaced the publication of the lament by highlighting that the letter had vividly illustrated the "worrisome" conditions of the Turkey-Syria border and their effect on the livelihoods of many citizens in the region:

> The other side of the border, in other words 1.7 meters away from it, is full of warehouses stocked with contraband goods. The situation has gone so far that a contraband merchant guarantees to deliver the ordered goods to anywhere the client wants on the other side of the border and does so with a 25 percent down payment. This guarantee is better understood probably as a deal offered from the Syrian side [of the border] to our contraband merchants. By observing this level of safety, envied even in the most orderly of countries, we could easily conclude that contraband commerce has emerged as the natural form of trade across our southern borders—and a natural form without precedence anywhere at that.[16]

The lament was indeed a moving one. Its author was too shy to plead for help but not too shy to name what he saw as a calamity that had befallen his business and his career as a merchant: *kaçak* goods and their merchants. The textile merchant of Mardin, Abdulrahman Veli Çelebizade, found himself writing the letter 350 miles away from home in the central Anatolian town of Sivas, where he was seeking employment. As he recounted his story of bankruptcy, Çelebizade remained worried not only about his family's "well-being" but also about that of the newly founded Republic of Turkey. He lamented the situation of the patriotic, tax-paying merchants caught up in the newly established and ineffective supply chains and formal procedures and driven out of business by the *kaçakçı* (contraband merchant):

> Everyone knows of those who, instead of defending the law of the state, have amassed large amounts of capital through trade across the border. Even before we get to these characters, [we should also mention] the women peddlers who are responsible for the perpetuation of contraband commerce within the city of Mardin. These women buy contraband goods from the merchants. They go in and out of everyone's house. Yet any of these women being caught while selling their contraband goods is unheard of. An upright merchant and an artisan with integrity like myself, on the other hand, is ruined and driven out of business for trying to sell the cloths and fabrics I have brought from Istanbul after a thousand problems [encountered] and a thousand assurances [given by the state].

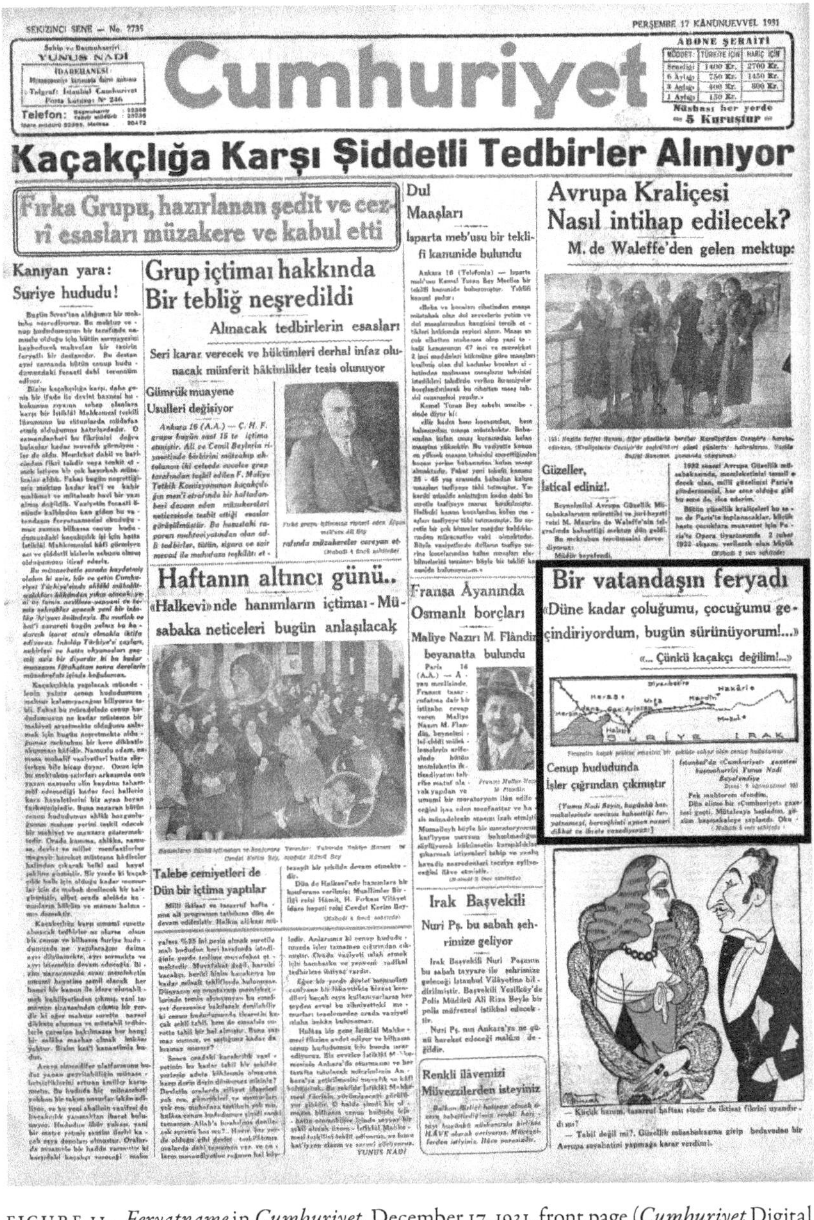

SEKİZİNCİ SENE — No. 2735

PERŞEMBE 17 KÂNUNUEVVEL 1931

Cumhuriyet

ABONE ŞERAİTİ

Nüshası her yerde 5 Kuruştur

Kaçakçlığa Karşı Şiddetli Tedbirler Alınıyor

Fırka Grupu, hazırlanan şedit ve cezaî esasları müzakere ve kabul etti

Kanıyan yara: Suriye hududu!

Grup içtimaı hakkında Bir tebliğ neşredildi

Alınacak tedbirlerin esasları

Seri karar verecek ve hükümleri derhal infaz olunacak münferit hâkimlikler tesis olunuyor

Gümrük muayene Usulleri değişiyor

Dul Maaşları

Isparta meb'usu bir teklifi kanunide bulundu

Avrupa Kraliçesi Nasıl intihap edilecek?

M. de Waleffe'den gelen mektup:

Güzeller, İstical ediniz!.

Haftanın altıncı günü..

«Halkevi» nde hanımların içtimaı - Müsabaka neticeleri bugün anlaşılacak

Fransa Âyanında Osmanlı borçları

Maliye Nazırı M. Flândin beyanatta bulundu

Bir vatandaşın feryadı

«Düne kadar çoluğumu, çocuğumu geçindiriyordum, bugün sürünüyorum!...»

«... Çünkü kaçakçı değilim!...»

Cenup hududunda İşler çığrından çıkmıştır

Talebe cemiyetleri de Dün bir içtima yaptılar

Irak Başvekili

Nuri Pş. bu sabah şehrimize geliyor

Renkli ilâvemizi Müvezzilerden isteyiniz

YUNUS NADİ

FIGURE 11. *Feryatname* in *Cumhuriyet*, December 17, 1931, front page (*Cumhuriyet* Digital Archives).

Çelebizade's letter also laid out how people in the former hinterlands of the Levant—such as Mardin, Antep, and Urfa—had to cope with costly and impractical supply routes of staple goods along the newly drawn border. With his days of commercial success and material wealth in Mardin now a distant memory because of the advent of the Syria-Turkey border and its *kaçak* markets, Çelebizade's lament was also for "those years when [he] paid one thousand *liras*" to the Turkish Republic in taxes. Curiously enough, Çelebizade held the "greed" of women peddlers (*bohçacı kadınlar*),[17] not the newly formed customs and taxation regimes in Turkey, responsible for his fall from Eden. To hold accountable those women and the ones who supplied them with contraband goods, Çelebizade had already set his eyes on a deterrent punishment mechanism: the newly established Courts of Independence (*İstiklal Mahkemeleri*), which had been established following World War I to convict "counterrevolutionary" forces. Ending his lament on a note of enthusiastic if opportunistic patriotism, Çelebizade called for the state execution of *kaçakçı* along with *asker kaçağı* (fugitives from compulsory military service, army defectors). His declaration of economic treachery as equivalent to political treason illuminates the force that the nationalist imaginary had acquired in less than a decade after independence in Turkey. Further, it yields a glimpse into the semantic domain of *kaçak*: in the dominant nationalist idiom of the freshly minted Republic of Turkey, fleeing from the legal obligations of citizenship, whether the obligation was to conduct economic transactions according to the laws or to serve in the military, constituted treason or treachery.

That same nationalist imaginary was in fact behind much more than the equation of political and economic transgression with treason or treachery. Particularly in Kurdish-majority areas and border zones, at the time subject to ongoing negotiations with the French and British Mandate regimes, *kaçak* had become a floating signifier co-opted by the state to regulate its territorial sovereignty and market integrity. Such nationalization of diverse places and the attendant formalization of diverse economic practices that had sustained these places became embedded in massive developmentalist transformations, particularly in the context of the "development" led by the industrializing state that undergirded the logics and logistics of a national economy. On the edges of such a national economy, and built over the specters of the Armenian genocide, commercial networks of (Gazi)antep had to be recategorized. Previous regional trade that had flowed across Anatolia and Great Syria under the Ottoman Empire was, with the help of national borders, divided into domestic and international trade, subject to a new set of regulations, including protective tariffs on commodities like tobacco, tea, oil, and sugar in Turkey.

As Mona pointed out in chapter 1, this motley assemblage in general, and the confluence of pilgrimage and commercial flows more specifically, gave no reason for theological alarm. It was rather a sign of the route's vitality.

The transformation of 'Aintab—from a provincial town on the outskirts of Aleppo in the early twentieth century into Gaziantep, an industrial hub of production and migration in the "developing" Turkey of the late twentieth century—is a case in point. In February of 1921, the Grand Assembly of the newly declared republic that would two years later officially become Turkey, modified the name of the town 'Aintab by adding the honorific prefix *gazi-* ("veteran"). It was bestowed upon the city to commemorate the resistance its inhabitants had shown against the French siege between April 1920 and February 1921.[18] Along with Maraş, renamed Kahramanmaraş ("heroic Maraş"), and Urfa, renamed Şanlıurfa ("renowned Urfa"), "veteran" 'Aintab— or to use its Latin-inscribed and Turkified name, Gaziantep—constituted the material grounds on which the so-called Turkish War of Independence was fought against the French and the British on the southern front. It was also a symbolically charged site marking the limits of the national body politic in Anatolia. While most of the Ottoman territories in the Mashriq and the Levant were being allocated to the British and French Mandates, these districts and their city centers with their newly glorified names were slated to become the new borderlands of a post-Ottoman Turkey. Antep therefore operated, and still does to this day, as an emblem of the successful national reconstruction and subsequent industrialization of Anatolia in Turkey.[19]

Prior to its emergence as a key site of national transformation, Antep was a rather insignificant town administratively tied, from the late sixteenth century until the late 1910s, to the provincial capital Aleppo, in what is now Syria. Prior to World War I, its population was about fifteen thousand—an estimate given after the city was ethnically cleansed of its Armenian population. In Turkish nationalist historiography, the city's historical transformation after the collapse of the Ottoman Empire and the Armenian genocide— indexed in the gradual change of its name from 'Aintab to Gazi Ayintab and finally Gaziantep—is often presented as a model success story in nation-state formation and industrialization.[20] Yet while these revisionist historiographies valorize 'Aintab's successful integration into post-Ottoman Anatolia and the newly founded Turkish Republic, what is often elided from view is that the transformation was gradual and involved extreme violence.[21] The rendering of the city's name on the 1932 front page of *Cumhuriyet* as "Gazi Ayintab" (while Maraş and Urfa were featured without their honorifics), on a map with railway tracks but no borders captures a city in transit between the provincial town it was and the industrial hub it would soon become.[22]

The republican project was not limited to changing the names of places in Anatolia in an attempt to reconstruct it as the Turkish homeland.[23] Name changes were often the discursive scaffolding of a spatial process that reclaimed Antep from the Levant, where it was a provincial town in the shadow of Aleppo, positioning it instead as the last post in "Turkish" Anatolia. Beyond Antep, it was implied in this spatial imaginary, one would cross into the Arab Levant to the south or into Turkey's Kurdistan to the east. This spatial process of economic and demographic restructuring, couched as national consolidation undertaken against French aggression and Arab collaboration, not only created a border where one had never existed but also completely altered the livelihoods of the producers, merchants, and inhabitants of Antep and its environs by changing the very routes of mobility and rearranging chains of trade and the supply of basic produce and goods.

As 'Aintab became Gaziantep, it also emerged as a laboratory of large-scale industrial development, urbanization, and infrastructural investment starting as early as the mid-1920s. The opening of the second textile factory in the country, Milli Mensucat Fabrikasi, in 1926, followed by the establishment of the Gaziantep Small Industrial Zone with a development and reconstruction loan from the United Nations Industrial Development Organization (UNIDO) in 1941, further accelerated Antep's development as *the* industrial city east of Ankara in Turkey. Particularly from the 1950s onwards, in no small part thanks to the expansion of the Small Industrial Zone and the subsequent establishment of the Gaziantep Organized Industrial District (GOID) in 1969 on its grounds, the city witnessed an exponential population increase due to labor migration drawing its travelers from the increasingly desolate and uncultivable countryside. As the GOID became Turkey's largest industrial zone through three expansions—in 1987, in 1994, and again in 1998—Antep's population grew accordingly. Doubling almost every twenty years since 1950, the city population reached 195,000 in 1960, 330,000 in 1970, and 642,000 in 1980. By 2001, its population had reached 1.2 million, making (Gazi)Antep the biggest city of the region.[24] The GOID, meanwhile, emerged as the premier export hub of Turkey's industrial production. Covering eleven million square meters, with eight hundred individual factories and firms that together employed 120,000 workers, the GOID exported $5.8B billion USD worth of products to more than 178 countries during my research there in 2012.[25] The state-led industrialization of Antep's economy was successful in "converting the commercial capital of the region into industrial capital," as one of its urban planners, Kemal Söylemezoğlu, put it in 1954.[26]

This process, however, did not simply transform the city's merchants into factory-owning capitalists and its agricultural producers into factory workers. As state and *Cumhuriyet* archives attest, massive industrialization efforts to "develop" the Antep economy had some unintended consequences. The high tariffs introduced to protect domestic textile and consumer goods in Antep's industrial zones continued to fuel the traffic in Syrian textiles and consumer goods into Turkey, where warehouses such as the ones described by Yusuf Nadi proliferated around the border. As Antep attempted to become a center of industry, in other words, it also grew as a hub for contraband commerce and cross-border trade. In fact, particularly in the context of massive urban and spatial transformation, the mutual imbrication of formal industry and contraband commerce defied the very terms of the development schemes that the state officials and urban planners such as Söylemezoğlu were so fond of implementing.

In an account that chronicles twenty-five days spent among the smugglers of Antep as an undercover investigative journalist for *Cumhuriyet,* the renowned novelist Yaşar Kemal captures the pervasiveness of contraband goods and commerce in the Gaziantep of the 1950s. He describes his struggle to locate contraband merchants: "On the street, or at the coffeehouse, I could have simply stopped a random man on the street and pitched: "Hi, my brother. How are you, my brother? I came to Antep to buy some merchandise. Some silk from Syria. My business used to be good in the past, now things have changed for the worse. My merchandise has been confiscated and I just got out of prison. Is there anything you could do for me? Let God keep you on your feet, and not let you fall like me. I too was a smuggler with a name, a reputation back in the day. Only God doesn't fall. What do you say, brother? I am a poor smuggler, brother. Kaçakçı Hasan of Adana. Would you be able to help a brother out?"[27] After having rehearsed this role as a self-deprecating attempt at crafting a persona for his investigation, he is quick to find out it might not have been that ridiculous after all. Kemal ends his reflections on that note:

"I should have just said that, and I would have been in."

Overwhelmed by the categories of people whose paths cross the contra-band bazaars of Antep, and particularly intrigued by the older women ped-dlers of the bazaar who sell textiles such as jackets and silk products and fabrics, Yaşar Kemal remarks: "I learned only later that the number of these women peddlers [bohçacı kadın] surpasses one thousand in Antep. In times that are known to be quiet and away from the watchful eyes of the zabıta [commercial police], they stuff their sack [bohça] and visit home after home." With his incisive description, Kemal highlights the ever-changing resource-fulness with which the mobile subjects least suspected of illegal trade carried most of the goods into homes. "Their way of working would change in response to the way the police worked. This time, they have wrapped up the whole roll of the silk fabric around their waist, and pulled a çarşaf [full-body covering, or chador] over it, and then they go off to the homes, to the women's bathhouses, to wherever a soon-to-be-bride is present. Wherever there is a wedding, there is one of them."[28]

The rapid industrialization of Antep's economy only deepened and fueled the informalization and contraband commerce in the region. This increasing informalization together with a growing population produced myriad plans to redesign the city to minimize the possibility of trafficking amid the bur-geoning sociality of traffic. In 1997, after Gaziantep's population surpassed one million, making it the fifth most populous city in Turkey, the municipal government initiated a series of infrastructural projects, including ones aimed at easing the city's clogged traffic. The locations of the two bus stations at the time—one on Ali Fuat Avenue serving those traveling to provinces throughout Turkey, and one on İnönü Avenue serving nearby villages and towns in Gaziantep Province—were cited as the main reasons for the old city's congested arteries. Under the leadership of the municipal governor at the time, Celal Doğan, and with corporate sponsorship from some of the biggest firms in the city's zone, the new Gaziantep bus station moved this bus traffic outside of the city center and next to the industrial zone to consolidate a hub for all buses serving within or beyond Gaziantep. Built on eight thou-sand square meters and serving more than seventy bus firms with a daily traffic of more than four hundred buses, the new station was completed in 2000. Thirteen years after its completion, it faced the same fate as its ances-tors in Antep—being engulfed by the expanding city.

The consolidation of bus traffic outside the city had evacuated large plots of industrial space in the city center. When a co-venture between two Antep businessmen to build a gas station and a mall failed to materialize, the bus

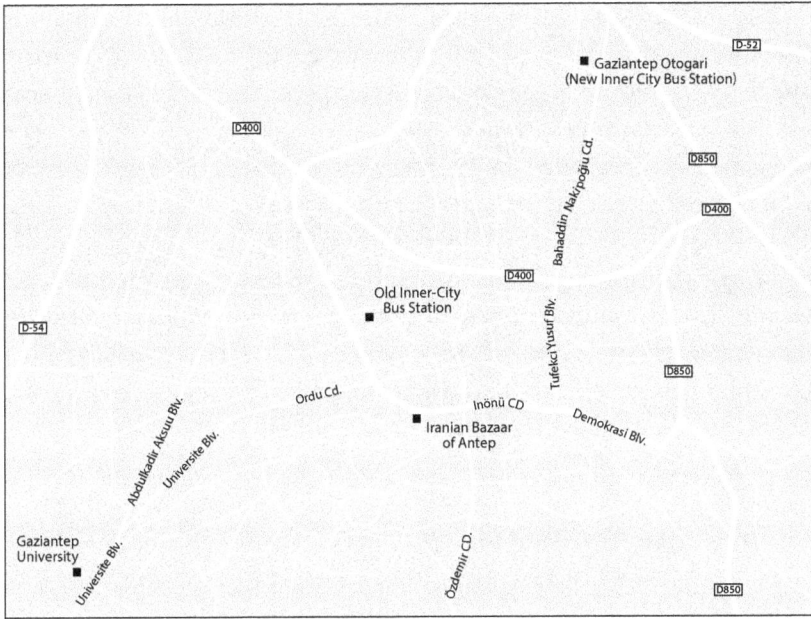

MAP 3. (Gazi)Antep (by Bill Nelson).

Map labels:
- D-52
- Gaziantep Otogari (New Inner City Bus Station)
- D400
- D850
- Bahaddin Nakipoğlu Cd.
- D400
- D400
- Old Inner-City Bus Station
- Tüfekçi Yusuf Blv.
- D-54
- D850
- Ordu Cd.
- İnönü CD
- Demokrasi Blv.
- Iranian Bazaar of Antep
- Abdulkadir Aksuu Blv.
- Üniversite Blv.
- Özdemir CD.
- Gaziantep University
- Üniversite Blv.
- D850

station on Ali Fuat Avenue was reclaimed as the grounds for an open-air market on Sundays. The former bus station on İnönü Avenue, on the other hand, was harder to market to real estate development. The cluster of mechanic shops initially set up to cater to the many buses and minibuses that passed through Antep, and the two-star hotels where long-distance travelers, local businessmen, and sex workers intermingled, "did not present the conditions most conducive to residential real estate development," as one municipal official described to me in 2012. It was on the grounds of this former bus station that the Iranian Bazaar would emerge. With no other parties interested in developing the vacant lot, this zone transformed into a terminal catering exclusively to Iranian pilgrimage buses en route to Syria. Although Iranian buses had been stopping here for years, it was only in the early 2000s, once the new bus station had opened and informal booths and mobile carts had started to proliferate around the bus station, that the mechanic shops and the hotels in the area received some new neighbors. While formal shops continued catering to Iranian pilgrims, the Gaziantep locals frequented the Iranian Bazaar for contraband goods, such as sugar, tea, and tobacco, often shuttled on the same buses that carried the Iranian pilgrims.

Because these pilgrims and their contraband companions on and under the buses made the bazaar what it is, the increasing popularity of the route and the steady growth of the bazaar in Antep put the site on city government officials' radar as a place whose revenue remained mostly off the city's tax-revenue accounting books. Once the Iranian Bazaar became a space of economic transaction on the scale of a formal shopping arcade in 2010, state-backed and bank-financed projects attempted to capitalize on those successes by bringing all bazaar transactions into the state's purview and onto its records. The enormity of the task did not escape the state official responsible for that record keeping: he was to bring the off-the-record economy of the bazaar into the registers of the state. "To the extent possible, of course," the municipal official added, qualifying his statement.

DEGREES OF FORMALIZATION: OSMAN AND YAŞAR'S LINGERIE SHOP IN THE ATATÜRK ARCADE

In mid-July of 2012, two weeks before Metin's monologue on contraband and formalization, Osman and Yaşar were keen to take the next big step and move their father's store to the newly constructed Atatürk Pasajı. According to the brothers, Metin's vehement opposition to the mall was driven more by what he did not know and by his generational difference than by what he did know.

Having grown up practically in their father's shop, Osman and Yaşar were no newcomers to the bazaar. Nor were they inexperienced merchants of a "new generation" mistaking themselves for "entrepreneurs" (*girişimci*), as Metin dismissively described them, while still admiring their ambition. Whenever doubts were voiced about their plans to move into the new arcade, the brothers were quick to point out that they had the best of both worlds: they had not only learned the bazaar business from their father also completed their university studies in marketing and business management. It was this combination of formal university training and practical know-how of the bazaar itself that positioned them as "organic businessmen," as they preferred to describe themselves.

When I spoke with them in 2010, Osman, the older of the two, reflected on their motivation, vision, and reasoning. Osman recounted: "Times are changing. I think Metin and others like him in the bazaar need to stop resisting change and just embrace it. Even the municipal government has woken up to the fact that the Iranian Bazaar is much more than a simple informal bazaar where locals shop for *kaçak* tea. There are a million other places that sell it on every corner!" Osman paused and waited for a reaction. I kept my eyes on my notes, nodding. Osman continued, "It is turning to the Iranian tourists and their demands that must guide our businesses here. Unlike Metin, who curses Iranians that do not fancy his inventory, we actively seek to adjust our merchandising according to our customers' demands. That is why we went out of our way to include Syrian lingerie along with other undergarments sourced from Istanbul. The days of waiting for *kaçak* cigarettes to pay for your rent because your formal shop is not doing good business with the pilgrims themselves are over." Osman had just made me understand the reasons behind the mixing of formal and informal business. Observing the intrigued look on my face, Osman scaled up: "After all these years spent inhaling the dust of the bazaar, I think we know where this marketplace is going. Unless something horrific happens and the pilgrimage ceases to exist, this place will turn into one of the most important touristic centers in Antep. And only then will the likes of Metin accept that they failed to get on with the times. And we are still merchants [*tüccar*], but not just merchants! We are also entrepreneurs. We don't see how one could claim to be one without the other, particularly in a bazaar like this, and particularly now when the market is saturated with the same goods, and the numbers of pilgrims keep growing."

As pilgrim after pilgrim asked for more elaborate and embroidered undergarments in their shop, Osman and Yaşar were naturally led to the Souq al-Hamidiyyeh in Damascus, where the particular style known as "Syrian lingerie" was invented.[29] "We could have done what Metin has been doing for decades with his pots and pans," Yaşar said sarcastically. Instead of ignoring the demands of the customers and losing them to the merchants of the Souq al-Hamidiyyeh, however, Osman and Yaşar put in their first request for a wholesale shipment of forty sets of Syrian lingerie. When the shipment, tucked into a secret compartment of a bus, finally arrived, Osman and Yaşar launched their Syrian line of undergarments with a promotion: for every two sets of Syrian lingerie, they included an Istanbul-produced set for free. With the Turkish *lira* strong against the Syrian pound and no tariffs to drive up their prices, the promotion caught on. "It was a way for us to move our older merchandise *and* test out the potential for Syrian lingerie in the bazaar," Yaşar explained. "And it worked!" The irony of their plan to formalize business through trafficked textile products was hard to miss: its entire success was made possible by evading taxes and moving the Syrian lingerie across the border in ways that were anything but formal. When I posed the question of whether this was all that different from smuggling cigarettes into Antep, Osman and Yaşar acknowledged the homology between the two circuits, but they also made sure to highlight the novelty of what they were doing in language adorned with market-speak—that made its rules as it went along.

To navigate the tenuously differentiated degrees of formality in the economy, bazaar merchants combined a set of formal and informal business practices. For Osman and Yaşar, combining the sale of kitchen appliances to pilgrims and contraband tea, sugar, and tobacco to the Antep locals was an outmoded and risky portfolio of bazaar business associated with small profit margins and an outdated mindset. At the same time, they did not formalize their business completely: becoming "formally" or officially "small-scale entrepreneurs" by moving their business to Atatürk Pasajı was logistically dependent on the contraband compartments of the buses and trucks that shuttled goods between Syria and Turkey.

It is through creating, exposing, policing, and fining contraband commerce that states link up their economies nationally and regionally, and reinforce them territorially under the rubric of "market integrity." Here I illustrate that that notion is always already bound up in territorial integrity and state formation in Anatolia and the Levant after the Ottoman Empire and the French and British Mandates. As we saw in Çelebizade's *feryatname,* this process of linking and unlinking the economy is an inherently political project that lies at the heart of state formation and hence of territorialization itself—a relationship I will examine more closely in the next chapter.

If anything, therefore, formalization is the state's attempt to perpetuate the mythical overlap between economic theory and practice while smuggling in a notion of territorial sovereignty that ensures both the territorial integrity of the nation-state and the market integrity of the national economy. It is a claim to territorial sovereignty and legality that relies upon contraband commerce as its constitutive outside. Actors interpolated into projects of formalization, like Osman and Yaşar, negotiate the terms of that interpolation by intermingling formality and informality and redrawing their boundaries, even in projects such as the Atatürk Arcade that aim at bringing off-the-record transactions onto the state's accounting books. Syrian lingerie trafficked through buses and turned into the only merchandise in Osman and Yaşar's store captures that intermingling in material form.

What none of the merchants in Antep had seen coming was the abrupt end of pilgrimage from Iran to Syria in February of 2012. In Gaziantep, the Atatürk Pasajı, erected to greet its Iranian customers with shops named after Tehran hotspots, remained mostly empty. More than 250 stores shut down, and twenty-five merchants declared bankruptcy when they were unable to pay off the loans they had taken out from Turkish banks in order to be part of the new arcade. Osman and Yaşar's worst nightmare had come true. With no other sources of income to compensate for their losses, they disappeared, leaving their guarantor-father to deal with the many bazaar merchants they were indebted to and the bank officials demanding immediate payment or foreclosure. By the time I returned to Antep for my long fieldwork stay, more than half of the merchants and mobile vendors I knew from earlier stays had dispersed across the city, if not the country, fleeing their debts. Meanwhile, the motley assemblage of the bazaar had generated new contingent conversions of value. The rooms of the two- and three-star hotels, most commonly associated with sex work in the area, were rented out as studios to the Syrian refugees who continued to flock to the city, causing an exponential surge in property prices. In addition, a few logistical firms and a travel agency, all specializing in transport from and to Iraqi Kurdistan, had already moved into Atatürk Pasajı—indexing yet another route born out of the arresting of mobility elsewhere.

CONCLUSION

Abdulrahman Çelebizade admitted in his letter that not only the *kaçak* goods but also the costly and unreliable nature of the officially sanctioned routes of commodity and supply chains (even of staples such as sugar) helped lay the foundation for the contraband trade to proliferate in Mardin, Urfa, Antep, and the broader border landscape across Iran, Iraq, Turkey, and Syria. For Çelebizade, the proliferation of contraband commerce and the social profile of those driving its proliferation revealed that the high-tariff customs regime had been established to guard the national sugar industry against competition from imported goods—making *kaçak* the "natural form" of commerce, as Yunus Nadi put it. And the procedures that aimed to tie Mardin to Istanbul for key commodity supply chains did not fare any better than the international customs regimes, according to Çelebizade. In fact, the slow and expensive procedure on the domestic front, which had then directed

Çelebizade and many others like him to Istanbul—as opposed to Aleppo or Mosul prior to the advent of national borders—came at added cost and with added risks. Even when merchants were able to secure the shipment of their orders from Istanbul, the transportation and taxation costs drove the prices of their goods so high that the domestic customers in the region had yet another reason to turn to *kaçak mal,* or fugitive goods. Çelebizade's choice of example was telling: "I had a neighbor who bought two crates of sugar by paying the custom taxes and put them in his store. He was able to sell it only slowly, and only to the temporary out-of-town clients at the price he had acquired then." Çelebizade continued, "Once he ran out, he once again applied to the Customs Office, declaring that he was going to send the two crates of sugar acquired at a given date to Diyarbekir. Not only did he recover his losses [from the initial two crates of sugar], but he even registered a substantial profit. He has continued since then to repeat [this operation]." Çelebizade had taken meticulous notes on everything and was ready and able to furnish evidence to make his point clear. "I had only one crate of sugar, for which I had paid the customs fee. I consumed half of that at home, and the remaining half I was able to sell only over the course of ten months. My honorable sir, all those who carry out contraband commerce, those who enable them, are all armed drunkards, monsters. Even the most merciful among them is the convict of a few murders. For them there is no homeland, no nation." Çelebizade was going for the kill to defend the nation, one market and commodity at a time: "There is only money. If the French were to give them money, they would attack us today. And those who are responsible for stopping them but instead look the other way, or ignore the regulation of our borders, are as much traitors as the contraband merchants themselves."

Çelebizade, as if he wanted to be mistaken for a municipally important local politician, ended his lamentation with a call for justice: "If the Courts of Independence [are called to bear on these crimes], all of them will be caught and hanged; the most terrible among them will be cleansed, and those predisposed to doing terrible things will stop out of fear, and maybe even their moral character could be ameliorated." Çelebizade was certain. "There is no other solution. In order to save and ensure the livelihood and future of fourteen million people, there is no sin, but rather merit in God's sight, in chopping off the heads of five to ten, or even fourteen thousand bandits, drunkards, and traitors."

In Çelebizade's logic, bringing goods produced in Syria to the newly demarcated territories of the Republic of Turkey and selling them there was tantamount to treason against the national body politic. The solution he proposed in order to stop contraband was as severe as his reaction to the growth and sustenance of the commercial ties across the border and their micro-operators under the new border regime, which demarcates two separate national regimes of sovereignty and, by extension, economies. The clash between the nationalist imaginary and the material conditions on the ground in the 1930s caused much pain, lamentation, and rage in actors in Anatolia and the Levant. The desperate measures proposed by Çelebizade could be productively approached as a lens through which to understand the politically charged nature of economic life under ideological and material construction. It is under these conditions of extreme uncertainty that the economic "wrongdoing" associated with *kaçak* economies and commodities is cast as being as despicable an act for the national body politic as the acts of those who refuse to serve the country as soldiers or those who tap into the state-laid grids of oil distribution to steal for private benefit what is meant to be a public good. The itineraries of merchants like Çelebizade and Metin, as well as those of Osman and Yaşar, and their differential embeddings at variegated scales in contraband circuits in Antep provide us with a point of entry into the broader cartography of the Turkish economy and the choreography that this cartography sets into motion.

Tracking histories of contraband from the 1930s to the present day as formations coeval with the advent of national borders and modern economies illustrates how informality or contraband needs to be approached historically and not reduced to instantiations of states failing to regulate economic life because of incompetence, corruption, or incapacity. Nor are *kaçak* commodities simply tokens of reinsertion into the modality of neoliberal economic arrangements, as resistant rural migrants and the urban poor are often presented as undertaking with their distinct cultural and moral economies. Neither contraband commerce, nor the intermingling of so-called formal and informal economic practices at the Iranian Bazaar, nor that of *ziyarat* and *tijarat,* is an anomaly; it is part and parcel of modern capitalism and its formal economies. As Timothy Mitchell instructs us: "Recall that even today, a century or more after the global consolidation of the capitalist order, half a century or more after the invention of the economy, a majority of people live hybrid lives, neither market nor subsistence, neither capital nor labor, neither within the national economy nor quite outside it, escaping the fixed categories of economic discourse."[30] Mitchell, expanding on the fugitives of these fixed categories also of law and political discourse, adds that "the undetermined identities of those whose lives place them at the edge of the economy represent neither a non-economic exterior, nor a temporary contradiction destined to resolve itself." Beyond providing grounds to rethink various alignments of capital accumulation and land development in minor urban environments and across modern state borders, the Iranian Bazaar of Antep helps us see *kaçak* and fugitive economic action for what they are: central and constitutive elements of the national economy in Turkey and more broadly of the social production of the region beyond national confines. It is to the relationship between the route and the border as the emblematic limits of those national confines that we now turn.

Muhsin's Pathways, or Mitigating Sanctions with Tobacco Seats

TWENTY MINUTES AFTER OUR arrival at Gaziantep's Iranian Bazaar, the bus was empty. Or so I thought. Alongside the other pilgrims, I had disembarked and made my way to the bazaar to surprise Metin and the Professor. The first one to pick me out among the pilgrims was Metin's apprentice. "Look who's coming!" he exclaimed and turned toward the Professor and Metin, who were taking a break from Gaziantep's punishing heat under a fig tree. "Where's the baklava?" asked the Professor, opening his arms wide to hug me. I realized that I had left the *sohan*, a saffron brittle originally from the city of Qom, on the bus. "I have something else for you from Iran," I replied. "Let me run back and get it."

I headed to the front door of the bus. It was locked. The back door, however, was open. I climbed in and was startled to find someone hastily moving things a few rows down from my seat. The man shoved whatever he had into a large plastic bag. Seeming even more startled than I was, he looked up and gave me an awkward smile. I nodded and made my way to my seat. As I passed, I saw that the leather sleeves of both seats had been removed, revealing hollow compartments inside. Two thin rectangular pieces of foam were sitting on top of the leather sleeves.

I opened the overhead compartment above my seat, took my backpack down, and unzipped the middle pocket. I grabbed the two *sohan* boxes I had picked up from the Tajrish bazaar in Tehran and made my way to the back of the bus. When I passed the man again, from the corner of my eye, I could see that the plastic bag contained a dozen or so cartons of cigarettes. I gave him an awkward smile of my own and hurried off to join the merchants with the promised sweets. Ten minutes later, I noticed the man with the bag make his way into the Atatürk Arcade across the street from Metin's store. He came out empty-handed.

An hour and a half later, when the bus was nearing the Syria/Turkey border, I felt a tap on my shoulder. I turned around and found the man with the plastic bag standing next to me. He produced a carton of Kents and extended it to me. Unsure of how to respond, I waited for an explanation. "You call it 'the right of the eye' [*göz hakkı*] in Turkish, don't you? You saw it, so you are entitled to a piece of the cake," he explained.

"You're too generous, but I cannot accept that. My eye didn't stay on it," I responded.

"Drop the etiquette of courtesy. Please, I insist," the man insisted.

"You're too kind, but I cannot possibly. Besides, I am trying to quit," I smiled in response.

He sighed under his breath and said, "Very well then. It was probably not too surprising to see that we carry contraband goods on the bus, was it? After all, this is a route known for both saint visitation and commerce [*ham ziyarat ham tijarat*]," and he forced a smile.

"Sure," I responded with the expected nod. I added, "But that looked like too much *tijarat* and not enough *ziyarat*."

"Ha! That was a good one, Agha-ye . . ."

"Yıldız. Emrah."

"I'm Muhsin. Pleased to meet you," Muhsin lowered his head with his right hand on his heart. Before I could squeeze in a "Likewise," Muhsin continued, "Feel free to visit us in the back. My wife and I would be glad to talk about not only *tijarat* but also *ziyarat*." I said I would love to take him up on his offer and followed him to the back of the bus.

Muhsin introduced me to his wife, Narmin. I could tell that Muhsin wanted to explain what I had seen. Wary of making him and Narmin uncomfortable, I just started with my default question. Turning to Narmin, I asked if they had something specific in mind that they wanted Hazrat-i Zainab's intercession on. Narmin did not skip a beat. "A roof over our heads that we can call our own. That's it. That is all I want from Zainab," she said. "I have been working for ten years, Mohsen for almost fifteen years," Narmin continued, "and yet what do we have to show for it? Nothing. We had come really close to having enough money to buy an apartment in 2009, but then you remember what happened?" She seemed to be referring to the postelection protest commonly associated with the "Green Movement."

Mohsen interjected, "Since then, we have been playing catch-up." He paused, then added, "If our tobacco is better than our money in crossing the border, then one is in trouble. And in Iran that's exactly where we are." I just listened. Mohsen was right.

Before Muhsin could continue, Narmin took over: "Please don't get the wrong idea. We are not smugglers [*ghachaghchi*]; we are not in this to make money. We are just tired of losing money. It is those who have unleashed these sanctions turning our worlds upside-down that are the real smugglers."

Seeing me nod in agreement, Muhsin picked up where Narmin dropped it. "No, actually we are. Everyone is. After more than forty years of living under sanctions, everyone in Iran, one way or another, has become a smuggler."

FOUR

Bordering Ziyarat

KAÇAK COORDINATES OF TERRITORY

THE *HAJJ-I FUQARA'* pilgrimage route has produced territory and sovereignty anew along the shifting borders of Persia, Anatolia, and the Levant.
Rather than mere physical demarcations of already territorialized regimes of
state sovereignty, borders have recently been conceptualized as "maelstrom[s]
of people, landscapes, and connections that both increasingly bind the region
into a new grid and also maintain links outside of it at the same time."[1] In the
case of the Turkey-Syria border, the spatial and temporal nesting of pilgrim
and merchant mobility on the route of the pilgrimage helped produce this
maelstrom on a regional scale. Extending Henri Lefebvre's dynamic and processual framing and his notion of spatial production to the Turkey-Syria border,[2] this chapter draws out how histories and geographies of *ziyarat* and
tijarat across the Middle East are unevenly superimposed onto one another
along the pilgrimage of the poor. That uneven superimposition constitutes the
possibility of mobility for a variety of social actors in Iran (and the region more
broadly). Such actors include contraband couriers who rode on pilgrim buses
while transiting through the Iranian Bazaar as well as pilgrims who construed
their journeys as both saint visitation (*ziyarat*) and commerce (*tijarat*). After
the route ceased because of the Syrian conflict, the same subjects had to find
different routes and vehicles of cross-border mobility in a dramatically shifting
geography. By *kaçak territorialization* here, I refer to these subjects' spatial
practices of crossing the terrestrial border within the context of the broader
spatial production of the Syria-Turkey borderlands. So while my analysis
remains attentive to the border as a key institution through which the state
apparatus exercises domestic sovereignty around the edges of its territory, and
international juridical sovereignty with what lies beyond, it is the border crossers of these spatial ecologies that this chapter aims to chronicle.

In the case of the Turkey-Syria border, the spatial production had bound a diverse set of people to a new grid through the *hajj-i fuqara'* route and beyond. What, I ask, was the relationship between the plans and uses of that grid and the traffic in goods and people that often diverged in their use from the planned spatial outcomes? Lefebvre's framework transposed onto the Turkey-Syria border helps us redefine the border as a palimpsest[3] of sovereignty, a layering of competing cartographies and their attendant regimes of mobility in the making of the Turkey-Syria border. Following the cross-border merchants that move across this dynamic process of border making, I suggest, provides us with an understudied method of centering the *kaçak* coordinates of territorialization in histories of border formation.

To parse out the layers that make up this palimpsest by way of following its fugitives (another meaning of *kaçak*), this chapter tracks shifts in the regulation, policing, and criminalization of cross-border mobility and the official designations of mobile subjects as pilgrims, tourists, merchants, or smugglers. These crossers of the Syria-Turkey borderlands—or in the language of Lefebvre, and more pointedly de Certeau, users of space—shaped patterns of modern state territorialization and border formation.[4] The routes and pathways they exploit are produced, contested, and transformed through a range of sociopolitical and discursive struggles over the precise coordinates of the region.

The pilgrimage of the poor and the pathways of moonlighting that it has opened up for its travelers are precisely what has allowed merchants and other patrons, including pilgrims themselves, to fully partake in these struggles. Through the confluence of *ziyarat* as religious mobility and *kaçak* as commercial mobility, the pilgrimage route has insinuated itself into the geographies it has traversed and connected. From the large "Welcome to Syria" placards written in Persian that greet people entering from Turkey at the Öncüpınar border to the bazaar in Gaziantep that is named after the closest Iranian territory some eight hundred kilometers away, the traces of *hajj-i fuqara'* in the border region are very visible indeed.

In order to understand visitation as a particular form of transnational mobility in the case of *hajj-i fuqara'*, however, we need to track what I refer to here as the *kaçak,* or fugitive, coordinates of territorialization that the pathways of Zainab have inscribed in the region. It is in that process of tracking the transformations of contraband commodities and circulators—and the state regulations concerning them—that we reveal the layering of the border as a palimpsest of sovereignty.[5] Each section in this chapter examines a particular history of sovereignty: the emergence of Iranian *ziyarat* in the Mashriq, the delineation of borders in the era of mandated nation-states, and state efforts to territorialize national space by policing contraband commerce and incarcerating its practitioners, while forming a more complex and selectively controlled mobility for the pilgrims.

TRANSIMPERIAL COORDINATES OF *ZIYARAT* ACROSS PERSIA, IRAQ, AND THE LEVANT

As discussed in the Introduction, *ziyarat,* pilgrimage to the tombs of holy persons, has long been practiced across the Islamic world. It has also remained a topic of theological debate among different schools of Islamic jurisprudence, revived time and again under different historical and political conditions. The emergence of *ziyarat* as a problem of diplomacy and the nexus of an imperial distinction to be drawn between the Ottomans and the Safavids dates back to the very first treaty between the two dynasties in 1555. This treaty included a clause specifically on pilgrimage mobility: in exchange for Safavid recognition of Ottoman sovereignty over Baghdad, Basra, and western Kurdistan, the Ottomans guaranteed Safavid subjects' safe transit over Ottoman lands to the Hijaz for *hajj*[6] and access to *'atabat* shrines in Najaf, Karbala, Kazemayn, and Samarra in current-day Iraq.[7]

Yet these Ottoman assurances of safe passage to the Hijaz did not generate a continuous traffic of Iranian pilgrims. Instead, at various points in Islamic history, and especially at times of strife between the Safavids and the Ottomans, "the visitation of Karbala substituted for the pilgrimage to Mecca."[8] This substitution ignited lively debates over *ziyarat*'s permissibility. After the Safavids designated Shi'i Islam the state religion, the substitution—born out of a historical conjuncture at a transimperial nexus—became the centerpiece of canonical theological debates. The Safavid formalization often lent the legitimacy of theological deliberation to certain ritual practices, the permissibility of which were contested among the Sunni schools of jurisprudence. Among such practices, *ziyarat* was arguably the most important.

The Shi'i endorsement of *'atabat* visitation, which was taken as akin to the *hajj* in religious value, was a result of processes of doctrinal differentiation refracted through imperial formations between Anatolia and Persia. What was at stake for the Sunni theologians—even for those who deemed *ziyarat* permissible—was nothing short of the singularity of *hajj* as *the* pilgrimage in Islam. If *ziyarat,* particularly *'atabat* visitation, was comparable to *hajj* in terms of the type of religious virtue that a traveler could potentially attain, then the canonical distinction between minor pilgrimages (*ziyarat*) and *the* pilgrimage (*hajj*) was hard to sustain. The value attached to the visitation of Imam Husayn's tomb in Karbala is apparent in a citation attributed to the sixth imam, Ja'far al-Sadiq, which states, "Whoever visits Husayn's tomb on 'Ashura is like one who performs pilgrimage to God's seat."[9] As Yitzhak Nakash notes, the connection between the distinctly Shi'i institution of the imamate and visitation lies at the heart of the long history of confessional differentiation, with the virtues of visitation for the pious Shi'a dating back to the eighth century. The following citation, attributed to the eighth imam, 'Ali al-Rida (d. 818), is a case in point: "Every Shi'i has a line of contact and an understanding [*'ahd*] with the imams. The visitation of tombs of the imams is one of the best means for fulfilling and being faithful to that contact and understanding. Whoever undertakes *ziyarat* of his own free will, thereby confirming the wish of the imams, for him the imams will intercede on the day of resurrection."[10]

The institutionalization and formalization of visitation, particularly in the nineteenth and early twentieth centuries—thanks in no small part to the relative improvement in Ottoman-Qajar relations after their last war in 1821–23—produced a rich archive of printed manuals of visitation throughout Iran. These manuals not only were formative of pilgrims' ritual practices but also operated as chronicles of the theological debates surrounding the cult of saints in Islam. They always featured quotations attributed to imams from the tenth to thirteenth centuries.[11] If one purpose of these *ziyarat* manuals was to claim the historicity of visitation within a particularly Shi'i genealogy of theological tradition, another was to preserve the importance of visitation in (re)producing a particularly Shi'i identity in the face of three challenges that emerged during the first three decades of the twentieth century: the criticism of visitation by Islamic modernists, the revival of the Wahhabi movement under 'Abd al-'Aziz ibn Sa'ud, and the formation of modern Iraq.

As Islamic modernists such as Muhammad Rashid Rida advocated giving scripture a greater place in the daily practices of Muslims and minimizing the ritualistic differences between the Sunnis and Shi'a, they specifically focused on the role of visitation, arguing that *ziyarat* was permissible only for the purposes of remembrance and paying respects to the dead. All other practices associated with *ziyarat*, Rida and his interlocutors argued, should be banned. These included "the glorification and worship of the dead and the tomb; the making of personal requests from the saint; the consideration of the tomb as possessing qualities capable of curing people from illness and disease; the recitation of poetry by the tomb; the placement of money boxes by the tomb for the benefit of its attendants; votive offerings and slaughtering by the tomb; the circumambulation of the tomb as if it were the Ka'ba; and the building or repair of mosques near the tomb."[12]

The emergence of puritanical Sunni Wahhabis in central Arabia posed the most violent challenge to the visitation practices of Shi'i subjects in both the Ottoman Mashriq and Qajar Iran. Inspired by a strict interpretation of Islamic jurisprudence associated with the Hanbali School and relying on a handful of scripturalist Hanbali scholars such Ibn Taymiyya, Wahhabis opposed the concept of *shafa'a* (seeking saintly intercession in worldly matters). They instead argued that the cult of saints and tomb veneration were incompatible with the monotheistic teachings of Islam. Their opposition, however, also took the form of physical destruction. In the name of opposing *shafa'a,* Wahhabis destroyed Shi'i tombs in Medina and Mecca in 1792, sacking Karbala and stripping the shrines of Imam Husayn and his half brother 'Abbas of all their gold and precious donations such as carpets. In 1803 and 1806, they targeted Najaf.[13] The structural elements resonate strongly here with the targeting of Sayyida Zainab shrine in postrevolutionary Syria. Whether for the purposes of mitigating or exacerbating the doctrinal differences between Shi'i and Sunni subjects, the routes of visitation were intimately linked to the control of traffic across transimperial borders— sedimented by the exercise of imperial sovereignty and embedded in a broader process of regional state formation.

The Ottoman state's political suspicion of Iranians on the move in Anatolia and the Mashriq outlived the Safavids and the Qajars alike, as Dr. Murtada briefly touched upon in chapter 2. Iranian complaints, submitted well into the early twentieth century, about the ill-treatment of pilgrims on their way to Hijaz and Iraq were often responded to with Ottoman objections to Iranian rituals of caliph condemnation.[14] What emerges in these historically constellated and regionally engulfing dynamics is that the permissibility of practices, such as *ziyarat,* that allegedly marked doctrinal differences was intimately tied to political contestation. Moreover, jurisprudential debates over *ziyarat* were most lively and polarized at times of political upheaval. We observe this, for instance, during the imperial battles across

Anatolia and Persia over the Qizilbash in the eighteenth century,[15] and during the mass conversions of Sunni Arab tribes to Shi'i Islam in the nineteenth and twentieth centuries in Iraq.[16] The shifting landscape of pilgrimage therefore must be understood in relation to the shifting regional landscape of state sovereignty.

Throughout the late 1890s and early 1900s, the archival record exhibits increasing concern on the part of Ottoman officials over the "spread of Shi'ism" in Hamidian Iraq.[17] Countless reports accumulated in Sublime Porte archives exhibit this concern. Coming precisely after the loss of most of its remaining Balkan possessions and their predominantly Christian populations as the result of the catastrophic war lost to Russia in 1877–78, the empire under Abdülhamit attempted to revive the sultan's claim to supreme religious leadership enshrined in his role as the caliph, or the *amir al-mu'minin,* of all Muslims worldwide.[18] The ideological retrenching of the empire on the basis of a universal Islamic identity, however, generated novel problems precisely because any challenge to Ottoman legitimacy arising from an Islamic context acquired new urgency.[19] The Ottoman-Qajar contestation over Iraq and the movement of Qajar subjects across Ottoman territory posed a doctrinally charged challenge.

In a report dated August 26, 1907, the Ottoman ambassador to Tehran, Ali Galip Bey, proposed a four-step plan to curb the "spread of Shi'ism" in Hamidian Iraq in particular, and within the Ottoman Empire more broadly.[20] First, Ali Galip called for the appointment of officially elected Sunni *'ulama* to counter the Shi'i propaganda that had taken Iraq "hostage." Only through investment in the education of the local populations, and a concerted counterpropaganda initiative undertaken by Sunni religious scholars, Ali Galip Bey maintained, could Sunnism and loyalty to the caliph be inculcated in Iraqis. Second, the ambassador urged that all *mujtahids,* students, and clerics (*akhundha*) of Qajar background be expelled from the shrine cities of Iraq. Third, he stressed that all Iraqis and Shi'a should acknowledge the generosity of the Ottoman caliph in making it possible for Shi'i men of learning to come to the holy shrines of Iraq to pay visits to the saints in the first place. He argued that a formal mechanism for controlling the movements of Iranian *zuwwar* to the holy shrines should be applied to restrict the time they were allowed to spend in Iraq and prevent their circulation among the population. Last, the ambassador proposed new border policies that would separate pilgrims from merchants and render redundant the Iranian middlemen who allegedly expedited the business of Shi'i merchants and pilgrims in Iraq, be it at the border, in the market, or around the holy shrines themselves. Only through such a comprehensive plan, Ali Galip concluded, could the Ottoman government undermine the credibility of Iranian propaganda, which claimed that the shah alone was the sole protector of all Shiʻi interests, and rein in the mass conversion of Iraq's Sunnis to Shiʻi Islam.

Another report by Ali Rıza Bey, the former Ottoman *şehbender* (consul) in the northern Iranian towns of Khoy and Salmas, highlighted that Ottoman efforts to curb the spread of Shiʻi Islam were doomed unless state officials grasped both the religious prestige of the Iranian mullahs and their financial and institutional independence from the Iranian state. Without understanding these two ways that the Ottoman and Qajar states differed in their relation to the *ʻulama*, Ali Rıza Bey concluded, Hamidian Iraq was ill equipped to distinguish the cleric from the citizen, let alone the pilgrim from the merchant: "The easiest thing in Iran is to become rich by joining the ranks of the mullahs. Once a poor man joins the learned profession and performs the pilgrimage to the holy shrines on foot, there receiving a diploma [*icazet*], in a few years he will be the owner of villages and farms." The social and physical mobility that came as a privilege of the learned class often served as the building block of economic exchange and commercial mobility as well.[21] As the Ottomans struggled to sort Iranian pilgrims from merchants, and learned men from lay couriers traveling across the borders of Hamidian Iran and Qajar Iran, disagreements over the rights of pilgrims were not only theologically and politically charged but economically charged as well. It was, then, not only overt political contestation that transformed the routes of *ziyarat* but also newly emerging methods of regulating economic mobility.

Iranian state representatives complained that the Ottomans were violating the terms of the treaty by taxing the pilgrims' carpets, rugs, and woven prayer mats as commercial goods, even though they were for personal use. Vehemently opposing such allegations of misconduct, Ottoman border authorities often retaliated by maintaining that merchants "pretending to be pilgrims" (*zuvvar kılığında*) crossed the Ottoman-Iran border. The same reports also relayed that these merchants made their fortune smuggling in *ʻaba* (cloaks), *firuze* (turquoise stone), and *safran* (saffron) to be sold in Karbala and Najaf bazaars. They were quick to emphasize that these merchants almost always traveled with the pilgrim caravans from Iran carrying bodies to be buried in the shrine city cemeteries. The Ottoman state apparatus was ill equipped to sort through the staggering numbers of pilgrims flocking to Iraq and filter out the contraband merchants. As Sabri Ateş notes, "around 100,000" Shiʿa hailing "primarily from Iran and India" visited the shrine cities in Iraq each year. "At that time," Ateş continues, "British officials estimated that the average amount spent by the Iranian visitors alone was 1,070,000 pounds."[22] These reports suggest, then, that Iranian pilgrims and/ or merchants were not only selling goods from Iran in Iraq but also buying in Iraq. In the traffic that was in part *ziyarat,* in part *tijarat,* and at times burial, the economic ties between Hamidian Iraq and Qajar Iran were far more developed.

The collapse of the Ottoman Empire and the designation of Iraq as a British Mandate state would ease the transimperial restrictions placed on the movements of Iranian pilgrims regionally. These movements underwrote the territorialization of *ziyarat* throughout Iran, to cities like Mashhad and Qom, while the Mandate Iraq remained deeply suspicious and regulated visitations of the ʿatabat in Iraq for decades to come.[23] Domestically within Iran, *ziyarat* undertaken to Zainab and other shrines in Syria remained unheard of or unrecorded until the Cultural Revolution. Reza Shah's son and successor, Mohammad Reza Pahlavi, who reigned between 1941 and 1979, likewise considered *ziyarat* to be a backward and superstitious practice and remained deeply suspicious of religious proceedings in general.[24]

In the 1980s, the visitation of Zainab became one of the few safe *ziyarat* routes outside of Iran. A combination of three factors contributed to this transformation. First, the sites of Karbala and Najaf remained inaccessible for prolonged periods of time during the Iran-Iraq War, cutting off Iranian access to ʿatabat shrines completely. Second, as Dr. Hani Murtada recounted in chapters 1 and 2, the state-backed Bunyad-i Shahid voucher program sent some two thousand Iranian pilgrims per week to Syria between 1986 and 1988. Third and finally, during the 1987 *hajj* season, Saudi police responded with disproportionate force to Iranian protests of Israeli policies in the Middle East. The skirmishes that ensued between the Iranian pilgrims and Saudi Arabian police left 275 Iranian pilgrims dead. The event led the Iranian regime to cut all diplomatic ties with Saudi Arabia. In retaliation and citing security concerns, Saudi Arabia imposed strict quotas for each country for the following year's *hajj,* holding the Iranian quota deliberately low at mere hundreds. The Iranian government in turn refused to send any pilgrims to *hajj* at all. These events dramatically shifted the possibilities of pilgrimage and further curtailed Iranian citizens' mobility, which was already constrained by visa regulations.

FIGURE 12. A hagiographical map of saint visitation (*ziyarat*) sites, Tehran, 1985–95. Middle Eastern Poster Collection, Box 6, poster 273, Special Collections Research Center, University of Chicago Library.

Historically Karbala had served as a substitute for *hajj* for Iranian pilgrims, and Sayyida Zainab provided a substitution for that substitution. Out of one arrested route of mobility, another emerged. As alternative routes of religious mobility proliferated both within and outside Iran, buses filled with Iranian pilgrims continued to traverse the borders between Iran, Turkey, and

Syria, adding an important destination to a regionally networked geography of visitation.

Meanwhile, in the wake of the second US invasion of Iraq in 2003, self-proclaimed Salafi and other Sunni revivalist militant groups increasingly targeted not only the shrines in Samarra and Karbala but also the buses shuttling pilgrims there from Iran. Their doctrinal pretext was that *ziyarat,* and seeking saintly intercession in worldly matters (*shafaʿa*) in particular, should be condemned as *bidʿa,* a noncanonical and heretical innovation. These attacks rippled through Iran, shaping the relationship between the various routes and destinations in the broader geography of visitation. The attacks on and around ʿ*atabat* shrines in Iraq, in other words, helped reroute Iranian pilgrims onto the ways of Zainab. And as *hajj-i fuqaraʾ* rose in popularity for pilgrims, its routes became a rare visa-free zone through which Iranian *zuwwar* could freely, if precariously, move. Yet that precarity also came with certain possibilities for travelers on the paths of Zainab—predominantly but not exclusively Iranians—to continue walking the thin line between pilgrim and merchant, tourist and smuggler, citizen and denizen. Let us now turn to the creative improvisations that these possibilities have engendered in the hands of Iranian travelers across Iran, Turkey, and Syria.

THE MANY CROSSERS OF THE BORDER: MUHSIN, NARMIN, AND THEIR SHOES OF GOLD

In early October 2011 *Yüksekova Haber,* a highly reliable media outlet operating out of Turkey's Kurdistan, reported that the Turkish antismuggling special forces had simultaneously discovered five kilograms of gold in two separate checkpoints along the Yüksekova İpekyolu Highway. The gold was recovered from a pilgrimage bus and two cars, all with Iranian plates. The vehicles had crossed into Turkish territory at the Gürbulak border crossing and were in transit to Syria. The article included a photograph of a one-kilogram brick of gold and the material in which it had been wrapped, placed atop the man's shoe in which the brick had been found (fig. 24).

When I interviewed some of the Turkish authorities at the Iran-Turkey border in 2012, they recounted how initially they had dismissed wrapped objects like these as amulets. Carrying lead or similarly heavy metals wrapped in written supplications is a common Islamic (and Islamicate) practice meant to guard the bearer of the amulet against evil. As awareness of gold smuggling grew, however, the secrets of these packages mistaken for amulets by the Turkish border guards came to light. The increasing number of reports of Iranian gold being sold in Turkey prompted border guards and antismuggling special forces to screen all Iranians crossing the borderland more thoroughly than before 2011. As visitors, they were on their way to the Sayyida Zainab shrine near Damascus, Syria. In the past they had also visited Konya, Turkey, to venerate Mawlana (Mevlana Jalaleddin Rumî in Turkish). Although the numbers of these pilgrims constituted just a fraction of all travelers between Iran and Turkey—estimated at 2.5 million in 2012 according to Ministry of Culture and Tourism records—their methods of evading border control and their material conduits of contraband commerce have come to condition how all Iranians on the move were perceived at border crossings with Turkey. According to Metin's estimates, every year around 200,000 of those 2.5 million Iranians transited through Gaziantep en route to the Sayyida Zainab shrine. Iranians, including some pilgrims, often traded gold for hard currencies like US dollars and Euros in Turkey, then took them back to Iran, where they proved to be in short supply. Finally the Turkish officials at the border figured it out: what they had thought were amulets slated to be touched by the saint's blessings (*baraka*) turned out to be good old gold bricks to be exchanged at the next *sarraf* (jewelry and currency merchant). After this realization, one such official relayed to me in anonymity, the number of Iranian nationals targeted by anti-*kaçak* operations also increased.[25]

The *Yüksekova Haber* article reported that as a result of these operations three Iranian nationals—Ismat Radmard, Isa Jommehpur, and Mahmud Gharabaghlu—were taken into custody and immediately deported from Turkey. The article ended on the panic-inducing note that this method of contraband commerce had become pervasive among Iranian nationals hoping to "cash in" on the stark price difference in gold between Iran and Turkey. At the time of the operation, in October 2012, a kilogram of gold cost around 60,000 Turkish *liras* (around $25,000 USD) in Iran, whereas the price for the same amount in Turkey started at 100,000 Turkish *liras* (approximately $37,000 USD).

The wrapping used to conceal the confiscated gold brick was a sleeve from a cassette of poetry by the famous contemporary Iranian poet Maryam Heydarzadeh. Heydarzadeh's quatrains (*ruba'iyat*) are wildly popular, particularly in the broader cultural topography of *zendegi-ye ranandegi* (life on the road), most intimately associated with truckers, bus and car drivers, and cabbies. In this particular case of the confiscated gold brick, the quatrains that had been repurposed to serve as the wrap-cum-"amulet" called into question the meaning of life and love:

> On the edge of your company I make my nest,
> I weave in my songs at its openings.
> To anyone who asks me for what I live,
> I give you as my excuse for life.

"That could have been my shoe!" was Muhsin's first reaction when, as we sat together in his Tabriz home in November 2014, I showed him the front page of *Yüksekova Haber*. "That gold is not my sole purpose in life," Muhsin immediately qualified, "but I do love Maryam Heydarzadeh!"

In addition to being an index of the social milieu from which the "golden shoes" hailed, the wrap had a much more immediate function: to the eyes of the border guards or the police tasked with regulating traffic across Turkey's eastern borders, the modified Arabic script and the stylized *nasta'liq* writing read as "Qur'anic," and hence spared them from inspection. Given the pervasiveness of carrying amulets with heavy metals (such as mercury and silver) and the relative ease with which Iranian visitors on their way to see Mawlana or Zainab could cross the border with Turkey, the wrapping of golden bricks was nothing novel, Muhsin's wife Narmin interjected; those traveling from Iran with gold were adopting and adapting a method of carrying personal possessions in a form that would temporarily evade police surveillance. Narmin asked rhetorically, "What better wrap than Iranian *nasta'liq*—a script that Turkish eyes on the border read as sacred?"

Walking on a gold brick "tucked away" into the sole of a shoe was certainly an uncomfortable task, according to Muhsin, a clerical worker for the state in his thirties living in a middle-class neighborhood of Tabriz, Iran. Muhsin explained that it was only through the security checks at the border that one had to "carry oneself well"—quite literally—taking care not to drag one's feet in the unlikely event that passengers were required to disembark from the bus. Yet the conversion of that gold into hard currency required a chain of conversions in value. The next big step in that process was finding a *sarraf*, who often served as an informal creditor in both Iran and Turkey.[26] Yet that *sarraf* had to be in an area far enough from the Iran-Turkey border that the markets remained relatively unexposed to Iranian gold. In other words, the *sarraf* should not be someone who would know all too well that the gold came from Iran and would therefore offer a price lower than the "national" market price.

Muhsin and Narmin were old hands at crossing the border, with a considerable amount of *kaçak* experience themselves. Hiding the gold that they had bought in Tabriz in their shoes, and tobacco in their seats, the couple embarked on their first trip to Syria in 2009. It was on this first trip that Narmin asked for saintly intercession to conceive a baby. Their second trip, almost two years later in 2011, was to thank Sayyida Zainab and Sayyida Ruqayya. My path first crossed with theirs when they were on their second journey to Syria. In the series of interviews I conducted with them in Tabriz in 2013 and 2014, they told me how they had previously shuttled cartons of Iranian cigarettes[27] to Gaziantep on their way to the Sayyida Zainab shrine. When we first met, they had just "branched out to gold," as they put it. By this time, and as a result of intensified sanctions, the plummeting value of their national currency, the *rial,* hit Iranian citizens even harder once they ventured abroad to locales such as Turkey, Syria, and Lebanon (which did not require them to have a visa for entry). As the effects of sanctions became all the more pressing with shortages in medical supplies, automotive parts, and refined oil,[28] Muhsin and Narmin decided that they were not going to let their *rials'* value diminish where it stood. Instead, they were going to start saving their money in gold, not unlike Iranian state actors, in order to acquire more stable foreign currencies, such as Euros or US dollars, in Turkey.[29]

Cognizant of the billion-dollar traffic in gold and older circuits of contraband commodities between Iran and Turkey, Muhsin and Narmin decided to diversify the commodities they traded to preserve the value of their monetary assets. "Once your money's value diminishes by the day, as if it had the half-life of uranium, what else can you do?" Muhsin asked rhetorically. Narmin picked up where her husband left off: "Once your normal is abnormal, like in our precarious case, who is to say carrying gold and tobacco is contraband? Sanctions are the actual smuggling. What Reza Zarrab, the Iranian middleman, in collaboration with the Turkish state officials, is doing—that's smuggling. Those who have reduced us to this role, leaving us no other option, are the ones to blame. Shame on them, not on the ones who see no other option! One cannot expect to level economic disenfranchisement as political punishment and expect that people will just follow suit."

For many Iranians who faced increasing physical, political, and economic confinement, the paths of Zainab offered a route out of Iran and its myriad internationally and regionally enforced restrictions. Though precarious, that route offered financially lucrative possibilities for contraband commerce. While some of the Iranian pilgrims such as Muhsin and Narmin took advantage of these possibilities themselves, the relative ease with which the buses crossed from Iran into Turkey and then from Syria back into Iran whetted the business appetite of contraband merchants in need of safe corridors or routes across Iran, Turkey, and Syria. Soon after this news of a new method spread, contraband merchants began recruiting bus drivers to move goods off the record. Then more "full-time" contraband merchants started making use of pilgrimage buses, where the elegies venerating Zainab alternated with discussions about the latest exchange rates and the price of gold. It was, after all, a journey of both visitation and commerce—*ham ziyarat ham tijarat*. Once contraband merchants started crossing the Iran-Turkey and Turkey-Syria borders as pilgrims, however, the pilgrimage buses came under the purview of the state.

THE MAKING OF THE BORDER AND THE *KAÇAKÇI* ACROSS TURKEY AND SYRIA: HIDIR'S STORY

After nine months behind bars for taking part in a small-scale smuggling network that operated across the Turkey-Syria border, Hıdır, a former police officer in his late thirties and father of three, was quick to reinvent himself. In his words, as a former "part-time" police officer caught collaborating with a contraband network, he was forced to become a "full-time" contrabander. As a former state official and border police officer convicted of corruption and aiding a smuggling network, Hıdır was unable to find other lines of employment. Pressed to provide for his extended family in the meantime, he turned to the opportunities that opened up to him through a different cross-border regime of patronage—that of his Kurdish kin, who lived on both sides of the Syria-Turkey border. Hıdır's identities were indeed many, and they blurred the lines between representing and defying sovereign authority, Turkish nationalism and Kurdish insurgency, and the legality and illegality of commercial activity.

Not unlike most of his colleagues working at the Öncüpınar border crossing in Kilis, Hıdır got involved in cross-border commerce as a state-employed border police officer charged with overseeing customs. In addition to preventing the illegal (*yasa dışı*) trafficking of people, drugs, and arms, he was responsible for keeping in check the informal (*kayıt dışı*—literally, "off the record") economy of sugar, tea, fuel oil, and cigarette trade across the visa-free Syria-Turkey border. These inspections often involved ignoring that many of the cars crossing the border had specially enlarged gas tanks that had been filled with Syrian oil in Aleppo, where oil cost a fraction of its cost in Turkey. In addition to moving passengers, the buses, trucks, and taxi shuttles that connected Gaziantep and Aleppo moved sugar, tea, and cigarettes in line with the trade quotas—at the time of research, two cartons of cigarettes and two kilograms of sugar per traveler. Hıdır soon found himself actively participating in, rather than merely ignoring, the very cross-border economy that he was employed to police.

Hıdır's positions as a self-described "part-time police officer" and *muhbir* (informer) for a cross-border contraband network earned him barely enough to provide for his nuclear family and his extended family in Kilis, whom he had been supporting for the past six years. These positions ended abruptly though in 2011 when the Syrian uprisings showed the first signs of turning into civil war. Decreased flow of formal traffic across the border meant fewer opportunities for trafficking. With few vehicles to "inspect" at the border, and pressed by others in his contraband network to inform them about other possible routes of passage between Turkey and Syria, Hıdır found himself seeking a new route for bringing sugar, tea, cigarettes, and oil from Syria to Turkey.

After a successful first run along this new route, a second and larger shipment was planned to deliver cigarettes and sugar to the Iranian Bazaar in Gaziantep, fifty kilometers north of the border. The second time around, things did not go according to plan. All the merchandise was confiscated in a police operation that had been tracking the activities of the network for the past month. Fifteen people—including Hıdır and another junior police officer who was also an ethnic Kurd native to the borderland between Turkey and Syria, as well as four Kurdish youths as young as sixteen from the border village of Karkamış—were convicted of smuggling and given prison terms ranging from nine months to four years.

Hıdır had never wanted to become a police officer. In fact, he had signed up to work for the state in order to honor his father's wish that he stay away from Kurdish insurgency politics, even though the state "had killed [his] brother." Hıdır's eldest brother, Deniz, had lost his life in a Turkish military operation in Şemdinli, Şırnak, as a rebel fighter for the PKK.[30] Hıdır's father, having already lost one son to the violent encounter between the Turkish state and the Kurdish insurgency, pressed Hıdır to avoid politics and instead become a pillar of economic stability for the family. And that is precisely what Hıdır had set out to do: "The border post was my second assignment as a police officer after having served in the Gaziantep police headquarters. I

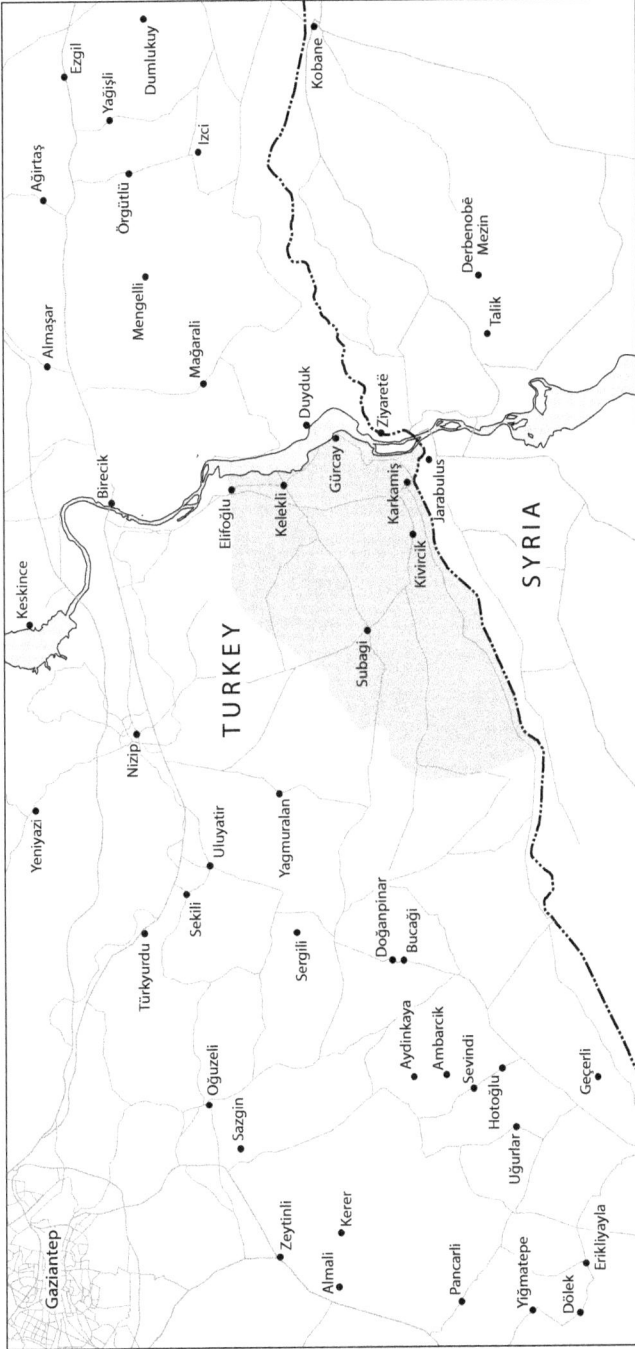

MAP 4. Turkey-Syria borderland. The Karkamış district, between Antep and Kobane, is marked in gray (by Bill Nelson).

had already worked as a police officer for five years when two vacancies opened up at the Öncüpınar border crossing in 2009, and I put in an application." Hıdır pulled out a cigarette and I reached out to light his cigarette. He gently tapped on my hand to gesture it was lit. He continued, "It was a double-pay position given that it was a high-security assignment, and my extended family was closer to the border than to Gaziantep. Given that my family and I really needed the money, I applied for the position, not thinking twice about it. Little did I know at the time that I was walking into a well-charted territory."

For the first four months in his new position, everything seemed to be going well for Hıdır. Except for rush hour, when they had to inspect large vehicles such as trucks and buses as well as taxis operating between Aleppo and Gaziantep, which were the most notorious vehicles for contraband commerce, the workload was lighter than at his previous assignment in the city of Gaziantep. The alignment between the state officials who were supposed to enforce border regulations and the smugglers who were committed to circumventing them left Hıdır jaded after four short months.

During one of these rush-hour inspections at the border, Hıdır met a taxi driver, a Kilis local himself, whose trunk upon inspection revealed five kilograms of sugar and ten cartons of cigarettes. The driver first argued that the merchandise was not above the duty-free quotas for the two passengers onboard. Upon closer inspection, though, it turned out that the passengers themselves had an additional three cartons of cigarettes in their suitcases. The quota math was off, but the taxi driver was insistent, even defiant, as if he knew that he need not worry about some rookie policeman stationed at the crossing. When the driver saw that his pleading only made Hıdır write out his fine slip faster, he demanded to speak with Hıdır's supervisor.

According to Hıdır's account, the *komiser* (commissioner) came out to talk to the taxi driver personally, which Hıdır had rarely seen during his tenure at Öncüpınar. Within fifteen minutes, the issue was declared resolved and the taxi driver drove off without a fine. At the time, the supervisor's handling of the ordeal puzzled Hıdır, so he asked what had been his mistake in assessing the taxi driver's case. This marked the beginning of the end for Hıdır at his Öncüpınar post. Komiser Ahmet warned him to remain content with what he had as a *Kurdish* police officer and not ask too many questions.

Hıdır indeed stopped asking the *komiser,* or anyone else, questions. He had already learned what he needed to know from the drivers he was tasked with inspecting. Not even a month after his tense encounter, Hıdır learned that Komiser Ahmet himself was implicated in a contraband network of his own. The network shuttled merchandise through "around twenty drivers" who would cross the border under the watch of the *komiser,* who collected a 15 percent commission off their profits. The network's fleet included a wide range of vehicles, from taxis and minibuses to logistical firm trucks and buses—including but not limited to pilgrimage buses that ran between Syria and Iran.

With a supervisor himself implicated in contraband, Hıdır reckoned that it was safe to form, slowly but surely, a cross-border network of his own. After all, many within his extended family hailed from villages on both sides of the Syria-Turkey border and had been engaged in cross-border trade. Hıdır recounted those early days: "Business for the first two months was pretty regular and good. Although the situation in Syria was getting worse, and there were more and more refugees fleeing, the border traffic remained rather busy. As long as the *komiser* had work, and I had work, no one else cared how much contraband was flowing through the border." Five months into being "a part-time police officer and a part-time contraband merchant," Hıdır thought he had found himself a way of being content at the border while being a "Kurdish police officer," as his supervisor put it. But when the cross-border traffic started to thin in late 2010, it became increasingly difficult for Hıdır to inform other members of his network about the best time to cross: "There were no good, let alone best, times left to inform anyone of. Even the *komiser*'s business was not going well."

A week after Hıdır realized that less traffic meant more trouble for his double role on the border, the bad news came: 3,838 cartons of cigarettes and 100 kilograms of sugar were recovered in an operation that searched through the seemingly empty back of a truck in Kilis. A carelessly tucked away piece of rope at the corner of the trunk had revealed the concealed compartment built into the ceiling and sides of the storage compartment. Carton after carton of cigarettes had been fed into these secret compartments with a rope mechanism to ensure their speedy recovery. The sugar was discovered in compartments built between the back wheels and the expanded gas tank. Because the *yükçü* juveniles and the driver occupied the lowest ranks of the network in terms of both earnings and authority, they were charged with the heaviest sentences, ranging from five to seven years, as they were deemed to be "committing" an illegal cross-border operation. By contrast, providing information and technical expertise to facilitate the actual crossing of the border was considered "aiding"; thus Hıdır as the *muhbir* of the network and another police officer received nine months each for their role providing information on the best times and routes of operation; the welder (*mimar*) who constructed the hidden compartments also was given a nine-month sentence.

"It was all the *komiser*'s doing, I am sure of it. He just could not share the border, definitely not with a Kurdish local like myself," recalled Hıdır. It was the competitive edge of his contraband business imbued with a perceived sense of Turkish entitlement, according to Hıdır, that had led to his arrest and the dismantling of his contraband network composed primarily of ethnic Kurds traversing the border landscape. Hıdır's theory remains impossible to prove, but where it led him after he served his prison sentence is more significant for our purposes. Confronted with an increasingly violent conflict in Syria and the pressing demands for contraband commodities back in Turkey as well as in Syria, Hıdır had to reinvent himself after his release. He became a full-time contraband merchant; yet this time around he was cut off from the border crossing that he knew so well. His search for work and his need for reinvention led him back to the Iranian Bazaar in Gaziantep, where we met. Hıdır explained, "Like everyone in Gaziantep, I knew that a lot of contraband passed through the bazaar thanks to the pilgrimage buses. But that was another well-charted territory. Most of the time the merchants had connections to the bus drivers and excluded all middlemen from their dealings." Hıdır was ready to share his secret this time around, and continued, "With pilgrims acting as shields, so to speak, whom the border officers often allowed to pass with no or minimal inspection, the buses were the perfect vehicles for moving anything heavy in value or light in weight. I thought at least I could travel on these buses and move my merchandise on my own."

Making inroads with the merchants of the bazaar revealed to Hıdır rather quickly that they were already well stocked with contraband goods shuttled on pilgrimage buses. In other words, unless he wanted to load and unload and do other kinds of menial work, the bazaar was not going to yield any "business" or new business partners for him. Two months after his first attempt to find work in the bazaar, there were no more Iranians or Iranian pilgrimage buses to speak of in Gaziantep: following a second abduction of a pilgrimage bus, the Iranian state issued a ban on all road travel from Iran to Syria.

By February 2012, the merchants of the Iranian Bazaar themselves had to find other ways to secure the contraband sugar, cigarettes, and tea that the local population demanded. This was another turning point where arrested mobilities generated a new pathway of mobility. They turned to Hıdır and others with connections to Kurdish border villages like Karkamış. The mules, the guide (*resan*), and the *yükçü* juveniles of these villages replaced the Iranian buses as the vehicles of contraband. But not only did the route and the vehicles have to be reconfigured; the direction and the contents of the contraband had to be adjusted according to the contemporary situation as well. Syria, most of which was mired in violence, faced fuel and electricity shortages as well as a life-threatening shortage of medicine and medical supplies. It was against this backdrop, and that of an autonomously operating Kurdish region in Syria, Rojava,[31] that new economic relations had to be forged between the "Iraqi" Kurdistan and the "Turkish" one. Merchants such as Hıdır had to stretch their operations into Iraqi Kurdistan to secure oil to sell in Turkey. In addition to taking advantage of the new opportunities created by the shifting economic demands, Hıdır asserted, his reinvention as a full-time contraband merchant was motivated by a political commitment to breaking the isolation of Syrian Kurdistan in general, and easing the living conditions of his relatives in Jarablus in particular.

The creation of the border between Turkey and Syria in the early twentieth century had rendered formerly legal economic networks "contraband commerce," imbuing them with additional economic and political value in the process. Even as newly delineated states sought to incarcerate populations politically and socioeconomically, actors such as Hıdır turned to enduring kinship networks and emergent spaces of political autonomy (such as the Kurdish-controlled areas of Syria) to forge new routes of mobility and secure new means of livelihood. What these networks carried across the border at a given time was dictated by the contingencies of social life. How border crossings were undertaken was intricately tied to both regimes of state sovereignty and networks of kinship. Hıdır imbued these networks with new economic and political functions once the Syrian conflict fundamentally altered the pathways of mobility across the Turkey-Syria border.

There was a widely recognized disconnect between the formal closing of the border and the flourishing of cross-border traffic in refugees, international aid, arms, and armed forces. "The border had never been more open," asserted Hıdır, referring to the now fully disclosed traffic in arms and medical supplies that had made their way from Turkey to mostly Sunni brigades within the Syrian opposition fighting against the regime. The Erdoğan administration in Turkey attempted to represent the border as open only in one direction—namely, that of the Syrian refugees fleeing into Turkey. But alternative media documented, and locals along the 957-kilometer border witnessed, not only a heavy traffic of refugees from Syria into Turkey but also a traffic in arms and medical supplies from Turkey into Syria. If the pilgrimage route itself could be taken as the traffic leaving its traces on the border, then the border itself could be understood as the palimpsest. Precisely because the territorial sovereignty of nation-states involved in bordering practices is uneven across its claimed territory, and almost always incongruous with the realities of borderlands, the mobile subjects who cross it or aim to transgress it become targets of constant regulation, criminalization, and incarceration.

Against the backdrop of an emergent sovereign region in Syria's Kurdistan, negotiations of economic transactions and political action are better conceptualized not around a scalar production of sovereignty but through a constant struggle of "autogestion," as proposed by Lefebvre: "Each time a social group (generally the productive workers) refuses to accept passively its conditions of existence, of life, or of survival, each time such a group forces itself not only to understand but to master its own conditions of existence, *autogestion* is occurring."[32] *Kaçakçı* uses of state territory show how that traffic itself, deemed marginal to spatial coordinates of state spaces, remains central to the perpetuation of state authority and the transgressions of it. However short-lived and precarious these transgressions might be, it is no coincidence that al-Jarablus and Kobane as well as the broader Rojava region were key sites of struggle in the production of the Syria-Turkey border almost a century ago under a different set of circumstances. So, what were the historical conditions of possibility for this type of autogestion? How did a border that had never existed come to divide Anatolia and the Levant into modern Turkey and Syria? It is to these conditions of possibility that we now turn.

STATES OF SOVEREIGNTY: TURNING THE FRANCO-TURKISH FRONTIER INTO THE SYRIO-TURKISH BOUNDARY THROUGH CONTRABAND COMMERCE (1921–59)

For four decades after World War I, the exact delineation of the border between Syria and Turkey would remain uncertain. Border formation, in other words, was a prolonged, contested process, and it continues to be contested to this day. It transformed an entire region into new grids of mandated and national sovereignties, while perpetuating a discourse of "artificiality"[33] among nationalists, anti-imperialists, imperialists, and,

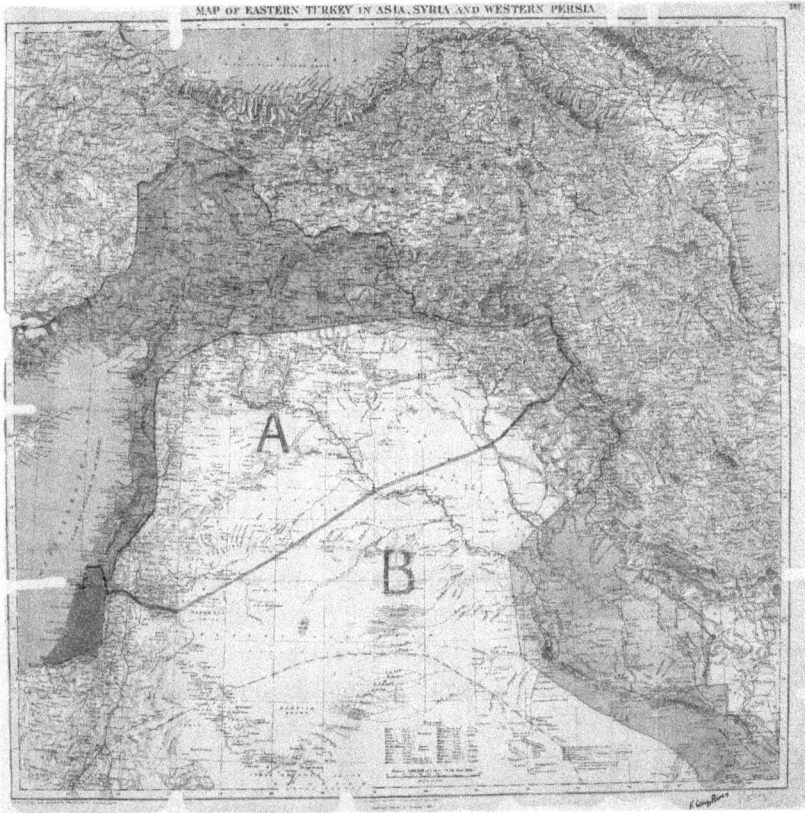

MAP 5. Sykes-Picot Agreement Map signed by Mark Sykes and François Georges-Picot, May 8, 1916 (UK National Archives, MPK1/426, FO 371/2777, folio 398).

most recently, jihadists alike. The Ankara government and the French Mandate authorities used the disagreement over where the border should lie as the pretext for a broader allocation of territory in the region to the French and British Mandates enshrined in the infamous Sykes-Picot Agreement of 1916.

With a project of establishing a colony in modern-day Turkey that consisted of a vast region extending from Adana and Cilicia on the eastern Mediterranean coast to Antep, Urfa, and Mardin in the east, the French used the zone commonly referred to as "the blue zone" as the grounds for the French incursion into Anatolia. French troops briefly occupied a large part of Cilicia and Alexandretta, territory also claimed by the Ankara government. The French accused the Ankara government of sending armed bands deep into Syria to stoke the anti-French opposition that was already smoldering, particularly in Aleppo. With the Franklin-Boullon Agreement of 1921, all fighting between the French and Turkish forces ceased. The territories of the newly founded Republic of Turkey and French Mandate Syria were opened to renegotiation and agreed upon in principle, with the exceptions of Alexandretta and Antioch in the west and the Nusaybin and al-Qamishli Districts of Mardin and Diyarbekir in the east.[34] Even though the territorial integrity of Syria and Turkey was established in the Treaty of Lausanne in 1923, the border between them changed again in 1939 when the Republic of Hatay, the independent state that existed for a year in the territory of the Sanjak of Alexandretta, was ceded to Turkey.[35]

Particularly after France's loss of oil-rich Mosul, Iraq, to the British, and Cilicia, a key port at the intersection of Levantine trade routes, to Turkey, the only remaining way to make Syria a profitable colony, members of the Parti Colonial reckoned, was through industrial agricultural cultivation.[36] Several reports on the economic prospects of the French Mandate state in Syria highlighted the urgency of taking control of the Orontes and Euphrates Valleys as well as the Jazira plain in Syria in order to implement this plan of rendering the Mandate profitable for the French administration.[37] As Seda Altuğ demonstrates in the case of the Jazira plain, located on the northeastern edge of Syria between the borders of Turkey and Iraq, the Mandate authorities "opened up the frontier region to cultivation through implanting Christian and Kurdish refugees [displaced from Turkey] conceived as the future peasants of the region."[38] While the French promoted this resettlement program to populate the frontier zone for projected economic gains, they also hoped that such a scheme would be useful politically by installing a buffer zone against both the Turkish nationalists in Turkey and the Arab nationalists in Syria.

These French Parti Colonial schemes to draw the Syria-Turkey border between the Levant and Anatolia and to populate the Syrian side primarily with Christian and Kurdish refugees fleeing Turkey further bolstered the claim that the allocation of territory disregarded the historical realities and mutual imbrication of communities on the ground. Thus emerged a large scholarship that explained away Syria's political volatility in the post-Ottoman, post-Mandate, and postcolonial periods as the predictable outcome of its territorial "artificiality."[39] It was, however, not only Orientalist scholars who perpetuated this narrative. Given that the very terms of these border negotiations were set by the French Mandate administration and the Turkish Republic, Syrian nationalists also spoke of Syria's borders as artificial—almost as frequently as Iraqi nationalists cited the artificiality of Iraq's. Yet the counterhegemonic historical discourse of Syrian Arab nationalists embraced the "artificiality" of Syria, with one qualification: in Ghassan Salama's words, most Arab nationalists viewed French Mandate Syria as "always less" (*du toujours moins*) than the historical territory of Balad al-Sham.[40] The spatial discrepancy between the territories claimed as the homeland of an ideal type of pan-Arabism on the one hand and the realities of the Mandate on the ground on the other set the conditions of possibility for Syrian nationalism.

The French schemes to turn the Jazira plain into the industrial agricultural hub of a new Syria, peopled with Christian and Kurdish refugees, generated extreme anxiety and diplomatic protests not only among the Syrian nationalists but also among the Turkish ruling elites. Wary of the possible formation of "an enclave of undesirables," in particular Armenians and Kurdish political refugees, to the immediate south of Turkey's border in Jazira, Turkish officials pressed the French Mandate authorities to control their side of the border more rigorously. Between 1925 and 1927, in particular, Franco-Turkish diplomatic correspondence was dominated by the Turkish state's complaints about Kurdish transborder incursions into Turkish territory and the resettlement of Armenian survivors and refugees of the genocide in the frontier zone, as evidenced by countless reports housed in the French Mandate archives in Nantes. When Turkish authorities condemned the French for sheltering Kurdish rebels and allegedly colonizing the frontier with "malicious elements," the Mandate authorities described the Turkish anxieties as misplaced and hyperbolic. A letter dated January 27, 1925, drafted in response to Turkish officials' allegations, is telling of the terms of this diplomatic back-and-forth:

> Since the beginning of the armistice, the biggest problem that the Mandate power is trying to resolve is the refugee problem. We have received 96,450 refugees since then and they are all impoverished people. France has made great economic sacrifices for them. Just for the sake of relieving pressure on the north of Syria, we have settled two-thirds of these poor people in inner Syria. The rest reside in Aleppo and in the Sanjak of Alexandretta and their settlements were realized calmly and in deference to the Muslim population.[41]

While the resettlement of refugees constituted one bone of contention between the Turkish and French authorities, political alliance with the

Kurdish notables constituted another. Contrary to what one might assume, both authorities forged alliances with these notables. In 1923, a joint Turkish-Kurdish force led by Hadjo Agha, the leader of the Kurdish Hevêrkan tribe, ambushed the French occupation forces in Bayandur. As a result, twenty-one French soldiers, most of them Senegalese recruits of the Légion Syrienne,[42] were killed. Once Hadjo Agha bowed to French rule in 1926, he explained in his letters addressing the Mandate authorities that after the French began their campaign in Syria, Turkish military and state officials encouraged him and some Arab tribal leaders to cause unrest in Jazira.[43]

Well before Hadjo Agha's confessions, however, the fatal ambush of the French forces, commonly referred to as the "Bayandur incident," had driven home the point for the French Mandate officials and strategists that neither their alliance with local and displaced Kurdish populations nor the Mandate itself was a given. Instead, the Mandate would be subject to constant negotiation. Following this ambush, and overwhelmed by the Druze revolt in southern Syria, the French Mandate authorities suspended their incursion deeper into Anatolia. Having faced fierce resistance in Urfa, Antep, and Marash, the French had to abandon all claims to Cilicia and the blue zone of the Sykes-Picot map. The French military force instead retreated to the Khabur River.

With the signing of the Convention of Good and Neighborly Relations between France and Turkey in February of 1926, the French Mandate military officers stepped up their reconnaissance tours with the declared aim of entering into negotiations with the Kurdish and Arab tribal shaykhs and winning them over to the French cause in Syria.[44] Concessions to engage in commerce through French posts proved to be the most effective method of recruitment. A well-known French Mandate officer of the time, Père Antoine Poidebard, commented in his notes on the situation of Kurdish refugees in Jabal al-Tur: "Some of them come to make trade in the frontier posts; a lot of them are originally from Mardin and the neighboring mountain, Jabal Tur. The young men of the Jabal are arriving with their families to join the Légion Syrienne, which has already recruited a small number of Assyrio-Chaldeans at Hassatche."[45] These concessions, however, did more than generate a rapprochement between the French Mandate and various Kurdish tribes—they also further galvanized the Turkish authorities. In an attempt to curb the movement of not only people but also goods, the Turkish state proposed a no-man's-land of one hundred meters on both sides of the border to arrest the mobility of native inhabitants of the borderland.

Both the tedious border delineation procedures and Turkish anxiety over Kurdish movement across the border meant a loss of land for the locals. Moreover, the land on the Syrian side was the most fertile in the area, and without access to it, locals were unable to engage in agricultural cultivation or raise livestock. Trade across the newly established border became the only possible way to secure a livelihood. The French concessions—which either actively encouraged or passively ignored the Kurdish traders—continued to be a topic of Turkish condemnation and French denial for another decade to come.

The Turkish state archives of the 1930s and '40s illustrate the anxiety that both the Kurdish "rebels" and these traders generated for the new republic, illuminating the great lengths to which the Turkish state went in order to curb the mobility of the inhabitants of its eastern border without offering any alternatives within the country itself. With most of their land either lost to the border zone or transferred to the direct jurisdiction of the military, the locals had no other option than cross-border commerce in order to sustain their livelihoods. A complaint letter that a group of grape farmers filed directly with the Kilis Chamber of Commerce,[46] and the subsequent report that the chamber drafted and forwarded to the central national authorities in October of 1933, is a case in point. In this letter, the grape farmers chronicled how their grapes, which were renowned in the region for *rakı* and wine production, were treated as second-rate produce within the Turkish market. The farmers' difficulties were compounded by the costly shipment of their produce from the border region into central Anatolia. To address these difficulties, the farmers presented two proposals to the state officials: "Either give us a fair price and include subsidies for the transportation of our produce to central Anatolia or give us permission to export our produce to Syria." While similar complaints about pistachio cultivation and livestock raising[47] form the backbone of these archives, state-level responses—if given at all—either misconstrued the facts (such as the prices offered to farmers) or downplayed the grievances of the local populations. Instead, the officials alleged that these complaints were evidence of how successfully the Turkish state had curtailed the funding of Kurdish insurgents in Syria. Despite all the self-congratulatory reporting on the part of state officials in the border zones, both cross-border trade and transhumance persisted in the region well into the 1950s. While the incarceration of primarily Kurdish locals for minor offenses, such as possession of contraband tobacco rolling papers known as Arabian papers, *Arap kağıdı,* became routine, cross-border commerce was named the "natural form of subsistence" in the region in contemporaneous media accounts.

Only in 1955 and through a massive international program that laid mines along the border was the Franco-Turkish frontier transformed into a Syrio-Turkish boundary. Initiated by the Menderes government in 1954 and executed by the NATO Maintenance and Supply Agency (NAMSA) between 1955 and 1959, the program laid 616,000 mines. The mines were evenly distributed along a 600-kilometer segment of the 957-kilometer border between Turkey and Syria, extending from Hatay through Kilis, Gaziantep, and Şanlıurfa, and ending at Mardin. The 350-meter-wide corridor of mines also meant yet another wave of dispossession from land vital for agricultural cultivation and livestock. The mining also resulted in around ten thousand people losing their lives and twenty thousand becoming disabled or debilitated as they attempted to cross the border.

The social history of the Turkey-Syria border is punctuated by a series of border delineation commission meetings between 1923 and 1960 that together reveal the fraught and incomplete process of separation that targeted not only land but also goods and people in the post-Ottoman Levant. This delineation project also cut off the Levantine commercial centers, Aleppo in particular, from their natural hinterlands such as Gaziantep and Şanlıurfa, which remained under Turkish sovereignty. It is no coincidence that the border that was meant to allocate sovereignty between the Turkish and Syrian states cut to the very heart of a Kurdish-majority geography,[48] rendering sovereignty itself as a "surplus" of state formation and subsequently producing two Kurdistans severed from each other by one of the most heavily mined borders in the world.

It is within this broader geography and the longer history of traffic that the pilgrimage route acquired its salience as a passageway unobstructed by visas or the possibility of sectarian violence. Goods and people were hard to contain, and cross-border trade between Turkey and Syria, deemed illegal by both states, continued to dominate the economic activities of the local inhabitants. These arrested mobilities continue to produce the historical and familial connections of Kurdish locals, such as Hıdır, who endured these punctuations of the border itself.

CONCLUSION

"We're leaving in three hours. If you still want to see the other side, this might be your best bet." I had been waiting to hear those words from Hıdır's lips for the past five months. It was a dry summer evening, around 7 p.m. on

August 14, 2012. As on many other summer evenings, I had joined a few of the merchants from the Iranian Bazaar in Antep in the coffeehouse off Turkmen Avenue, where the unemployed of the bazaar waited for a gig to present itself. Over the course of those five months, Hıdır had told me his entire life story twice over, recounting his family tree that spanned from Mardin into Jazira on his father's side and to the gardens of Kilis and eventually Karkamış on his mother's side. At a wedding ceremony in Antep, he had introduced me to his immediate family as his "journalist" friend from Istanbul. To his partners in business, however, I had remained a stranger.

Until that day, the only person from Hıdır's business circles I knew was the *mimar*, "the architect," whose specialization within the network was the building of compartments into cars and other vehicles to carry contraband goods. He was the one behind the rope mechanism that was used to hide thousands of cigarette cartons at a time. The last time it had been used, however, was when the police arrested Hıdır and the others. Most of the *mimar*'s business was from building expanded gas tanks in a mechanic shop next to the Iranian Bazaar. These tanks, as well as informal pipelines connecting gas stations between Şanlıurfa and Diyarbekir, were the main arteries for the *kaçak petrol* (contraband fuel oil) that constituted 25 percent of all fuel oil consumed in the country.

"A Turk of Kilis," the *mimar* worked more and spoke less, as Hıdır described him. Beyond the *mimar*, Hıdır's contraband network consisted mostly of his kin from a border village, who provided the manual labor power to load and unload the contraband items. That evening they were in Birecik, packing bandage material, canned goods, and other emergency supplies into large blue plastic barrels, which they would then move across the border by way of the Euphrates. Hıdır explained that the barrels loosely tied to each other would simply float on the Euphrates to the other side of the border, where they would be picked up by his kin near al-Jarablus. Three people, including Hıdır and myself, were across from a section of the border that had been cleared of mines thanks to an enraged livestock merchant of Antep who had ushered a hundred of his sheep across the mined border to clear a segment of it after the Turkish state prohibited him from selling them in Aleppo. Now using the *kuzu geçidi*, or the "sheep passage," as this segment was known among the locals, we were to cross into Syria, while the barrels filled with bandages and canned goods floated on the Euphrates toward al-Jarablus. The barrels would then be filled with fuel oil and shipped back into Syria in trucks along the "sheep passage." Once the barrels were secured on the

Turkish side, they would be transferred to an oil tanker to be distributed to local providers of *kaçak* petrol in the region.

Everybody on the team knew the script and acted their part. In addition to Hıdır and the *mimar,* the team included five manual laborers (*yükçü*). Ranging in age between twelve and eighteen, the *yükçü* are recruited to be trained in the craftsmanship of *kaçak*. They are paid at most fifty Turkish *lira,* approximately twenty US dollars, for each part of the move. These young apprentices carried, moved, loaded, and unloaded contraband goods according to the *mimar*'s designs and Hıdır's supervision. They were the most vulnerable to the immediate threats posed by the police and military; but given the lack of opportunity for making a livelihood otherwise, they had no other option than "going to *kaçak*." And in the language of the *yükçü* and others too, "going to *kaçak*" (*kaçağa gitmek*) was distinct from being a *kaçakçı* (a smuggler). The latter term they reserved for the Turkish state itself. Confiscation of land and property and economic isolation and forced migration were the ways in which the state smuggled value out of these youths' lives, as they saw it. That was the difference for them between the real smugglers and "going to smuggling."

In the *feryatname* of Çelebizade and the writings of Yaşar Kemal discussed in the previous chapter, the figure of the woman peddler (*bohçacı kadın*) emerged time and again as the ultimate transgressor of a national economic imaginary. The thirty-six-hour trip I took across the border with Hıdır and his partners confirmed for me that in 2013 the Kurdish *yükçü* can be seen as that disruptive figure. What provided a corridor of mobility for the oil was more than the waters of the Euphrates on our brief journey. It was the labor of those *yükçü* and the compartments of the *mimar.* It was the local merchant who had blown up his sheep in protest of his inability to sell his livestock in Aleppo in the 1940s like his father in the 1920s. It was also Hıdır's extensive family networks—including cousins with Syrian national ID papers, which at the time provided relative ease of movement on the Syrian side—that completed the circuit at its Syrian end.

Hıdır, the *mimar,* and their *yükçü* regrouped with a much smaller group of workers to carry out the actual moving of merchandise across the border. The short period during which they were able to use the pilgrimage buses from Iran to cross the border with those *parti* (loads) of contraband goods had ended, but they did not despair. Reverting back to his kinship ties, Hıdır reclaimed the border as a corridor of mobility and source of sustenance. Thanks to the hospitality that his cousin from his father's side provided to the entire group who crossed the border, we were able to sleep and eat. This distant cousin, Soresh, highlighted the intimate relationship between kin and business across the border, which was now mired in multiple conflicts. Hıdır's cousin would correct me as I was recording their pedigree: "The war in Syria made us brothers, not cousins!" *Kaçak*, then, not unlike *ziyarat*, was the grounds on which kinship was remade. Soresh was only half-joking, given not only that they were distant cousins but also that the addition of their being business partners in *kaçak* made them more than cousins alone.

On our way back to Birecik after having spent fifteen hours in al-Jarablus making sure the barrels were filled properly with fuel oil and loaded onto the back of black Tacomas, the *kamyonet* tasked to carry them across the border, Hıdır described the career of *kaçak* in these border landscapes: "There was *kaçak* before the buses; there will be *kaçak* after the buses. You cannot stop. Even over where we dropped the barrels in the river, they tried to insert fish-nets to stop the flow. As if these were fish, how are you going to stop barrels with nets? Let's even imagine that they stop the fish and the barrels. How are they going to stop the Euphrates? That's why *kaçak* will endure . . . because even if you are the state, one cannot draw lines on water."

Even though Hıdır's portfolio of spatial transgression and categorical defiance is not the norm in the region, he is not exceptional either in having invented another route of mobility out of arrested mobility. To put it differently, both the *kaçakçıs* and the pilgrims of the border are resourceful users of the borderland ecology.

The Syria-Turkey border and its crossers' spatial practices reveal the process of layering on the palimpsest. The regional history of Iranian *ziyarat* in the broader Levant as well as the transformation of the Turco-French frontier into the Turco-Syrian boundary informs how the travelers, merchants, pilgrims, and smugglers are assembled on the paths of Zainab in the contemporary era. *Kaçak* and *ziyarat* come to intersect in the Iranian buses on their way to Sayyida Zainab. The Syria-Turkey border as a palimpsest of sovereignty carries some of its deepest traces from the era of mandated nation-states. These traces give us new analytical purchase on how nation-states' efforts to territorialize their national space have often involved policing contraband commerce and incarcerating its practitioners, while forming selectively porous mobility regimes for pilgrims and tourists.

·   ·   ·

In his essay titled "Space and the State," Lefebvre articulates the particularity of the state-territory relationship through the concept of state space (*l'espace étatique*):

> The modern State is confronted with open spaces, or rather, spaces that have burst open on all sides: from apartments to buildings to the national territory by way of institutions (the school, the neighborhood, the city, the region). As historical products of previous epochs, carrying within themselves the various remnants of those periods (analogical, symbolic, etc.), these spaces are devastated, disintegrated, and ripped apart; at the same time, they overflow their borders. This is just one part of the catastrophic picture being sketched here. Apartments and buildings form open links with collective infrastructure, neighborhoods with the city. . . . The nation itself no longer has any borders— not for capital or technology, for workers and the workforce, for expertise, or for commodities. Flows traverse borders with the impetuosity of rivers.[49]

Whether in the golden shoes of Muhsin and Narmin or in the floating barrels of Hıdır across the waters of the Euphrates, the state spaces of Turkey and Syria had indeed burst open. And in Hıdır's case, cross-border traffic flowed with the impetuosity of rivers—only to be arrested by the ebb of figurative and literal droughts. If we understand territory "at once as a historically specific form of politico-spatial organization, as a key modality of modern statecraft and as a strategic dimension of modern politics,"[50] the process of territorialization can unfold only as a historical product of previous epochs unevenly layered over each other, leaving their distinct traces on the border.

Tracing the spatial and temporal overlaps of pilgrim and merchant mobilities and their confluence on the paths of Zainab provides a chronicle of territorialization in the post-Ottoman and post-Mandate Middle East. That historical process and its attendant regime of mobility produced not only different spaces as distinct and endowed with quantifiable and hence abstractable features but also different social actors of transborder mobility. *Ziyarat,* however, is even more than the interarticulation of the religious and the economic, or the religious and the political. At the interarticulating triangulation of the religious, the economic, and the political—and how people choreograph their valuations through that triangular relationship on the paths of Zainab— *ziyarat* emerges as a kinship-making and region-making social practice. It is with a fuller sense of this triadic relationship, forged in routes of arrested mobilities and their implications, that this chapter now concludes.

Karam and Sahand's Pathways, and a Khayyam Quatrain on Breath

AFTER MY CLUMSY INTRODUCTION over the bus microphone to the entire bus, while I was making my way to the back, my eyes met those of Karam and Sahand. I acknowledged them with a nod and smiled. They smiled back. My eyes fixated on Sahand's NP baseball cap—a rather niche queer fashion brand, short for *Nasty Pig*. Both in Iran and Turkey, I was used to seeing brand-festooned clothing among young men, turning themselves, often proudly, into walking billboards. That said, seeing NP sported on a pilgrimage bus was a first. My surprise impaired my already-limited subtlety to such an extent that it took me a second to catch myself staring. Karam's smile had morphed into a chuckle, and Sahand's into a can-I-help-you look. I nodded again, this time apologetically, and averting my eyes hurried to the back of the bus.

About four hours later, somewhere between Tatvan and Bitlis, the bus pulled into a rest stop and the driver declared that we would have thirty minutes before moving on. Although there had been no shortage of food making its rounds in the bus, almost everybody got off to see what the rest stop restaurant had in store. I thought some fresh air and tea might do me good. The "restaurant" had three kinds of paninis and a soup of the day. I ordered a cheese panini and a glass of tea. "*Kaçak* or *Rize*?" asked the cashier taking my order before he slammed a tray down on the laminated counter. Before I could figure out that he was asking me whether I wanted contraband or domestic tea, he spoke again, reaching out for one of the two samovars brewing to his right. "It seems *Rize* would suit you just fine. Anything else?" he followed up.

"No, that is it," I responded.

While I ordered, another intercity bus, a Turkish one operating between Kars and Istanbul, pulled up. All but one of the dozen tables set up under a long tarpaulin were taken by pilgrims. I hurried to the one remaining table and put my tray down before anyone else could claim it. Mildly satisfied with my small win, I took a bite of my cheese panini, which had more of the latter and less of the former. When I looked up with a soured face, Sahand was staring at me and holding up his own cheese panini, grinning. Karam joined him in mocking the panini they were sharing and motioned me to the chair next to him. I happily complied.

After exchanging pleasantries, I asked what brought them to the road to Zainab. Karam and Sahand exchanged glances, and Sahand responded after a nod from Karam. "Well, we aren't going to Zainab's shrine actually. We will get off the bus in Gaziantep." Registering my confused look, Karam took over, and when I probed what was for them in Gaziantep, he replied: "Well, we will continue to Ankara from there and file for asylum. We just needed cover to leave Iran in the least suspicious way possible." Observing my confusion growing, Sahand took over and explained. Karam, an affluent and self-employed interior designer, and Sahand, a graduate student of architecture at the University of Tehran, had lived together in northern Tehran, and in their words, quite happily. During the first five years of their monogamous relationship, they had considered the restrictions imposed on their desire to live a public life of love and intimacy to be no different from those imposed on heterosexual couples. But their ability to pass, in part due to their masculine gender expression and upper-class position, ended abruptly in their sixth year together. Karam and Sahand decided to embark on their journey to Turkey when a house party, organized by their friend Pouya in upscale northern Tehran, was raided by the morality police.

The party was in fact just a social gathering with no sex in sight, but its attendees were *hamjinsha* (literally, "same-sexers"). Pouya had periodically organized such gatherings, and complaints about previous parties had generated only increasingly high bribes to keep the officers at bay. This time the penalties were higher: the police opted to interrogate the attendees and record their personal information. Karam and Sahand hoped that the moral police would not follow up with them, but a week later two officers showed up at their door with a warrant. They confiscated alcohol from their bar and pornographic DVDs from their bookshelves. The officers searched their computers, copying their IP address and duplicating temporary files and Internet cookies, which showed visits to gay social networking websites as well as other websites with banned content, including political commentary and bear pornography. Karam and Sahand were informed that this was their first and last warning to come to their senses and return to the "straight path" of Islamic morality. In line with the norms of masculinity in Iran that they were asked to uphold, "at least in appearance," they were commended for looking like respectable men and not like some other *kuniha* (faggots). The moral police advised them to take this warning seriously and change their ways by praying. They added, "Otherwise, we will teach you ourselves." This encounter was the last straw, Karam said. "And here we are, a week later, on our way to Zainab," Sahand added, completing Karam's narrative.

I was flabbergasted. Both had also grown quiet. I tried to come up with an encouraging follow-up. Could I think of some LGBTQ organizations in Istanbul that could provide some help, Sahand inquired. I was running through names in my head when my thoughts were interrupted by an announcement over the megaphone. Our bus was ready for departure. Seeing that I was failing to produce any names, Karam got up. "Shall we?" he asked, turning toward the bus. We walked in silence. Karam continued, "Maybe we should indeed stay on the bus and enlist Hazrat-i Zainab's help." "It would confirm for the moral police that we had indeed repented and found the right path," Sahand responded. Then he began reciting poetry that I could at the time comprehend only superficially. It must have been clear from my noncommittal smile that I didn't know the poem, because Karam said he would write it out for me on the bus. It was a quatrain from Omar Khayyam:

From the station of disbelief to that of belief is but a breath.
And, but one breath, from the station of doubt to that of faith.
This precious breath, let us pass it gayly.
Since the harvest of our lives is but that very breath.

Conclusion

I WAS RETURNING HOME to Sa'adat Abad from the Majlis Library in northern Tehran on an early November afternoon in 2013 when one of my interlocutors, Sima, called me. A master's student of sociology interested in studies of religion herself, she had sent several references my way before. This time, she was calling to say that she had happened upon a particularly well-attended *ta'ziyeh* proceeding near 'Allamih Tabata'i University—a fifteen-minute walk from my apartment—and wanted to invite me.

Twenty minutes later, Sima and I were standing at the university gates. The *ta'ziyeh* booth was set up just beyond the entrance, in the yard leading to the main building. Posters of Imam 'Ali, Supreme Leader Khamenei, and Khomeini hung alongside those of Hazrat-i Fatima and Hazrat-i Zainab sketched by none other than Nasser Palangi (discussed in chapter 1). "It's like Christmastime in the US," Sima commented. "It starts earlier every year and gets flashier and flashier." Muharram—a period of commemorative mourning for Shi'i Muslims around the world—had just begun.

As Sima and I stood talking, we noticed two groups of men. The first, under the influence of some stimulants, were deep in the literal ecstasies of commemorative ritual a few meters from the booth. Closer up front, another group had lost themselves without the drug induction. For some, the very recitation of supplications (*ad'iyya,* sing. *du'a'*) for those martyred on the grounds of Karbala was more than stimulating enough. Sima and I moved toward some women who seemed to be reciting supplications. In the hands of one young woman was a guidebook I recalled having seen on the pilgrimage bus. After sending her supplication to the prophet and the imams, the middle-aged leader of the supplication circle moved on to Hazrat-i Zainab. The woman extolled her courageous outspokenness and sensitive care, then expressed her regret over not having visited Syria before the Sayyida Zainab shrine near Damascus came under heavy bombardment from rocket fire.

While the leader of the supplication circle sent another elegy Zainab's way, I thought of others I had come to know since I started my research in 2008 and how they were now immobilized in different ways in different locales that four years ago had been connected. Merchants in the Iranian Bazaar in Turkey, like Metin Abi, were now lamenting the interruption of their access to the women in the circle in front of me as potential customers. Dr. Hani Murtada remained in self-imposed exile in Beirut. His guardianship over the shrine had transformed from a badge of prophetic genealogy to a life-threatening liability as Hizballah moved into the shrine town and the outskirts of Damascus to prop up the Syrian state's forces.

Even if the situation in Syria were to improve, it was unknown whether Iranians would be able to travel in the same large numbers to Syria under the current regime of sanctions. By 2013, the sanctions had led Iran's national economy into a self-perpetuating cycle of exponential inflation and increasing unemployment. Iranians felt the arresting effects of the sanctions across a variety of sites in their social lives, including lack of access to medicine to treat the chronically ill and barriers to transnational religious journeys. As the corner of the major highway near the university continued to fill with ecstatic bodies in commemorative ritual, my mind kept returning to the ailing stores of Gaziantep in the blighted Iranian Bazaar. I thought of Dr. Murtada again and speculated how he would have commented on these rituals if he were next to me.

The leader of the recitation circle finished recitations devoted to Hazrat-i Ruqayya and passed the lead to another woman in the circle. She was deep in conversation with Sima when I noticed Sima point in my direction. I hesitantly walked over and greeted the recitation leader. "This is Fatima Khanum," Sima announced as I approached, introducing us. Sima had already told her about my research, and she seemed curious to hear what I had seen in the course of my fieldwork. "You must be an exceptionally fortunate soul," she said with a friendly smile. She continued quickly, without allowing me to thank her for her kindness. "After all, you have been able to spend so much time around our lady, Hazrat-i Zainab. So, what did you see? Did you manage to find out what *ziyarat* is about? Why do we go on it, and why do they attack it?" I confirmed that the "we" in her question were the Shi'a, suffering again from immobility, and that the "they" were the fighters of the Islamic State, targeting shrines in Iraq and Syria. As I had explained to others before, I said my research was not concerned with what *ziyarat* was and was not about, but rather what people made it to be about. I added that I was in no position to pass judgment as an authority, given the diversity of motivations that moved many pilgrims on the paths of Zainab. Fatima Khanum pressed further: but did I, as a Sunni, think of *ziyarat* as a virtuous religious practice? I reiterated that I aimed to better understand how the route, in part due to the diverse motivations of those who traveled it, forged historical and geographical connections in the region. As in some of the previous conversations in which this question arose, I could feel Fatima Khanum's disappointment in my answer. I imagined her thinking, "What a waste—after so many years of research this is the answer you reach?"

That was neither the first nor the last time I was asked these questions. It was, however, the last time I tried to avoid answering them by refusing their very terms. That day I finally conceded. I told Sima that if anything the fact that so many people asked these very questions *now* should be significant in and of itself. At the time, I had no better response. I had a few ideas that meditated on the frequent description of the pilgrimage route as a path of both visitation and commerce, but nothing that I found satisfactory as an answer to "What did I see? What is *ziyarat* about? And why do people go on it and others attack it?"

That was not the last time Fatima Khanum and I met either. She graciously kept in touch with me over the years and hosted me for an overwhelmingly rich Ramadan feast in her Shahrak-i Gharb apartment in Tehran during the summer of 2014. When everyone else was sitting quietly after breaking the fast or simply dozing off, Fatima Khanum quickly retreated to the kitchen to tidy up. This was the time to do it. I reminded her of those three questions she had posed when we first met. Of course, she remembered them, she said. I told her that I wanted to give the answer a second try. And I said I wanted to recite a quatrain as a part of my answer. An informally taught student of Qur'anic recitation and now a teacher of girls interested in reading the Qur'an, Fatima Khanum, I thought, would at least appreciate my efforts at getting the meter and intonation right. I recited:

From the station of disbelief to that of belief is but a breath.
And, but one breath, from the station of doubt to that of faith.
This precious breath, let us pass it gayly.
Since the harvest of our lives is but that very breath.

I proceeded to explain to Fatima Khanum that on the pathways of Zainab I came to describe *ziyarat* through Omar Khayyam's breath. Pathways of Zainab, as I encountered them, were where the distance between the sacred and the profane, the secular and the religious, supplication and Syrian lingerie was indeed but a breath. And that entanglement of *ham ziyarat ham tijarat* that prompted in some a sectarian dismissal of the religious virtues of the route itself—a route that spanned three countries and insinuated itself into the territories it traversed—was nothing if not that breath. Some called it the pilgrimage of the poor; and precisely because the pilgrims were not economically impoverished but deprived of mobility, it was not about the destination but the journey. So I ended my answer in Fatima Khanum's kitchen. She seemed excited. But she also could not hide that she was surprised to be excited about my answer. She said, with an unusual smile, "You might have found your answer, I suppose. But Khayyam? I presume the Wahhabis would not disagree. But about the importance of the journey, you might just be right."

I cannot claim that for all pilgrims the journey itself and the spaces it has opened up for political, economic, and personal maneuvering were the reason why they poured onto the pathways of Zainab. Not unlike the *ta'ziyeh* proceedings where I met Fatima Khanum, *ziyarat* too had its motley crew. For some, it was a search for questions otherwise left unanswered; for others, a pursuit of ambitions otherwise stalled. Still others were after a remedy for suffering otherwise unabated. I thought perhaps it was precisely this plurality offered to Iranians by the journey itself that attracted not only a diverse set of travelers but also physical attacks by brigades intent on violently inscribing their theological convictions—which deemed *ziyarat* impermissible and all saint veneration blasphemous—onto territory by destroying, among other things, any place of worship devoted to saint veneration. The theory of theological deliberation was being presented to justify the practice of political violence in the name of Islam once again—and once again *ziyarat* was in excess of the religious.

Ziyarat indeed is better conceived as a social field of force. Within that field and in the hands of diverse subjects, different notions of religious authority, economic opportunity, and political possibility battled for discursive and material hegemony. In its contemporary constellation, the historically sedimented and creatively improvised grounds of *ziyarat* have transformed into an archive of sectarianization as a historical process. Among the formerly mobile cast of characters associated with the pilgrimage route, the only ones that continued moving across the border were Hıdır and his network of cross-border *kaçak* trade. If the pilgrimage route had emblematized the vitality of regional mobility just a few years ago, its abrupt cessation in 2012 was the canary in the mine for the emergence of the Islamic State as a regional force, if not a calamity to come. Maybe "they," as Fatima Khanum suggested, would have agreed that the journey was why they attacked its destination.

ARGUMENTS

In this book, I have made three key arguments. First, I drew out the importance of histories of visitation and the regional cartography of Shiʻi saint veneration as the grounds for contemporary *ziyarat* routes such as *hajj-i fuqara'*. The pathways of Zainab and their entanglements with *kaçak* showed discernible continuities with the confluence of *'atabat* pilgrimage and trade between Iran and Iraq. Although *ziyarat* at times became a contested topic of theological debate among different schools of Islamic jurisprudence, the regulation of *ziyarat* routes was intimately linked to regional state formation and the exercise of imperial sovereignty. Indeed, jurisprudential debates over *ziyarat* were most lively and polarized at times of political upheaval. We see this, as explicated in chapter 4, for instance, in the imperial battles fought across Anatolia and Persia over the Qizilbash in the eighteenth century, and the mass conversions of Sunni Arab tribes to Shiʻi Islam in eighteenth- and nineteenth-century Iraq. We saw in these dynamics—as well as in others, including the Wahhabi attacks on centers of commerce and religious learning in Ottoman Iraq, as a tactic for gaining legitimacy in the revival of the movement in the early nineteenth century—that doctrinal difference was intimately tied to political contestation over space. The shifting landscape of pilgrimage, therefore, has to be understood in relation to the shifting landscape of state sovereignty. As Simon Coleman has noted, shifting grounds of sovereignty are intimately tied to religious rituals' capability to underwrite sheer physical movement.[1] What Zainab's traffic reveals is that those powers include not only mobilizing bodies but geographies and histories into genealogically instituted grids of connectivity. Thinking of Islamic religious practice in these more historical, processual ways allows us to reconceptualize Islamic ritual. In this reconceptualization, ritual emerges as a generative sphere of political and socioeconomic negotiation—or what Pierre Bourdieu has called "regulated improvisation"—rather than the reiteration of a hermetically sealed discursive tradition.

The second main argument, concerning the relationship between arrested mobility and value, is that a historical approach to the circuits of commodity trade that are deeply interwoven with those of *ziyarat* gives us new analytical purchase on formations of the economy and markets as well as transformations of sovereignty and borders. Circuits of the Iranian Bazaar provide us a view into how contraband is constructed as external and secondary to formal economies yet in reality remains primary and central to the constitution of bazaars and borders alike. From cigarettes produced domestically, exported to Iran, and then smuggled back into the country to evade taxation in Turkey, to the guaranteed contraband tea and crafty women peddlers of Antep, *kaçak* emerges as a central thread in the very formation of markets and states on the paths of Zainab.

This traffic in value was not limited to cross-border trade in goods and commodities. Property regimes tied to land use and tenure also were transformed through the *hajj-i fuqara'* traffic. As we observed in chapter 2, the guardians of the Sayyida Zainab shrine, the Murtada family, gradually converted the landed assets tied to their family's charitable trust into private property slated for real estate development. The involvement of the *waqf dhurri* associated with the shrine in a diverse portfolio of real estate development and service industry projects provided us with a case study to rethink the place of patriliny in studies of genealogy and to approach patronage as a generative modality of kinship-making.

Approached differently, the Murtada family's conversion of their patrimonial assets to private property was also a traffic in excess of the economic realm altogether. Acting as real estate developers while being *sayyids,* or as an embedded informant for a contraband network while serving as a police officer like Hıdır, seems to point to a common practice of value generation among various actors along the *hajj-i fuqara'* who transvalued across different regimes of value. Turning theoretical exclusions assumed between the different regimes of value of religion, economy, and polity into thresholds of conversion between them, the Murtada family exploited their *sayyid* renown to bolster the value of their property, Hıdır used police intelligence for contraband strategy, and Osman and Yaşar leased a formal store to sell contraband goods. The diagonal cuts that these actors made across regimes of value, in other words, made transvaluation a particularly generative practice across Iran, Turkey, and Syria.

Finally, I have argued for an understanding of spatial and transnational mobility in relational and processual terms. Rather than see pilgrims as pawns in a larger game of state-orchestrated missionization or as iterative devotees of scriptural Islam alone, I have argued for placing their journeys at the center of our analysis and for tracing how they formed themselves as subjects in a dialectical relationship between multiple and nested hegemonies—whereby contestation over space and access to mobility emerge as both the technology of regulation and a technique of improvisation to circumvent those regulations.

Pilgrims on the paths of Zainab have utilized *ziyarat* to lay claim to new routes of movement in the rapidly shifting political landscapes of their region. This pattern of veneration and visitation reflects pilgrims' awareness of their political embeddedness within larger structures of state authority, their recognition of the creative gap between myth and ritual, and their sense of agency in bridging that gap. In Iranian pilgrims' mobility across Iraq and the Levant, we not only observed creatively improvised invocations of Islamic traditions of pilgrimage and visitations but also saw how their claims to transnational mobility belied a sharp distinction between religion and other realms of social life.

The particular transnational constellation of regional dynamics that put Sayyida Zainab on the map of Shiʿi visitation animated the genealogy, iconography, and history of the saint and the shrine in significant but selective ways. These selective contemporary collages of Zainab and her figuration in fact made it possible to reimagine *ziyarat* as both an increasingly sectarianized religious practice and the grounds on which to forge a geography of mobility for Iranian citizenry. In an international regime mined with arduous visa application processes, Iranian nationals—who described themselves as poor of mobility even as Syrians feared their overwhelming numbers—had made the ways of Zainab into journeys of their own.

Epilogue

CHICAGO, ILLINOIS

August 12, 2023

4,542 DAYS AFTER THE SYRIAN REVOLUTION
4,217 DAYS AFTER THE PILGRIM ABDUCTIONS
4,796 DAYS AFTER THE DEADLIEST ISIL ATTACK ON THE SHRINE
18 DAYS AFTER THE LATEST ISIL ATTACK ON THE SHRINE

Karam and Sahand, after an arduous process with the Office of the United Nations High Commissioner for Refugees, have been granted asylum as queer bears and have resettled in Cologne, Germany. Sahand, in part, holds Sayyida Zainab's blessing responsible for their resettlement.

Mohsen and Narmin gave up on buying an apartment in Tabriz, Iran. After Turkey introduced a golden passport scheme for those who buy $250,000 USD worth of property, they bought an apartment in Antalya, Turkey, instead in 2020. At the time of writing in 2022, they have their Turkish passports.

Banu never had a baby. She completed her residency and specialized as a neurologist. Within two years of the trip to Sayyida Zainab, Banu and Payam decided to divorce. Two years after the divorce, Banu relocated to Paris, France.

Fariba Khanum passed away, peacefully and at her house, on September 29, 2019. The family contemplated burying her in the Sayyida Zainab cemetery as she had wished in her will. Because the war didn't allow it, the family decided that she would stay permanently in Tehran—the Tehran that she, originally tracing her roots back to the northern city of Ardabil in Iran, had always known, after each trip to pay visits elsewhere, as home.

The Professor "informally" retired from full-time work at the *mimar*'s mechanic shop. He enjoys rereading his social theory books from his time at Mimar Sinan University. He occasionally meets with Metin—who also retired—at a teahouse near the former Iranian Bazaar to enjoy a glass of *kaçak* tea and reminisce.

The shrine itself stands, despite periodic attacks. The latest of these was in July 2023, when six people were killed and over twenty wounded in a massive explosion just a day ahead of 'Ashura—the date on which Shia Muslims remember the death of the Islamic Prophet's grandson Husayn ibn Ali and the captivity of the Prophet's granddaughter Sayyida Zaynab in Damascus.

Parastoo, now a mother of twins, is planning another trip to Sayyida Zainab shrine, this time with Umid and via Iraq. The new route between Iran and Sayyida Zainab now meanders through Iraq's Anbar Province. Thus the Iranian *ziyarat* to Zainab reemerges in yet another reincarnation, as the arresting of mobility begets other routes of mobility.

NOTES

INTRODUCTION

1. On sectarianism as an analytical paradigm rather than an object of inquiry, see Shakman Hurd 2015. On use of sectarian difference that "masks other forms of social difference," see Deeb 2020. On intersectional approaches to sect alongside class and gender, see Joseph 1975; Joseph 2011; and Mikdashi 2022. For the formative role Shi'i courts have played in the sectarian design of the Lebanese nation-state, see Weiss 2010 and Makdisi 2000.

2. Bayoumi 2006; Li 2019; Mamdani 2002; Naber 2008; Rana 2011; Wadud 2011.

3. Alatas 2016; Coleman 2002; Coleman 2014; Elfenbein 2015; Scheele 2013.

4. Granovetter 1985. The neoclassical conceptualization of economic action, according to Granovetter, assumes an undersocialized actor who chooses to engage in utilitarian pursuit of self-interest untethered by social relationships or institutional contexts (484). In this book I contend that the anthropology of Islam after the ethical turn similarly operates with an undersocialized notion of religious action, whereby the social atomization of the pious individual, outside of social institutions, remains the premise to reduce ritual to a method of ethical cultivation.

5. Ho 2004.

6. "Khanum" is a Persian honorific used like "Ms." or "Mrs." in English.

7. A multiplicity of orthodox and heterodox religious communities that would align under the umbrella of Shi'i Islam believed that sovereign leadership for the Prophetic State was hereditary and had been left by the Prophet Muhammad to his son-in-law and cousin, Imam Ali, and to his descendants. Those committed to this hereditary genealogy of rightful leadership named Ali and his descendants as "imams." Sunni Muslims instead followed the caliphate as the legitimate institution of leadership, conceiving of its sovereign genealogy as a nonhereditary lineage stemming from Prophet's companion (Deeb 2009a, 252). Considering this fundamental difference in tracing genealogies for legitimate leadership, venerating the members

of the Ahl al-Bayt (the Family of the Prophet) and women saints in the same family, like Hazrat-i Zainab, became a jurisprudentially integrated ritual in most Shiʿi traditions. While it continued to be practiced widely among those religious communities under the "umbrella" of Sunni Islam, it escaped similar jurisprudential work except for first Wahhabi and later Salafi condemnations of the practice as a heretical innovation in Islamic tradition. For Iranians, whose possibilities for transnational mobility, including pilgrimages and saint visitation (*ziyarat*), have been methodically diminished through interstate visa policies since 1979, this "hagiographic" history with its important genealogical questions provided one more deep-history layer in the jagged landscape of saint visitation across Southwest Asia.

8. On the embodiment of this model of modern pious womanhood in the Lebanese context, see Deeb 2009a. For an erudite analysis of sainthood around Zainab, see Szanto 2012b.

9. Asad 1993; Asad 2003. See also Scott and Hirschkind 2006.

10. Fadil and Fernando 2015. For moral ambivalences of pious living, see Schielke 2009.

11. Mahmood 2005. As Samah Selim points out in her review of *Politics of Piety*, *daʿwa* is not the "natural" expression of an ontological form of Egyptian women's agency grounded in Islamic sentiments and sensibilities that are ultimately untranslatable in terms of progressive "Western" ideals of feminism but rather an active political movement that silences the past of a long history of women's struggles. It is indeed Mahmood's analytical indifference to the entire range of the piety movement's institutional and pedagogic activities that allows her to define the women's piety movement as a fundamentally, if not purely, ethical project of personal cultivation and to ignore its function as a politically prescriptive project in its own right. See Selim 2010. On engagements with Saba Mahmood's framework of ethical cultivation, see also Bangstad 2011; Mittermaier 2012.

12. Fernando 2014, 15.

13. Osella and Soares, 2010, 11.

14. Deeb 2009b.

15. Caton 2006, 54.

16. On symbols in ritualistic action and ritual as process, see Turner 1969. On liminality and *communitas* in ritual, see Turner and Turner 1978. On pilgrimage and ritual, see also Eickelman and Piscatori 1990. On discursive regimes built around rituals of pilgrimage, see Lahiri 2007.

17. Weston 2009.

18. Tarde [1899] 2008; Latour 2005.

19. On the morality of exchange and cultural approaches to value regimes and networks of exchange, see Bloch and Parry 1989. On intersections of economy and Islam in particular, see Maurer 2006; Rudnyckyj 2009; Ismail 2013.

20. Guyer 2004, 28.

21. Roitman 2005.

22. Appadurai 1986.

23. Malinowski [1922] 1961.

24. Munn 1986.

25. Saussure [1916] 2006.

26. Caton 2006, 56.

27. A. Subramanian 2006.

28. On the intellectual history of the concept of space, see Harvey 2006; Soja 1989. For Lefebvre's paradigm of the production of space scaled to state formation, see Lefebvre 2009c, 110–13. On territory as state space, see Brenner and Elden 2009, 358. On territory as a methodological assumption rather than an object of investigation in state formation, see Agnew 1994.

29. Silverstein 1976; Caton 2006.

30. Marcus 1995. On multiscalar ethnography, see Xiang 2013. On scaling as social praxis in the context of sanctions, see Yıldız 2021.

OF WAYS AND TRAFFIC

1. Rubin 1975.

2. Coleman 2015. Also see Bajc, Coleman, and Eade 2007; Eade and Sallnow 2000.

3. Rubin 1975, 209.

4. Rubin 1975, 158.

1. ZAINAB'S TRAFFIC

1. Throughout I refer to the same historical figure by her honorifics: Sayyida Zainab in Arabic, and Hazrat-i Zainab in Persian and Turkish.

2. While *ziyarat* is jurisprudentially endorsed in Twelver Shiʿism and jurisprudentially condemned in most literalist revivalist Sunni traditions like Wahabi or Salafi interpretations, none of the *canonized* schools of Islamic *fiqh* (jurisprudence) to date has endorsed or condemned the practice of saint visitation. *Ziyarat* remains a widely observed ritual among Alevis, ʿAlawites, and Bektaşis, as well as among some Hanafi Sunni practitioners throughout Turkey, Kurdistan, and Syria in addition to the majority Twelver Shiʿi practitioners across Azerbaijan, Iran, and Iraq.

3. Zamzam water is sourced from the Zamzam well in Mecca, the holiest city in Islam. It is believed to be sacred with purifying and healing properties. Therefore most pilgrims bring back home some Zamzam water and gift it to extended kin and loved ones.

4. Durkheim [1912] 1995; Douglas [1966] 2002.

5. On the moral economy of tourism and *ziyarat,* see Adelkhah 2009. On Syria-based markets of religious objects making "Shiʿism" transnational, see Pinto 2007.

6. Sayyida Ruqayya was Imam Hussein's youngest daughter. She died at the age of four in Yazid's prison. For an art historical study of the Ruqayya Mosque's

expansions, see Tabaa 2007. On the shrine town, Sayyida Zainab, see Mervin 1996; Szanto 2014.

7. For a conception of tradition as a "historically extended, socially embodied argument," see MacIntyre 2012, 222. For an ethical explication of this conception in the anthropology of Islam, see Asad 1986. For a reworking of this ethical conception in Islamic occult practices among Iranians, see Doostdar 2019. Here I follow Bourdieu ([1980] 1990, 10–15), who in his practice theory locates the historical dynamism of social formations, like saint visitation, as effects of regulated improvisations (10–15). Instead of projecting the habitus of those improvisations inwards (Mahmood 2001), my approach follows the connections outwards. By "Zainab's traffic" here, I refer to the aggregate spatial production of these regulated improvisations into a social ecology of movement built around the figure of Hazrat-i Zainab.

8. Cresswell 2010, 17. On cross-class and cross-gender potentials of interactions across multiple vehicles in urban traffic as an object of analysis, see Truitt 2008; on cross-class and cross-gender encounters in congested traffic in Istanbul, see Yazici 2013; on nested temporalities and variegated intensities of cross-border and highway traffic, see Yeh 2018.

9. See Xiang 2013; Yıldız 2021.

10. Dating back to the 1930s in their operations, the Ittila'at publishing conglomerate produced a variety of magazines, including one specifically dedicated to women but better known for its eponymous daily newspaper. Another daily, *Kayman,* also had an affiliated women's weekly at the time; it was called *Zan-i Ruz,* roughly translatable to "Today's Woman."

11. Ahl al-Bayt (lit. "People of the Household") is a designation in Islam for the Prophet's family, particularly his daughter Fatima, her husband the fourth caliph and first imam Imam Ali, their sons Imams Hussain and Hasan, and their daughter Hazrat-i Zainab.

12. Nasser Palangi is a practicing multimedia artist. During the Iran-Iraq War, he was a prolific illustrator and muralist who produced several state-commissioned and publicly circulated images of Zainab on postrevolutionary streets of Tehran. The image sampled here by my interlocutor was his contribution to the magazine *Zainab's Way.*

13. Moallem 2005, 96.

14. Dr. Hani Murtada, interview by author, 2018, Beirut.

15. Hedayat [1943] 1962, 11–57. For a critique of "superstitious practices" of religion among Iranians, see Kasravi 1943. Cf. Fischer [1980] 2003. On the relationship between piety and reconstitution of gendered notions of class and modernity in Sadegh Hedayat's work, see Moallem 2005, 71–73.

16. On the remedies of modern psychiatric medicine in postwar Iran, see Behrouzan 2016. On practices of seeking cures through the occult sciences, see Doostdar 2018.

17. *Rowzah* and *ta'ziyeh* are distinct sets of ritual, performed to venerate those of the Ahl al-Bayt lineage and those fallen in Karbala. Cf. Aghaie 2004.

18. Tambar 2011.

19. Honarpisheh 2013.

20. Muharram processions are a set of commemoration rituals observed primarily by Shi'i and Sufi Muslims. Falling in the first month of the Islamic calendar, *Muharram*, the processions mark the Battle of Karbala.

21. Turner 1973; Coleman 2002.

22. Yıldız 2021.

23. MacIntyre 2012.

24. Cohen 1992; Coleman 2014.

25. Moallem 2005, 95–96.

26. Deeb 2009b.

PARASTOO'S PATHWAYS AND OBSERVANT PARTICIPATION

1. *Ayna-kari,* literally "mirror-work," is a Persianate form of interior decoration where finely cut pieces of mirror are assembled together into geometric, calligraphic, or foliage templates.

2. CRAFTING PATRONAGE

1. Before the Syrian conflict, and up until 2012, one US dollar was worth forty-seven Syrian pounds. Since the conflict started, however, the Syrian pound has depreciated 166 percent.

2. The following scholarship on Sayyida Zainab reproduces this conspiracy about the shrine as an Iranian state satellite in some shape or form: Mervin 1996; Adelkhah 2009; Pinto 2007; Szanto 2014.

3. Another way that the history of construction is marginal to pilgrims' experience of the shrine is the erasure or convenient overlooking of the construction itself. The anachronistic collage of architectural features associated with different eras and places of Islamic architecture further complicates any attempt to place the shrine in a particular period. Its features—particularly the golden dome, the exterior use of tiles, and the interior use of mirrored ceilings—mark the shrine as Persianate in style.

4. *Zakat* is an obligatory almsgiving for all Muslims possessing a certain minimum income (*nisab*). Religious charitable organizations are one of the primary recipients of donations in the form of *zakat*.

5. Ateş 2010; Nakash 1995. For an alternative account of the Ottoman-Safavid negotiations of Iraq's borders, see Matthee 2003. For memoirs and travelogues penned by colonial officers moving across Ottoman and Qajar territories, and the place of corpse traffic in the spatial development of the cemeteries of Karbala, see Ussher 1865; Cowper 1894, 372.

6. Moumtaz 2021, 47.

7. Moumtaz 2021, 3.

8. For a historical overview of *waqf* studies, see Crecelius 1995; Hoexter 1998. For earlier works on *waqf* in Ottoman studies, see Köprülü 1942. For the role of imperial *awqaf* in Ottoman economy, see İnalcık 1969; Gerber 1983; Hoexter 1997.

9. Khoury 1987. For more recent studies that rethink territorialization outside the nation-state paradigm in Syria and the broader Levant, see Schayegh 2011.

10. *Al-Mawsem* 1997.

11. Ottoman Archives of Turkey's Prime Ministry (hereafter BOA) 490 36 748 1312 R08 1, Mustafa Emin Effendi to Sublime Port, March 28, 1896.

12. *Al-Mawsem* 1997 features a selection among the *waqfiyya* documents that chronicle the Murtada family genealogy, including a brief history of the properties placed under the patrimony of the *waqf*.

13. This discrepancy might be due to a marriage that the family did not approve of one generation removed that resulted in the splitting of the *waqf dhurri* rights between Sayyid 'Abbas and Sayyid Rida as two sons of the same father with different mothers, yet another formative matriarchal twist in an otherwise patriarchally told family story known as Prophetic genealogy.

14. BOA SD185 27 1326 M10 1, "Inheritance Verdict on the Hazrat-I Zainab Shrine and Its Waqf," June 12, 1910. Şura-yı Devlet was a high court formed by Sultan Abdülaziz in 1868. A direct product of the 1839 reforms, known as Gülhane Hatt-ı Hümayun of 1839, Şura-yı Devlet functioned as the highest judiciary court in the Ottoman Empire until 1922. The fact that the Murtada inheritance case was decided in this court indicates that establishing the inheritance of the Sayyida Zainab shrine was a process filled with contestation that made its way through the court hierarchy. The Ottoman files give no clue as to what the initial dispute was that moved the case through the hierarchy of courts within the pluralistic legal regime of the empire.

15. The institution of the *marja' al-taqlid* (literally, "source of emulation"; pl. *maraji' al-taqlid*) is often traced back to a major Shi'i doctrinal debate between rationalists (*al-usuliyun*) and traditionalists (*al-akhbariyun*) in the eighteenth and nineteenth centuries. The institution ushered in by the rationalists formalized a hierarchy of scholars ('ulama), the top echelons of which are reserved for a handful of scholars, who then serve as *maraji' al-taqlid*. Shi'a who do not attain the level of *mujtahid* (i.e., one capable of independent legal reasoning) are required to perform *taqlid* or emulate one who has—the *marja' al-taqlid*. See Litvak 1998; Khamenei 1997, 9; S. Shirazi 2008, 7.

16. Louër 2008, 88–89, 91.

17. Both *khums* and *zakat* are obligatory taxes on acquired wealth for Muslims. While different confessions calculate these taxes differently, they could be understood as means to purify wealth by giving a compulsory and regular donation to good causes. *Zakat* is most often taken to be 2.5 percent of a Muslim's wealth, after they have paid for what is necessary to support themselves and their families. It constitutes the third pillar across Sunni Islam denominations, and the third of the

Ten Obligatory Acts across Shi'i ones. *Khums* (lit. "a fifth") constitutes the sixth of the Ten Obligatory Acts for Shi'i Muslims and is paid on any *profit* earned.

18. Szanto 2012a, 56.

19. Anthropologists and historians of Iran such as Michael Fischer and Nikki Keddie grappled with the politicization of Shi'i Muharram practices and discourses at the hands of the *'ulama* and Shi'i intellectuals, such as 'Ali Shari'ati. In 1981, Fischer coined the term *the Karbala paradigm* in order to distinguish Shi'i Muharram practices from those of Catholic Penitentes. The paradigm, according to Fischer [1980] 2003, 21, "provides models for living and a mnemonic for thinking about how to live." See also Aghaie 2004; Deeb 2006. These selective mobilizations of the figure of Zainab took on important political and social issues in creative ways across a vast geography from Lebanon to Iran and South Asia. See Deeb 2009a. The revolutionary hagiography, often created with the financial and political support of the Iranian state, in the print and visual media of revolutionary Iran, is explored in chapter 4.

3. ARRESTED MOBILITIES AND FUGITIVE MARKETS

1. On temporary marriages in Iran, see Haeri 1989.

2. A rich literature on marketplaces in the Middle East and the cultural form of the bazaar exists in anthropology. I do not explicitly engage with this literature in this chapter, but my argument about contraband being central to the constitution of economies should sever the ties assumed between bazaars as precapitalized spaces of economic exchange on the one hand and informality as a cultural or historically residual practice on the other, or alternatively one that is governed not by an excess of information but by its scarcity. See in particular Geertz 1979; Geertz 1978. Geertz's earlier work (1963) on peddlers in Indonesia is instructive here as well. See also Keshavarzian 2007, particularly 39–74.

3. Rize, located in the Black Sea region of Turkey in the northeast, is renowned for tea cultivation in the country. Çaykur Rize, the former state-led industrialization project, was converted to Turkey's National Wealth Fund in 2007, yet it continues to control about 60 percent of the formal tea market in Turkey.

4. De Soto [1986] 1989; Hart 1987; Lomnitz, 1988.

5. Elyachar 2003; Gandolfo 2013.

6. Galemba 2017; Matthew 2016; Mezzadra and Neilson 2013; Schayegh 2011.

7. Callon 1998; Callon and Koray Çalışkan 2009. Also see Mitchell 1998; McFall and Dodsworth 2009.

8. Mitchell 1991. Also see Hull 2008; Navaro 2007.

9. Beritan and Yildirim 2013; also see Mendi 2018.

10. Mendi 2018, 261.

11. According to data published by the World Health Organization in 2012, only three years after adopting tough antismoking measures, Turkey's tobacco consumption was down 15 percent. The same bulletin entry also states, "According to a

government survey of tobacco use conducted in 2006, some 33% of adults were daily smokers, including just over half of all men and approximately 16% of women aged 18 and over. In a Gallup poll conducted in 100 countries the following year, two out of three Turkish men said they had lit up the day before they were surveyed, as did one out of three women. That was, Gallup said, 'by far the highest incidence reported.' It also confirmed a stereotype common across Europe: that to smoke heavily was 'to smoke like a Turk'" (Adams 2012, 408).

12. Appadurai 1986; Kopytoff 1986; Bronislaw Malinowski [1922] 1961; Mauss [1925] 2000; Munn 1986.

13. Chakrabarty 2007.

14. Callon 2021; Callon 1998; Callon and Çalışkan 2009; Mitchell 1998.

15. Elyachar 2005; Gandolfo 2013; Hull 2012; Kalir and van Schendel 2017.

16. "Citizen's Lament" 1932.

17. The figure of the *bohçacı kadın,* the woman peddler, reveals the gendered anxieties of the newly founded Republic of Turkey in 1930s, as exemplified by Çelebizade's vilification of these women. Even more remarkably, it shows that contraband networks turn the exclusions of the formal economy into unexplored means for generating economic value: by moving between the seemingly separate realms of the marketplace and the household, the *bohçacı kadın* make it possible for contraband to make its way into the very houses of consumers. On women peddlers and the relationship between gendered informality and nationalism, see Baron 2007; Davis 1986.

18. Jorum 2014. Also see Altuğ 2011.

19. Gültekin 2011, 32.

20. Aydın 2008; Güngor 2004; Uzel 1952.

21. For a historical analysis of sixteenth-century Antep and its legal landscape, see Pierce 2003.

22. As Kurt (2021, 33) shows, land confiscation and population transfer made new wealth available, when prosperous Armenians—who worked in sizable numbers across manufacturing, agriculture, and trade—were ejected from Antep. While the forced removal of the Armenians during the genocide was rationalized on national security grounds, the prospect of material gain, as Kurt shows, had been a key motivator of support for the Armenian genocide among the local Muslim gentry and the Kurdish and Turkish publics it mobilized in expropriation of Armenian wealth and property. These new merchant classes that would industrialize Antep hence jump-started their post-Ottoman national careers in early Republican Turkey with a genocidal primitive accumulation.

23. Balta 2010.

24. Yüksel 2011, 379.

25. *Gaziantep Organized Industrial Zone Almanac* 2012, 2.

26. Karadağ 2011, 400.

27. Kemal 2011, 32.

28. Kemal 2011, 40.

29. A more detailed discussion on circulations of Syrian lingerie and Iranian women pilgrims as customers can be found in chapter 1. For a fascinating art historical approach to Syrian lingerie, see Halasa and Salam 2008.

30. Mitchell 1998, 100.

4. BORDERING *ZIYARAT*

1. Tagliacozzo 2007, 5.

2. As Manu Goswami (2004, 35) notes in *Producing India: From Colonial Economy to National Space*, Lefebvre's work on the social production of space and his emphasis on treating space as a modality of political and economic power provide us with important insights into "the uneven and differentiated character of global space, the reciprocal liaison between spatial practices and representation and the dynamic relationship between the modern state and space." Although Lefebvre's rigorous processual analysis of the triadic relationship between state, space, and capital has not been extended beyond studies of urban environments to studies of borders, his 1954 dissertation research conducted on peasant communities in the Pyrenees is instructive for such a fruitful engagement. See Lefebvre [1965] 2000. For more on borders, see Lefebvre 2009c, 110–13. On territory as state space, see Brenner and Elden 2009. On territory as a methodological assumption rather than an object of investigation in state formation, see Agnew 1994.

3. *Palimpsest* was introduced to scholarly parlance thanks to Gerard Genette's usage in *Palimpsestes: La littérature au second degré* (1982) to explicate the process of the layering texts and to draw out *hypertextuality* in literary production and criticism. See Genette 1997 for English translation. On the intellectual history of palimpsest as an analytic, see Dillon 2007. In this work, Dillon distinguishes between *palimpsestic,* which "refers to the process of layering that produces a palimpsest," and *palimpsestuous,* which "describes the structure that one is presented with as a result of that process" (57). This chapter provides a palimpsestic account for palimpsestuous borders as the latter intersect with saint visitation routes.

4. I borrow the term *borderland* from Anzaldúa 1987. Also see Grimson and Vila 2002; Flynn 1997. On circuits of migration and space, see Rouse 1991.

5. Following Agnew 2020, I understand territorial sovereignty as a political fiction wherein "the territory of a state represents both the exclusive zone of effective control that state exercises and the only focus for political and cultural loyalty" (2). While my focus is on the historically sedimented and, to this day, contested claims to territorial sovereignty of what is now Syria, Turkey, and their Kurdistans, I depart from the premise, following Krasner 2010, that sovereignty itself should be approached as operating in at least three overlapping and often conflicting modalities: (1) international legal sovereignty, understood as juridical equality among states under international law; (2) Westphalian sovereignty, understood as the absence of submission to external rule in a territory and the 1648 mantra of *Cuis regio, euis*

religio (To whom is the region/territory, his is the religion); and (3) domestic sovereignty, understood as a state's exercise of power and monopoly over means of violence in that state's territory, including and especially over cross-border mobility (96).

6. In *Pilgrims and Sultans: The Hajj under the Ottomans*, Suraiya Faroqhi chronicles how, as early as the sixteenth century, Ottomans devised a Hijaz route for Iranians in order to curtail the numbers of *'atabat* visitors and minimize the time Safavid subjects spent around Baghdad. Along this Hijaz route, Aleppo served as the meeting point between the pilgrims traveling over land from the Balkans and those traveling from Iran and Central Asia. After the congregation of the Balkan, Anatolian, and Iranian pilgrims in and near Aleppo, the *hajj* candidates would travel down to the Hijaz through territory that is now Syria and Jordan (Faroqhi 1996, esp. 128, 134–45).

7. Al 'atabat Al-Aliyat (lit. "sublime doorsteps") refers to the burial places of six Shi'i imams across four cities in current-day Iraq: namely Karbala, Kadhimiya, Najaf, and Samarra.

8. Nakash 1995, 154.

9. Quluwahy 2008, 147–49.

10. al-Muzaffar 1962, 93.

11. Nakash 1995 identifies *Kamil al-Ziyarat* by Ibn Quluwayh (d. 980/81) as the first major attempt to regulate the dates of visitation of the imams and to emphasize the rewards to be gained from it. Nakash also mentions classical jurists who have examined *ziyarat,* such as Abu al-Salah al-Halabi (d. 1055/56), Muhammad ibn al-Hasan al-Tusi (d. 1067), and Muhammad ibn Idris al-Hilli (d. 1202).

12. Nakash 1994, 45–46.

13. Iranian genealogies of *ziyarat* do not, however, include only episodes of sectarian violence in the production of intra-Islamic difference. Nadir Shah further attempted to bridge the widening doctrinal divide between Sunni and Shi'i Islam by proposing that the Ottomans accept Iranian Shi'ism as a fifth *madhab* (school of thought in Islamic jurisprudence): *madhab-i Ja'fari.* For a detailed discussion of contestation over *ziyarat* between different schools of jurisprudence, see Meri 2001. For *ziyarat* in Egypt, see Taylor 1999.

14. Deringil 1990, 47.

15. Karakaya-Stump 2008.

16. Ottoman Archives of Turkey's Prime Ministry (hereafter BOA), Yıldız Peraknede Başkitabet Dairesi Maruzatı (Y PRK BŞK), 57/16, 19, "Report on Spread of Shi'ism in Iraq," August 1, 1898. The reports in this collection were written by a commission of five clerics sent to the region to assess the allegations of Sunni Iraqis' mass conversions to Shi'ism. In an attached commentary accompanying the record, as Sabri Ates also notes (2010, 519), Vahap Bey, a local state official in Baghdad, argues that the reports confirm "the immediate need to counter the spread of Shi'ism and the proselytizing of *akhunds* [clerics]." Also see BOA, "Yıldız Mutenevvi Maruzat" (Y MTV), 73/71, "Report on Shi'ism in Iraq," July 21, 1894.

17. BOA Yıldız Esas Evraki, 14/212/26/3–7, "Spread of Shi'ism in Iraq," July 20, 1907.

18. Aydin 2017.

19. Dugid 1973; Deringil 1990, 54; Salibi 1979, 72, also quoted in Deringil 1990.

20. Republican Archives of Turkey's Prime Ministry (hereafter BCA), BBA, Yıldız Esas Evraki, 14/257/126/8, "Ali Galip Bey's Report on the Spread of Shiʿism in Hamidian Iraq," August 26, 1907.

21. BCA, BBA, Yıldız Esas Evraki, 14 212/126/7, "A Report by Major Ali Rıza Bey" (an officer with the Imperial General Staff and former consul to Khoy and Selmas), n.d.

22. Ateş 2010, 560.

23. The formation of modern Iraq and its relationship to *ziyarat* under the Mandate regime remains beyond the purview of this study. Here the Mandate Period in Iraq refers to the period of formal British rule between 1921 and 1932 as well as the period of proxy rule that lasted until the 1958 coup.

24. Despite his dismissive attitude toward public displays of religious ritual, Mohammad Reza Pahlavi undertook *ziyarat* to Qom in 1950 and to Mashhad in 1953 in an attempt to reclaim religious legitimacy.

25. As I will explore in greater detail below, the methods used by the special forces to counter cross-border trade—such as embedded agents traveling on the same buses, tasked with recording the array of hidden compartments or highway checkpoints—are not alien to these landscapes and were not invented to control Iranian populations. In fact, most of these methods that the Turkish security forces have unleashed on "golden shoes" (*altın ayakkabılar*), as they have come to be known in the area, were perfected on the Kurdish populations of the same geographies.

26. See L. Subramanian 1991.

27. I explore in chapter 3 the emergence of tobacco as one of the main contraband commodities in Turkey.

28. In international relations scholarship on global governance, the employment of sanctions—defined as unilateral or collective action taken against a state considered in violation of international law—has been celebrated as a diplomatic technology designed to compel the targeted country to conform to global norms. On sanctions as a technology of international governance, see Cortright and Lopez 2000; Eckert 2010. As temporary measures of international security, sanctions have long been considered less costly than military intervention in punishing deviation from international guidelines. Yet unlike military action, which has legal codes regarding the conduct of belligerents and third-party actors, sanctions have escaped such codification. Indeed, they continue to lend themselves to further weaponization. In the case of Iran, sanctions are better approached as an ever-expanding arsenal of "low-intensity" coercion that has exacerbated already-vexed relations between Iran and sanctioning states (Daoudi and Dajani 1983, 163). Further, as attempts to turn Iranians against their own government, sanctions have resulted in the collective punishment of the most vulnerable within Iran. They have also allowed the regime to claim that it is defending the country's national security against imperialist and capitalist conspiracy, revealing once again the recursive and

nested shapes that technologies of security and experiences of insecurity take in the context of sanctions. As security measures, then, sanctions are better understood as exercises in collective punishment that generate lived insecurities and bolster, rather than weaken, a targeted regime's power. Although the United States has levied a series of sanctions on Iran since 1979, their effects intensified between 2006 and 2012, when the United States succeeded in pushing through a series of UN Security Council resolutions that forced Iran to halt its uranium-enrichment program. Together, these resolutions delivered the biggest blow to the Iranian economy: banning banks worldwide (with cooperation of the Brussels-headquartered SWIFT) from processing all transactions out of Iran. When a total ban on Iranian oil exports to the EU went into effect in July 2012, the Iranian *rial* fell to a record low against the US dollar in less than two months. By September 2012, the *rial* had lost more than 80 percent of its value in less than a year. Iranians felt the immediate effects of sanctions in their lives through foreign capital flight, high unemployment, exponential inflation, and arrested supply chains. With a growing and young population's ever-increasing demand for consumer goods, however, sanctions also produced new configurations of exchange. On sanctions in Iran, see Yıldız 2021.

29. In December of 2014, I got a Skype call from Muhsin. In haste, he asked if I had heard about the scandal. Without skipping a beat, Muhsen explained that he had just listened to a recording "breaking" the Iranian internet. The source of the leaked recording was a Turkish police investigation. The police had tapped the phone of Zafer Çağlayan, Turkey's former economy minister. In the recording, Çağlayan, tasked with managing Turkey's $800 billion economy, was heard advising his collaborators on the other end of the line to find a way to increase exports by at least $1 billion a month for the remainder of the fiscal year. His collaborators, in response, reassured Çağlayan that what might seem like an unlikely source, the sanctions on Iran, was going to deliver to Turkish state coffers that amount, "if not more." "Fast-forward to the end," Mohsen interjected as I was taking notes. "There [Çağlayan] describes the network trading gold between Iran and Turkey via the United Arab Emirates. It spans as far as China and Ghana. It is *ghachagh* gone global!" Mohsen exclaimed. After I got off the call, I started digging into the recording on the internet myself. The operation's ringleaders were Reza Zarrab, an Iranian businessman, and Mehmet Hakan Atilla, the deputy CEO of Halkbank, a Turkish state-owned bank where the Iranian government parked payments for natural gas and oil exports to Turkey. According to the Turkish police investigation, Çağlayan, Zarrab, and their associates undertook gold trade with Iranian state functionaries and businesspeople, which swelled into a multi-billion-dollar operation: hundreds of tons of gold flowed from Turkey to Iran, much of it via Dubai. That freed up Iranian money—oil payments for Turkey's imports trapped at the same bank due to sanctions—while in turn boosting Turkish exports, as Çağlayan initially directed his addressee in the tapped phone conversation. The surge in gold exports, according to Turkish records, was markedly rapid and extensive—gold transfers to Iran jumped from $53 million in 2011 to $6.5 billion in 2012, drastically reducing Turkey's

budget deficit, which ran at approximately 10 percent of the country's GDP. See Parkinson and Peker 2012. The gold transfers boosted overall exports to $153 billion—up by almost 13 percent in 2012 from the previous year. They failed, however, to offset the Turkish appetite for imports, and the country ended FY2012 with a $65 billion budget deficit, up by almost $20 billion since 2011.

30. Partiya Karkeren Kurdistan (PKK), or Kurdistan's Workers Party, is a Marxist-Leninist insurgency formed in the early 1980s to fight the Turkish state for Kurdish sovereignty, and later cultural rights and autonomy of the Kurdish-majority regions of Turkey. On the PKK and political economy of the region, see Yarkin 2015; Ercan 2013.

31. Graeber 2014; Dicle 2013.

32. Lefebvre 2009a, 135.

33. Pursley 2015a; Pursley 2015b.

34. Burke 1973; Khoury 1987, 110–15. As we observed in the case of 'Aintab's historical and urban transformation into Gaziantep, the French invasion and the local opposition to it were enshrined in the very names of the places included in the "original" blue zone of the Sykes-Picot Agreement: Adana, Marash, Antep, Urfa, Diyarbekir, and Mardin. Khoury mentions Syria's loss of not only Aleppo's agricultural hinterland to Turkey but also its Mediterranean port in Alexandretta in the late 1930s as the most critical impetus for the anti-Mandate and the pro-Ottoman factions in Aleppo to unite with those seeking independence in Damascus.

35. On Alexandretta and its Turkish annexation, see Watenpaugh 1996.

36. Andrew and Kanya-Forstner 1971.

37. See the reports of Père Poidebard, MAE, E-Levant Syrie-Liban, vol. 299; Père Poidebard, *Notes sur la Haute Djezireh,* 1926, CADN, Cabinet Politique, Fonds Beyrouth, box 571, "Rapport du Père Poidebard du 6.01.1928 sur la Situation des Réfugiés en Haute Jézireh en Octobre 1927."

38. Altuğ 2011.

39. Owen 2002; Esman and Rabinovich 1988; Zisser 2006; Raymond 1980. The 1946–58 period after British formal rule ended is often called "the struggle for Syria," as in Patrick Seale's *The Struggle for Syria: A Study of Post-war Arab Politics, 1945–1958* (1965).

40. Salama 1999, 59, also quoted in Altuğ 2011, 66.

41. MAE, Série Syrie-Liban, vol. 177, Relation Turquie-Française, also quoted in Van Bruinessen 1991 and in Altuğ 2011, 59–60.

42. "Légion Syrienne" refers to the French troops recruited exclusively from West Africa. Troops were primarily Senegalese, but the legion also counted non-Muslim and non-Arab Syrians among its ranks. It was renamed Troupes Auxiliaires, and then Troupes Spéciales du Levant in 1930.

43. CADN, Fonds Ankara, Ambassade, no. 104, Compte Rendu no. 2539 du Général Billotte, représentant Haut Commissaire à M. l'Envoyé extraordinaire à Damas, Alep, September 21, 1926, 1–3.

44. Thomas 2002.

45. CADN, Syrie-Liban, Cabinet Politique, box 569, "Situation des Refugies en Haute Djézireh," October 1927, Père Poidebard, no. 327/K2.

46. Republic of Turkey Ankara State Archives, Basbakanlik Cumhuriyet Archives [BCA], 30.10, 155-90-10, "Grape Producers Complain about Collected Customs," March 26, 1932.

47. BCA, 30.10, 265-787-81, "Complaint Letter from Tobacco and Pistachio Producers," March 7, 1933.

48. On regional fragmentation and the fourfold minoritization that Kurdish people have suffered in the post-Ottoman, post-Mandate Middle East, see Beşikçi 2004.

49. Lefebvre 2009b, 240.

50. Brenner and Elden 2009, 356.

CONCLUSION

1. Coleman 2021.

REFERENCES

Adams, Patrick. 2012. "Turkey's Transformation." *Bulletin of the World Health Organization* 90 (6): 408–9.

Adelkhah, Fariba. 2009. "Moral Economy of Pilgrimage and Civil Society in Iran: Religious, Commercial and Tourist Trips to Damascus." *South African Historical Journal* 61 (March): 38–53.

Aghaie, Kamran. 2001. "The Karbala Narrative: Shīʿi Political Discourse in Modern Iran in the 1960s and 1970s." *Journal of Islamic Studies* 12:151–76.

———. 2004. *The Martyrs of Karbala: Shīʿi Symbols and Rituals in Modern Iran.* Seattle: University of Washington Press.

Agnew, John. 1994. "The Territorial Trap: The Geographical Assumptions of International Relations Theory." *Review of International Political Economy* 1 (1): 53–80.

———. 2020. "Taking Back Control? The Myth of Territorial Sovereignty and the Brexit Fiasco." *Territory, Politics, Governance* 8 (2): 259–72.

Akhavi, Shahrogh. 1980. *Religion and Politics in Contemporary Iran.* Albany: State University of New York Press.

Alatas, Ismail Fajrie. 2016. "The Poetics of Pilgrimage: Assembling Contemporary Indonesian Pilgrimage to Hadramawt, Yemen." *Comparative Studies in Society and History* 58 (3): 607–35.

Altuğ, Seda. 2011. "Sectarianism in the Syrian Jazira: Community, Land and Violence in the Memories of World War I and the French Mandate (1915–1939)." PhD diss., Utrecht University.

Alvarez, R. 2012. "Borders and Bridges: Exploring a New Conceptual Architecture for (U.S.-Mexico) Border Studies." *Journal of Latin American and Caribbean Anthropology* 17 (1): 24–40.

Andrew, C. M., and A. S. Kanya-Forstner. 1971. "The French Colonial Party: Its Composition, Aims and Influence, 1885–1914." *Historical Journal* 14 (1): 99–128.

Anzaldúa, Gloria. 1987. *Borderlands/La Frontera: The New Mestiza.* San Francisco: Aunt Lute Book Company.

Appadurai, Arjun. 1986. "Introduction: Commodities and the Politics of Value." In *The Social Life of Things: Commodities in Cultural Perspective,* edited by Arjun Appadurai, 3–63. Cambridge: Cambridge University Press.

———. 1996. *Modernity at Large: Cultural Dimensions of Globalization.* Minneapolis: University of Minnesota Press.

Arjomand, Said Amir. 1984. *The Shadow of God and the Hidden Imam: Religion, Political Organization and Societal Change in Shiite Iran from the Beginning to 1890.* Chicago: University of Chicago Press.

Arrighi, G. 1988. *The Turban for the Crown: The Islamic Revolution in Iran.* Oxford: Oxford University Press.

———. 1999. "Globalization, State, Sovereignty and the 'Endless' Accumulation of Capital." In *States and Sovereignty in the Global Economy*, edited by David A. Smith, Dorothy J. Solinger, and Steven C. Topik, 53–73. London: Routledge.

Asad, Talal. 1986. *The Idea of an Anthropology of Islam.* Washington, DC: Center for Contemporary Arab Studies, Georgetown University.

———. 1993. *Genealogies of Religion: Discipline and Reasons of Power in Christianity and Islam.* Baltimore: Johns Hopkins University Press.

———. 2003. *Formations of the Secular: Christianity, Islam and Modernity.* Stanford, CA: Stanford University Press.

Ashraf, Ahmed. 1981. "The Roots of Emerging Dual Class Structure in Nineteen-Century Iran." *Iranian Studies* 14:5–27.

Ateş, Sabri. 2010. "Bones of Contention: Corpse Traffic and Ottoman-Iranian Rivalry in Nineteenth Century Iraq." *Comparative Studies of South Asia, Africa and the Middle East* 30 (3): 512–32.

Aydin, Cemil. *The Idea of the Muslim World: A Global Intellectual History.* Cambridge, MA: Harvard University Press, 2017.

Aydın, Suavi. 2008. *Terzinin biçtiği bedene uymazsa: Türk kimliğinin yaratılması ve ulusal kimlik sorunu* [What if the measure doesn't fit the body: The invention of Turkish identity and the problem of national identity]. Ankara: Özgür Üniversite Kitaplığı.

Bajc, Vida, Simon Coleman, and John Eade. 2007. "Introduction: Mobility and Centring in Pilgrimage." *Mobilities* 2 (3): 321–29.

Bakhtin, M. M. 1981. "Forms of Time and Chronotope in the Novel." In *The Dialogic Imagination: Four Essays*, edited by Michael Holquist, 83–84. Austin: University of Texas Press.

Balta, Nevin. 2010. *Gaziantep yer adlari üzerine bir inceleme* [An investigation into naming places in Gaziantep]. Gaziantep: Gaziantep Valiliği Il Kültür ve Turizm Müdürlüğü.

Bangstad, Sindre. 2011. "Saba Mahmood and Anthropological Feminism after Virtue." *Theory, Culture and Society* 28 (3): 28–54.

Baron, Beth. *Egypt as Woman: Nationalism, Gender and Politics.* Oakland: University of California Press, 2007.

Bayly, C. A. 1986. "The Origins of Swadeshi (Home Industry) Cloth and Indian Society, 1700–1930." In *The Social Life of Things: Commodities in Cultural*

Perspective, edited by Arjun Appadurai, 285–322. Cambridge: Cambridge University Press.

Bayoumi, Moustafa. 2006. "Racing Religion." *CR: The New Centennial Review* 6 (2): 267–93.

Bear, Laura, Karen Ho, and Sylvia Yanagisako. 2015. "Generating Capitalism." Society for Cultural Anthropology, Fieldsights, Editors' Forum: Theorizing the Contemporary, March 30. https://culanth.org/fieldsights/650-generating-capitalism.

Behdad, Sohrab, and Farhad Nomani. 2002. "Workers, Peasants, and Peddlers: A Study of Labor Stratification in the Post-revolutionary Iran." *International Journal of Middle East Studies* 34:667–90.

———. 2009. "What a Revolution! Thirty Years of Social Class Reshuffling in Iran." *Comparative Studies of South Asia, Africa and the Middle East* 29 (1): 84–104.

Behrouzan, Orkideh. 2016. *Prozak Diaries: Psychiatry and Generation Memory in Iran.* Stanford, CA: Stanford University Press.

Benton, Lauren. 2009. *A Search for Sovereignty: Law and Geography in European Empires, 1400–1900.* Cambridge: Cambridge University Press.

Beritan, Saim, and Emre Yildirim. 2013. "Introduction." In *Proceedings of Rize Development Symposium: Tea, Logistics and Tourism,* edited by Saim Beritan and Emre Yildirim, 10–12 [in Turkish]. Rize: Recep Tayyip Erdogan University Press.

Beşikçi, Ismail. 2004. *International Colony Kurdistan.* London: Taderon Press.

Betteridge, Anne. 1985. "Specialists in Miraculous Action: Some Shrines in Shiraz." In *Sacred Journeys: The Anthropology of Pilgrimage,* edited by E. Alan Morinis, 189–209. Westport, CT: Greenwood Press.

Bloch, Maurice, and Jonathan Parry. 1989. Introduction to *Money and the Morality of Exchange,* edited by Jonathan Parry and Maurice Bloch, 1–32. Cambridge: Cambridge University Press.

Bourdieu, Pierre. [1980] 1990. *The Logic of Practice.* Translated by R. Nice. Stanford, CA: Stanford University Press.

Brenner, Neil, and Stuart Elden. 2009. "Henri Lefebvre on State, Space and Territory." *International Political Sociology* 3 (4): 353–73.

Burbank, Jane, and Frederick Cooper. 2010. *Empires in World History: Power and the Politics of Difference.* Princeton, NJ: Princeton University Press.

Burke, Edmund. 1973. "A Comparative View of French Native Policy in Morocco and Syria, 1912–1925." *Middle Eastern Studies* 9 (3): 175–86.

Butler, Judith. 2010. "Performative Agency." *Journal of Cultural Economy* 3 (2): 147–61.

Callon, Michel. 1998. *The Laws of Markets.* Oxford: Blackwell.

———. 2010. "Performativity, Misfires and Politics." *Journal of Cultural Economy* 3 (2): 163–69.

———. 2021. *Markets in the Making: Rethinking Competition, Goods and Innovation.* Princeton, NJ: Princeton University Press.

Callon, Michel, and Koray Çalışkan. 2009. "Economization, Part 1: Shifting Attention from the Economy towards Processes of Economization." *Economy and Society* 38 (3): 369–98.

———. 2010. "Economization, Part 2: A Research Programme for the Study of Markets." *Economy and Society* 39 (1): 1–32.

Caton, Steve. 2006. "What Is an 'Authorizing Discourse'?" In *Powers of the Secular Modern*, edited by David Scott and Charles Hirschkind, 31–56. Stanford, CA: Stanford University Press.

Chakrabarty, Dipesh. 2007. *Provincializing Europe: Postcolonial Thought and Historical Difference.* Princeton, NJ: Princeton University Press.

Chalfin, Brenda. 2010. *Neoliberal Frontiers: An Ethnography of Sovereignty in West Africa.* Chicago: University of Chicago Press.

Chelkowski, Peter J. 2005. "Iconography of the Women of Karbala: Tiles, Murals, Stamps, and Posters." In *The Women of Karbala: Ritual Performance and Symbolic Discourses in Modern Shi'i Islam*, edited by Kamran Scot Aghaie, 119–38. Austin: University of Texas Press.

"A Citizen's Lament." 1932. *Cumhuriyet,* December 17. *Cumhuriyet* digital archives. https://egazete.cumhuriyet.com.tr/.

Cohen, E. 1992. "Pilgrimage Centers: Concentric and Excentric." *Annals of Tourism Research* 19:33–50.

Coleman, Simon. 2002. "Do You Pilgrimage? Communitas, Contestation and Beyond." *Anthropological Theory* 2 (3): 355–68.

———. 2014. "Pilgrimage as Trope for an Anthropology of Christianity." *Current Anthropology* 55 (10): 281–91.

———. 2015. "Anthropological Tropes and Historical Tricksters: Pilgrimage as an 'Example' of Persuasion." *Journal of the Royal Anthropological Institute* 21 (1): 144–61.

———. 2021. *Powers of Pilgrimage: Religion in a World of Movement.* New York: NYU Press.

Comaroff, Jean, and John Comaroff. 1999. "Occult Economies and the Violence of Abstraction: Notes from the South African Colony." *American Ethnologist* 26 (2): 279–303.

Cortright, David, and George Lopez. *The Sanctions Decade: Assessing UN Strategies in the 1990s.* Boulder, CO: Lynne Rienner, 2000.

Cowper, H. Swainson. 1894. *Through Turkish Arabia: A Journey from the Mediterranean to Bombay by the Euphrates and Tigris Valleys and the Persian Gulf.* London: H. Allen.

Crawford, David. 2008. *Moroccan Households in the World Economy: Labor and Inequality in a Berber Village.* Baton Rouge: Louisiana State University Press.

Crecelius, Daniel. 1995. "Introduction." *Journal of the Economic and Social History of the Orient* 38 (3): 247–61.

Cresswell, Tim. 2010. "Towards a Politics of Mobility." *Environment and Planning D: Society and Space* 28 (1): 17–31.

Dalakoglou, Dimitris. 2010. "An Ethnography of the Albanian-Greek Cross-border Motorway." *American Ethnologist* 37 (1): 132–49.

Daoudi, Mohammed, and Munther Suleiman Dajani. 1983. *Economic Sanctions: Ideals and Experience*. London: Routledge.

Das, Veena. 1984. "For a Folk Theology and a Theoretical Anthropology of Islam." *Contributions to Indian Sociology*, n.s., 18 (2): 293–900.

Davis, Fanny. *The Ottoman Lady: A Social History (1718–1918)*. London: Greenwood Press, 1986.

Deeb, Lara. 2005. "From Mourning to Activism: Sayyedeh Zaynab, Lebanese Shiʿi Women, and the Transformation of Ashura." In *The Women of Karbala: Ritual Performance and Symbolic Discourses in Modern Shīʿi Islam,* edited by Kamran Scot Aghaie, 241–66. Austin: University of Texas Press.

———. 2006. *An Enchanted Modern: Gender and Public Piety in Shiʿi Lebanon.* Princeton, NJ: Princeton University Press.

———. 2009a. "Emulating and/or Embodying the Ideal: The Gendering of Temporal Frameworks and Islamic Role Models in Shiʿi Lebanon." *American Ethnologist* 36 (2): 242–57.

———. 2009b. "Piety Politics and the Role of Transnational Feminist Analysis." *Journal of the Royal Anthropological Institute* 15:112–26.

———. 2020. "Beyond Sectarianism: Intermarriage and Social Difference in Lebanon." *International Journal of Middle East Studies* 52:215–28.

Deguilhem, Randi. 1995. *Le waqf dans l'espace islamique: Outil de pouvoir socio-economique*. Damascus: Institute Francais d'Etudes Arabes de Damas.

Deringil, Selim. 1990. "The Struggle against Shiism in Hamidian Iraq: A Study in Ottoman Counter-propaganda." *Die Welt des Islams* 30 (1.4): 45–62.

de Soto, Hernando. [1986] 1989. *The Other Path: The Invisible Revolution in the Third World*. Translated by June Abbott. New York: Harper and Row.

Dicle, Amed. 2013. "Rojava's Political Structure." *Jadaliyya,* September. www .jadaliyya.com/pages/index/14272/rojavas-political-structure.

Dillon, Sarah. 2007. *The Palimpsest: Literature, Criticism, Theory*. New York: Bloomsbury.

Doostdar, Alireza. 2018. *Iranian Metaphysicals: Explorations in Science, Islam, and the Uncanny*. Princeton, NJ: Princeton University Press.

———. 2019. "Impossible Occultists: Practice and Practice in an Islamic Tradition." *American Ethnologist* 46 (2): 176–89.

Douglas, Mary. [1966] 2002. *Purity and Danger: An Analysis of Pollution and Taboo*. London: Routledge.

Dugid, Stephen. 1973. "The Hamidian Politics of Unity." *Middle Eastern Studies* 9 (2): 139–55.

Durkheim, Émile. [1912] 1995. *Elementary Forms of Religious Life*. New York: Free Press.

Eade, John, and Michael J. Sallnow. 2000. "Introduction." In *Contesting the Sacred: The Anthropology of Christian Pilgrimage*, edited by John Eade and Michael J. Sallnow, 1–30. Urbana: University of Illinois Press.

Eckert, Sue. 2010. "United Nations Nonproliferation Sanctions." *International Journal* 65 (1): 69–83.

Eickelman, Dale F., and James Piscatori. 1990. *Muslim Travelers: Pilgrimage, Migration and the Religious Imagination*. Los Angeles: University of California Press.

Elfenbein, Caleb. 2015. "Contingency in the Age of Religion: The Hajj and Religion-Making in Colonial and Postcolonial India." *Method and Theory in the Study of Religion* 27 (3): 247–77.

Elyachar, Julia. 2003. "Mappings of Power: The State, NGOs, and International Organizations in the Informal Economy of Cairo." *Comparative Studies in Society and History* 45 (3): 571–605.

———. 2005. *Markets of Dispossession: NGOs, Economic Development, and the State in Cairo*. Durham, NC: Duke University Press.

Erami, Narges, and Arang Keshavarzian. 2015. "When Ties Don't Bind: Smuggling Effects, Bazaars and Regulatory Regimes in Postrevolutionary Iran." *Economy and Society* 44 (1): 110–39.

Ercan, Harun. 2013. "Talking to the Ontological Other: Armed Struggle and the Negotiations between the Turkish State and the PKK." *Dialectical Anthropology* 37 (1): 113–22.

Esman, Milton J., and Itamar Rabinovich. 1988. *Ethnicity, Pluralism and the State in the Middle East*. Ithaca, NY: Cornell University Press.

Fadil, Nadia, and Mayanthi Fernando. 2015. "Rediscovering the 'Everyday' Muslim." *HAU: Journal of Ethnographic Theory* 5 (2): 59–88.

Faroqhi, Suraiya. 1996. *Pilgrims and Sultans: The Hajj under the Ottomans*. London: I. B. Tauris.

Ferguson, James, and Akhil Gupta. 2002. "Spatializing States: Toward an Ethnography of Neoliberal Governmentality." *American Ethnologist* 29 (4): 981–1002.

Fernando, Mayanthi. 2014. *Republic Unsettled: Muslim French and the Contradictions of Secularism*. Durham, NC: Duke University Press.

Fischer, Michael. [1980] 2003. *Iran: From Religious Dispute to Revolution*. Madison: University of Wisconsin Press.

Fischer, Michael, and Mehdi Abadi. 1990. *Debating Muslims: Cultural Dialogues in Postmodernity and Tradition*. Madison: University of Wisconsin Press.

Flynn, Donna K. 1997. "We Are the Border! Identity, Exchange and the State along the Benin-Nigeria Border." *American Ethnologist* 24 (2): 311–30.

Galemba, Rebecca. 2017. *Contraband Corridor: Making a Living at the Mexico-Guatemala Border*. Palo Alto, CA: Stanford University Press.

Gandolfo, Daniella. 2013. "Formless: A Day at Lima's Office of Formalization." *Cultural Anthropology* 28 (2): 278–98.

Gaziantep Organized Industrial Zone Almanac [in Turkish]. 2012. May. Gaziantep: Gaziantep Municipality.

Geertz, Clifford. 1963. *Peddlers and Princes: Social Change and Economic Modernization in Two Indonesian Towns*. Chicago: University of Chicago Press.

———. 1973. "Religion as a Cultural System." in *The Interpretation of Cultures: Selected Essays*, 87–125. New York: Basic Books.

———. 1978. "The Bazaar Economy: Information and Search in Peasant Marketing." *American Economic Review* 68:28–32.

———. 1979. "Suq: The Bazaar Economy in Sefrou." In *Meaning and Order in Moroccan Society,* edited by Clifford Geertz, Hildred Geertz, and Lawrence Rosen, 123–313. Cambridge: Cambridge University Press.

Genette, Gerard. 1997. *Palimpsests: Literatures in the Second Degree.* Translated by Channa Newman and Claude Doubinsky. Lincoln: University of Nebraska Press.

Gerber, Haim. 1983. "The Waqf Institution in Early Ottoman Edirne." *Journal of Asian and African Studies* 17:29–45.

———. 1985. *Ottoman Rule in Jerusalem, 1890–1914.* Berlin: K. Schwarz.

Gilsenan, Michael. 1983. *Recognizing Islam: Religion and Society in the Modern Arab World.* New York: Pantheon Books.

Glover, William. 2007. *Making Lahore Modern: Constructing and Imagining a Colonial City.* Minneapolis: University of Minnesota Press.

Goswami, Manu. 2002. "Rethinking the Modular Nation Form: Toward a Sociohistorical Conception of Nationalism." *Comparative Studies in Society and History* 44 (4): 770–99.

———. 2004. *Producing India: From Colonial Economy to National Space.* Chicago: University of Chicago Press.

Graeber, David. 2014. "Why Is the World Ignoring the Revolutionary Kurds in Syria." *The Guardian*, October 8. www.theguardian.com/commentisfree/2014/oct/08/why-world-ignoring-revolutionary-kurds-syria-isis.

Granovetter, Mark. 1985. "Economic Action and Social Structure: The Problem of Embeddedness." *American Journal of Sociology* 91 (3): 481–510.

Grimson, Alejandro, and Pablo Vila. 2002. "Forgotten Border Actors: The Border Reinforcers, A Comparison of the U.S. Mexico-Border and South American Borders." *Journal of Political Ecology* 9:70–89.

Gültekin, Mehmet Nuri. 2011. "Antep imgesinin zaman içindeki dönüşümü" [Transformation of the symbol of Antep across time]. In *Ta ezelden taşkındır Antep* [Since time immemorial Antep has been wild], edited by Mehmet Nuri Gültekin, 29–73. Istanbul: İletişim.

Güngor, M. Birol. 2004. *Antep harbi* [The Antep War]. Istanbul: Eren Press.

Guyer, Jane. 2004. *Marginal Gains: Monetary Transactions in Atlantic Africa.* Chicago: University of Chicago Press.

Haeri, Shahla. 1989. *Laws of Desire: Temporary Marriage in Shi'i Iran.* Syracuse, NY: Syracuse University Press.

Halasa, Malu, and Rana Salam, eds. 2008. *Secret Life of Syrian Lingerie: Intimacy and Design.* San Francisco: Chronicle Books.

Hart, Keith. 1987. "Informal Economy." In *The New Palgrave: A Dictionary of Economics*, vol. 2, edited by John Eatwell, Murray Milgate, and Peter Newman, 845–46. London: Macmillan, 1988.

Harvey, David. 2006. "Space as a Key Word." In *Spaces of Global Capitalism: A Theory of Uneven Geographical Development*, 117–48. New York: Verso.

Hedayat, Sadegh. [1943] 1962. "Alaviyeh Khanum" [Madame Alaviyeh]. In *Alaviyeh Khanum va Velengari*, 11–57. Tehran: Amir Kabir.

Hirschman, Albert. 1978. "Exit, Voice, and the State." *World Politics* 31 (1): 90–107.

Ho, Engseng. 2004. "Empire through Diasporic Eyes: The View from the Other Boat." *Comparative Studies in History and Society* 46 (2): 210–46.

———. 2006. *The Graves of Tarim: Genealogy and Mobility across the Indian Ocean.* Los Angeles: University of California Press.

Hoexter, Miriam. 1997. "Adaptation to Changing Circumstances: Perpetual Leases and Exchange Transactions in Waqf Properties in Ottoman Algiers." *Islamic Law and Society* 4:319–33.

———. 1998. "Waqf Studies in the Twentieth Century: The State of the Art." *Journal of the Economic and Social History of the Orient* 41 (4): 474–95.

Honarpisheh, Dona. 2013. "Women in Pilgrimage: Senses, Places, Embodiment, and Agency. Experiencing Ziyarat in Shiraz." *Journal of Shi'a Islamic Studies* 6 (4): 383–409.

Hourani, Albert. 1968. "Ottoman Reform and the Politics of Notables." In *Beginnings of Modernization in the Middle East: The Nineteenth Century*, edited by William Roe Polk and Richard L. Chambers, 41–68. Chicago: University of Chicago Press.

Hull, Matthew. 2008. "Appropriation of Land and Misappropriation of Lists in Islamabad." *American Ethnologist* 35 (4): 501–18.

———. 2012. *Government of Paper: The Materiality of Bureaucracy in Urban Pakistan.* Berkeley: University of California Press.

İnalcık, Halil. 1969. "Capital Formation in the Ottoman Empire." *Journal of Economic History* 29 (1): 132–35.

Ismail, Salwa. 2013. "Piety, Profit and the Market in Cairo: A Political Economy of Islamization." *Contemporary Islam* 7 (1): 107–28.

Jorum, Emma Lungren. 2014. *Beyond Syria's Borders: A History of Territorial Disputes in the Middle East.* London: I.B. Tauris.

Joseph, Suad. 1975. "The Politicization of Religious Sects in Borj Hammoud, Lebanon." PhD diss., Columbia University.

———. 2011. "Political Familialism in Lebanon." *Annals of the American Academy of Political and Social Science* 636 (July): 150–63.

Kalir, Barak, and Willem van Schendel. 2017. "Introduction: Nonrecording States between Legibility and Looking Away." *Focaal: Journal of Global and Historical Anthropology* 77:1–7.

Karadağ, Meltem. 2011. "Gaziantep'te kentsel mekanın ve kültürel coğrafyanın değişimi" [Transformations of urban space and cultural geography in Gaziantep]. In *Ta ezelden taşkındır Antep* [Since time immemorial, Antep has been wild], edited by Mehmet Nuri Gültekin, 293–335. Istanbul: Iletisim.

Karakaya-Stump, Ayfer. 2008. "Subjects of the Sultan, Disciples of the Shah: Formation and Transformation of the Kizilbash/Alevi Communities in Ottoman Anatolia." PhD diss., Harvard University.

Kasravi, Ahmad. 1943. *Pendarha* [Thoughts]. Tehran: Payman.

Katz, E. 1997. "The Intra-household Economics of Voice and Exit." *Feminist Economics* 3 (3): 25–46.

Kemal, Yaşar. 2011. "Kaçakçılar arasında 25 gün" [25 days among the smugglers]. In *Röportaj yazarlığında 60 yıl* [60 years in journalistic interviews], 31–83. Istanbul: Yapı Kredi Yayınları.

Keshavarzian, Arang. 2007. *Bazaar and State in Iran: The Politics of the Tehran Marketplace.* Cambridge: Cambridge University Press.

Khamenei, Sayyid 'Ali Hosseini. 1997. *Practical Laws of Islam* [in Persian]. Tehran: Islamic Cultural and Relations Organization.

Khoury, Philip S. 1987. *Syria and the French Mandate: The Politics of Arab Nationalism, 1920–1945.* Princeton, NJ: Princeton University Press.

———. 1991. "Continuity and Change in Syrian Political Life: The Nineteenth and Twentieth Centuries." *American Historical Review* 96 (5): 1374–95.

Köprülü, Fuad. 1942. "Vakıf müessesesinin hukuki mahiyeti ve tarihi tekamülü" [The legal significance and historical transformation of the *waqf* as institution]. *Vakıflar Dergisi* 2:1–35.

Kopytoff, Igor. 1986. "The Cultural Biography of Things: Commoditization as Process." In *The Social Life of Things: Commodities in Cultural Perspective,* edited by Arjun Appadurai, 64–91. Cambridge: Cambridge University Press.

Krasner, Stephen. 2010. "The Durability of Organized Hypocrisy." In *Sovereignty in Fragments: The Past, Present and Future of a Contested Concept,* edited by Hent Kalmo and Quentin Skinner, 96–113. Cambridge: Cambridge University Press.

Kurt, Ümit. 2021. *Armenians of Aintab: The Economics of Genocide in an Ottoman Province.* Cambridge, MA: Harvard University Press.

Lahiri, Smita. 2007. "Rhetorical Indios: Propagandists and Their Publics in the Spanish Philippines." *Comparative Studies in Society and History* 49 (2): 243–75.

Latour, Bruno. 2005. *Reassembling the Social: An Introduction to Actor-Network Theory.* Oxford: Oxford University Press.

Lefebvre, Henri. [1965] 2000. *Pyrénées.* Pau: Cairn.

———. 2009a. "Comments on a New State Form." In *State, Space, World: Selected Essays,* edited by Neil Brenner and Stuart Elden, 124–37. Minneapolis: University of Minnesota Press.

———. 2009b. "Space and the State." In *State, Space, World: Selected Essays,* edited by Neil Brenner and Stuart Elden, 223–53. Minneapolis: University of Minnesota Press.

———. 2009c. "The State in the Modern World." In *State, Space, World: Selected Essays,* edited by Neil Brenner and Stuart Elden, 95–123. Minneapolis: University of Minnesota Press.

Li, Darryl. 2015. "A Jihadism Anti-primer." *Middle East Report* 276 (Fall). www.merip.org/mer/mer276/jihadism-anti-primer.

———. 2019. *The Universal Enemy: Jihad, Empire and the Challenge of Solidarity.* Palo Alto, CA: Stanford University Press.

Lipset, David. 2015. "On The Bridge: Class and the Chronotope of Modern Romance in an American Love Story." *Anthropological Quarterly* 88 (1): 163–85.

Litvak, Meir. 1998. *Shi'i Scholars of Nineteenth Century Iraq: The 'Ulama' of Najaf and Karbala.* Cambridge: Cambridge University Press.

Lomnitz, Larissa. 1988. "Informal Exchange Networks in Formal Systems: A Theoretical Model." *American Anthropologist* 90:42–54.

Louër, Laurence. 2008. *Transnational Shia Politics.* New York: Columbia University Press.

MacIntyre, Alasdair. 2012. *After Virtue: A Study of Moral Theory.* 3rd ed. Notre Dame, IN: University of Notre Dame Press.

Mahmood, Saba. 2001. "Feminist Theory, Embodiment, and the Docile Agent: Some Reflections on the Egyptian Islamic Revival." *Cultural Anthropology* 16 (2): 202–36.

———. 2005. *Politics of Piety: The Islamic Revival and the Feminist Subject.* Princeton, NJ: Princeton University Press.

Makdisi, Ussama S. 2000. *The Culture of Sectarianism: Community, History and Violence in Nineteenth-Century Ottoman Lebanon.* Los Angeles: University of California Press.

Malinowski, Bronislaw. [1922] 1961. *Argonauts of the Western Pacific.* London: E. P. Dutton.

Mamdani, Mahmood. 2002. "Good Muslim, Bad Muslim: A Political Perspective on Culture and Terrorism." *American Anthropologist* 104 (3): 766–75.

Manalansan, Martin, IV. 2003. *Global Divas: Filipino Gay Men in the Diaspora.* Durham, NC: Duke University Press.

Ma'oz, Moshe. 1968. *Ottoman Reform in Syria and Palestine, 1840–1861: The Impact of Tanzimat on Politics and Society.* Oxford: Oxford University Press.

Marcus, George. 1995. "Ethnography in/of the World System: The Emergence of Multi-sited Ethnography." *Annual Review of Anthropology* 24:95–117.

Matthee, Rudi. 2003. "The Safavid-Ottoman Frontier: Iraq-i 'Arab as Seen by the Safavids." *International Journal of Turkish Studies* 9:157–73.

Matthew, Johan. 2016. *Margins of the Market: Trafficking and Capitalism across the Arabian Sea.* Berkeley: University of California Press.

Maurer, Bill. 2006. *Mutual Life, Limited: Islamic Banking, Alternative Currencies, Lateral Reason.* Princeton, NJ: Princeton University Press.

Mauss, Marcel. [1925] 2000. *The Gift: Forms and Functions of Exchange in Archaic Societies.* Translated by Ian Cunnison. New York: Norton.

Al-Mawsem: A Quarterly Illustrated Magazine of Archaeology and Tradition. Special issue. Edited by Mohammad Saeed Al-Touraihi. Netherlands: Mohammad Saeed Al-Touraihi, 1997.

McFall, Liz, and Francis Dodsworth. 2009. "Fabricating the Market: The Promotion of Life Assurance in the Long Nineteenth Century." *Journal of Historical Sociology* 22 (1): 30–52.

Mendi, Arif Furkan. 2018. "Tea Industry in Turkey: A Sectoral and Empirical Study" [in Turkish]. *International Journal of Social Sciences and Education Research* 4 (2): 252–73.

Meri, Josef. 2001. "A Late Medieval Syrian Pilgrimage Guide: Ibn Al-Hawrani's Al-Isharat Ila Amakin al-Ziyarat." *Medieval Encounters* 7 (1): 3–15.

Mervin, Sabrina. 1996. "Sayyida Zaynab, banlieue de Damas ou nouvelle ville sainte chiite?" *Cahiers d' Études sur la Mediterranée Orientale et le Monde Turco-Iraniene: Arabes et Iraniens* 22:149–62.

Mezzadra, Sandro, and Brett Nelson. 2013. *Border as Method, or, The Multiplication of Labor.* Durham, NC: Duke University Press.

Mikdashi, Maya. 2022. *Sextarianism: Sovereignty, Secularism, and the State in Lebanon.* Palo Alto, CA: Stanford University Press.

Mintz, Sidney. 1985. *Sweetness and Power: The Place of Sugar in Modern History.* New York: Penguin.

Mitchell, Timothy. 1991. "The Limits of the State: Beyond Statist Approaches and Their Critics." *American Political Science Review* 85 (1): 77–96.

———. 1998. "Fixing the Economy." *Cultural Studies* 12 (1): 82–101.

———. 1999. "State, Economy and the State-Effect." In *State/Culture: State Formation after the Cultural Turn,* edited by George Steinmetz, 76–97. Ithaca, NY: Cornell University Press.

Mittermaier, Amira. 2012. "Dreams from Elsewhere: Muslim Subjectivities beyond the Trope of Self-Cultivation." *Journal of the Royal Anthropological Institute* 18 (2): 247–65.

Moallem, Minoo. 2005. *Between Warrior Brother and Veiled Sister: Islamic Fundamentalism and the Politics of Patriarchy in Iran.* Berkeley: University of California Press.

Monroe, Kristin. 2016. *The Insecure City: Space, Power and Mobility in Beirut.* New Brunswick, NJ: Rutgers University Press.

Montazeri, Hossein Ali. 2000. *Khaterat* [Memories]. www.scribd.com/doc/13584945/Khaterate-Ayatollah-Montazeri. Tehran.

Moumtaz, Nada. 2021. *God's Property: Islam, Charity, and the Modern State.* Berkeley: University of California Press.

Mundy, Martha. 1996. *Domestic Government: Kinship, Community and Polity in North Yemen.* London: I. B. Tauris.

Munn, Nancy. 1986. *The Fane of Gawa: A Symbolic Study of Value Transformation in a Massim (Papua New Guinea) Society.* Cambridge: Cambridge University Press.

al-Muzaffar, Mohammed Rida. 1962. *'Aqa'id al-imamiyya* [The basic tenets of the Imamate]. 2nd ed. Cairo: Al-Najah.

Naber, Nadine. 2008. "'Look, Mohammed the Terrorist Is Coming!': Cultural Racism, Nation-Based Racism and the Intersectionality of Oppressions after 9/11." In *Race and Arab Americans before and after 9/11,* edited by Amaney Jamal and Nadine Naber, 276–304. Syracuse, NY: Syracuse University Press.

Nakash, Yitzhak. 1995. "The Visitation of the Shrines of Imams." *Studia Islamica,* no. 81, 153–64.

———. 2003. *The Shiʿis of Iraq.* Princeton, NJ: Princeton University Press.

Navaro, Yael. 2007. "Make-Believe Papers, Legal Forms and the Counterfeit." *Anthropological Theory* 7 (1): 79–98.

Osella, Filippo, and Benjamin Soares. 2010. "Islam, Politics, Anthropology." In *Islam, Politics, Anthropology,* edited by Filippo Osella and Benjamin Soares, 1–22. Oxford: Wiley-Blackwell.

Owen, Roger. 2002. *State, Power and Politics in the Making of the Modern Middle East.* London: Routledge.

Pakniya, Abdulkarim. 2009. *Sayyida Zainab and Visitation in Kufah and Greater Syria.* Tehran: Irshad Publications.

Panitch, L. 1996. "Rethinking the Role of the State in an Era of Globalization." In *Globalization: Critical Reflections,* edited by J. H. Mittelman, 83–113. Boulder, CO: Lynne Rienner.

Parkinson, Joe, and Emre Peker. 2012. "Turkey Swaps Gold for Iranian Gas." *Wall Street Journal,* November 23.

Peirce, Charles. 1992. "How to Make Our Ideas Clear" [1878]. In *The Essential Peirce,* edited by N. Houser and C. Kloesel, 1:124–41. Bloomington: Indiana University Press.

Pierce, Leslie. 2003. *Morality Tales: Law and Gender in the Ottoman Court of Aintab.* Los Angeles: University of California Press.

Pinto, Paulo G. 2007. "Pilgrimage, Commodities, and Religious Objectification: The Making of Transnational Shiʿism between Iran and Syria." *Comparative Studies of South Asia, Africa and the Middle East* 27 (1): 109–25.

Povinelli, Elizabeth. 2006. "Feminism as a Way of Life." *Women's Studies Quarterly* 34 (1–2): 438–41.

Pursley, Sara. 2015a. "'Lines Drawn on an Empty Map': Iraq's Borders and the Legend of the Artificial State (Part 1)." *Jadaliyya,* June 2.

———. 2015b. "'Lines Drawn on an Empty Map': Iraq's Borders and the Legend of the Artificial State (Part 2)." *Jadaliyya,* June 3.

Quluwahy, Ibn. 2008. *Merits and Method of Visiting Holy Tombs (Kamil al-ziyārat).* Ontario: Shiʿa Books.

Rana, Junaid. 2011. *Terrifying Muslims: Race and Labor in the South Asian Diaspora.* Durham, NC: Duke University Press.

Raymond, André. 1980. *La Syrie d'aujourd'hui* [Syria today]. Paris: CNRS.

Rice, D. S. 1955. "A Muslin Muslim Shrine in Harran." *Bulletin of the School of Oriental and African Studies* 17 (3): 436–48.

Roitman, Janet. 2005. *Fiscal Disobedience: An Anthropology of Economic Regulation in Central Africa.* Princeton, NJ: Princeton University Press.

Rosenau, J. 1995. "Sovereignty in a Turbulent World." In *Beyond Westphalia? State Sovereignty and International Intervention,* edited by Gene M. Lyons and Michael Mastanduno, 191–227. Baltimore: Johns Hopkins University Press.

Rouse, Roger. 1991. "Mexican Migration and the Social Space of Postmodernism." *Diaspora: A Journal of Transnational Studies* 1 (1): 8–23.

Rubin, Gayle. 1975. "The Traffic in Women: Notes on the 'Political Economy' of Sex." In *Toward an Anthropology of Women*, edited by Rayna R. Reiter, 157–210. New York: Monthly Press.

Rubin, Gayle, and Judith Butler. 1997. "Sexual Traffic: Interview." In *Feminism Meets Queer Theory*, edited by Elizabeth Weed and Naomi Schor, 68–108. Bloomington: Indiana University Press.

Rudnyckyj, Daromir. 2009. "Spiritual Economies: Islam and Neoliberalism in Contemporary Indonesia." *Cultural Anthropology* 24 (1): 104–41.

Salama, Ghassan. 1999. *Al-Mujtamaʿ wa al-dawla fi al-Mashriq al-ʿarabi* [State and society in the Arab Levant]. Beirut: CAUS.

Salibi, Kamal. 1979. "Middle Eastern Parallels: Syria-Iraq-Arabia in Ottoman Times." *Middle Eastern Studies* 15 (1): 70–81.

Saussure, Ferdinand. [1916] 2006. *Writings in General Linguistics*. Oxford: Oxford University Press.

Schayegh, Cyrus. 2011. "The Many Worlds of ʿAbud Yasin; or, What Narcotics Trafficking in the Interwar Middle East Can Tell Us about Territorialization." *American Historical Review* 116 (2): 273–306.

Scheele, Judith. 2013. "A Pilgrimage to Arawan: Religious Legitimacy, Status, and Ownership in Timbuktu." *American Ethnologist* 40 (1): 165–81.

Schielke, Samuli. 2009. "Being Good in Ramadan: Ambivalence, Fragmentation and the Moral Self in the Lives of Young Egyptians." *Journal of the Royal Anthropological Institute* 15:S24–S40.

Schneider, David. 1980. *American Kinship: A Cultural Account*. Chicago: University of Chicago Press.

———. 1984. *A Critique of the Study of Kinship*. Ann Arbor: University of Michigan Press.

Scott, David, and Charles Hirschkind. 2006. *Powers of the Secular Modern: Talal Asad and His Interlocutors*. Stanford, CA: Stanford University Press.

Seale, Patrick. 1965. *The Struggle for Syria: A Study of Post-war Arab Politics, 1945–1958*. London: Oxford University Press.

Selim, Samah. 2010. Review of *The Politics of Piety: The Islamic Revival and the Feminist Subject,* by Saba Mahmood. *Jadaliyya,* October 13. www.jadaliyya.com /Details/23539.

Seyed-Gohrab, Ashghar. 2011. "Martyrdom as Piety: Mysticism and National Identity in Iran-Iraq War Poetry." *Der Islam* 87 (1–2): 248–73.

Shakman Hurd, Elizabeth. 2015. "Politics of Sectarianism: Rethinking Religion and Politics in the Middle East." Special issue, "Research and Methodology in a Post-Arab Spring Environment: Challenges for the Field," *Middle East Law and Governance* 7 (1): 61–75.

Shariʿati, ʿAli. [1971] 1998. *Fatima Is Fatima*. Translated by Laleh Bakhtiar. Tehran: Shariati Foundation Publications.

Shirazi, Faegheh. 2005. "The Daughters of Karbala: Images of Women in Popular Shīʿi Culture in Iran." In *The Women of Karbala: Ritual Performance and Symbolic Discourses in Modern Shīʿi Islam*, edited by Kamran Scot Aghaie, 93–118. Austin: University of Texas Press.

Shirazi, Sayyid Sadiq Husayn. 2008. *Islamic Law*. Washington, DC: Fountain Books.

Shryock, Andrew. 2007. Review of *The Graves of Tarim: Genealogy and Mobility across the Indian Ocean*, by Engseng Ho. *Anthropological Quarterly* 80 (1): 265–70.

———. 2013. "It's This, Not That: How Marshall Sahlins Solves Kinship." *HAU: Journal of Ethnographic Theory* 3 (2): 271–79.

Silverstein, Michael. 1976. "Shifters, Linguistic Categories, and Cultural Description." In *Meaning in Anthropology*, edited by Keith Basso and Henry A. Selby, 11–55. Albuquerque: University of New Mexico Press.

Soja, Edward. 1989. *Postmodern Geographies*. New York: Verso.

Subramanian, Ajantha. 2006. *Shorelines: Space and Rights in South India*. Stanford, CA: Stanford University Press.

Subramanian, Lakshmi. 1991. "Banias and the British: The Role of Indigenous Credit in the Process of Imperial Expansion in Western India in the Second Half of the Eighteenth Century." *Modern Asian Studies* 21 (3): 473–510.

Szanto, Edith. 2012a. "Following Sayyida Zaynab: Twelver Shīʿism in Contemporary Syria." PhD diss., University of Toronto.

———. 2012b. "Sayyida Zainab and the State of Exception: Shīʿi Sainthood as 'Qualified Life' in Contemporary Syria." *International Journal of Middle East Studies* 44 (2): 285–99.

———. 2014. "Sex and the Cemetery: Iranian Pilgrims, Shrine Visitation and Shīʿi Piety in Damascus." *Syrian Studies Association Bulletin* 19 (2): 2–9.

Tabaa, Yasser. 2007. "Invented Pieties: The Rediscovery and Rebuilding of the Shrine of Sayyida Ruqayya in Damascus." *Artibus Asiae* 67 (1): 95–112.

Tagliacozzo, Eric. 2007. *Secret Trades, Porous Borders: Smuggling and States along a Southeast Asian Frontier, 1865–1915*. New Haven, CT: Yale University Press.

Takim, Liyakat. 2004. "Charismatic Appeal or Communitas? Visitation to the Shrines of Imams." *Journal of Ritual Studies* 18 (2): 106–20.

Tambar, Kabir. 2011. "Iterations of Lament: Anachronism and Affect in a Shīʿi Islamic Revival in Turkey." *American Ethnologist* 38 (3): 484–500.

Tarde, Gabriel. [1899] 2008. *Social Laws: An Outline of Sociology*. [US]: Hicks Press.

Taylor, C. S. 1999. *In the Vicinity of the Righteous: Ziyara and the Veneration of Saints*. Leiden: Brill.

Thomas, Martin. 2002. "French Intelligence-Gathering in the Syrian Mandate, 1920–40." *Middle Eastern Studies* 38 (1): 1–32.

Trouillot, Michel Ralph. 2001. "The Anthropology of the State in the Age of Globalization: Close Encounters of the Deceptive Kind." *Current Anthropology* 42:125–38.

Truitt, Allison. 2008. "On the Back of a Motorbike: Middle-Class Mobility in Ho Chi Minh City, Vietnam." *American Ethnologist* 35 (1): 3–19.

Turner, Victor. 1969. *The Ritual Process: Structure and Anti-structure.* Ithaca, NY: Cornell University Press.

——. 1973. "The Center Out There: Pilgrim's Goal." *History of Religions* 12 (3): 191–230.

Turner, Victor, and Edith Turner. 1978. *Image and Pilgrimage in Christian Culture.* New York: Columbia University Press.

Ussher, John. 1865. *A Journey from London to Persepolis.* London: Hurst and Blackett.

Uzel, Galip. 1952. *Gaziantep Savaşının içyüzü* [The internal face of the War of Gaziantep]. Ankara: Doğuş Press.

Van Bruinessen, Martin. 1991. *Agha, Sheikh, and State: The Social and Political Structures of Kurdistan.* London: Zed Books.

Wadud, Amina. 2011. "American by Force, Muslim by Choice." *Political Theology* 12 (5): 699–705.

Watenpaugh, Keith D. 1996. "Creating Phantoms: Zaki al-Arsuzi, the Alexandretta Crisis and Formation of Modern Arab Nationalism in Syria." *International Journal of Middle East Studies* 28:363–89.

Weiss, Max. 2010. *In the Shadow of Sectarianism: Law, Shiʿism, and the Making of Modern Lebanon.* Cambridge, MA: Harvard University Press.

Weston, Kath. 2008. *Traveling Light: On the Road with America's Poor.* Boston: Beacon Press.

Wolf, Eric. 1982. *Europe and the People without History.* Berkeley: University of California Press.

Xiang, Biao. 2013. "Multi-scalar Ethnography: An Approach for Critical Engagement with Migration and Social Change." *Ethnography* 14 (3): 282–99.

Yanagisako, Sylvia Junko. 1978. "Variance in American Kinship: Implications for Cultural Analysis." *American Ethnologist* 5 (1): 15–29.

Yarkin, Güllistan. 2015. "The Ideological Transformation of the PKK Regarding the Political Economy of the Kurdish Region in Turkey." *Kurdish Studies* 3 (1): 26–46.

Yazici, Berna 2013. "Towards an Anthropology of Traffic: A Ride through Class Hierarchies on Istanbul's Roadways." *Ethnos* 78 (4): 515–42.

Yeh, Rihan. 2018. "Three Types of Traffic in Tijuana: Heteronomy at the Mexico-US Border." *Public Culture* 30 (3): 441–64.

Yıldız, Emrah. 2021. "Of Nuclear Rials and Golden Shoes: Scaling Commodities and Currencies across Sanctions on Iran." *International Journal of Middle East Studies* 53 (4): 604–19.

Yüksel, Ayşe Seda. 2011. "Bir şehir efsanesi: Göç ve değişen Antep" [An urban legend: Migration and transforming Antep]. In *Ta ezelden taşkındır Antep* [Since time immemorial Antep has been wild], edited by Mehmet Nuri Gültekin. Istanbul: Iletisim.

El-Zein, A. H. 1977. "Beyond Ideology and Theology: The Search for an Anthropology of Islam." *Annual Review of Anthropology* 6:227–54.

Zisser, Eyal. 2006. "Who's Afraid of Syrian Nationalism? National and State Identity in Syria." *Middle Eastern Studies* 4 (2): 179–98.

INDEX

'Abd al-'Aziz ibn Sa'ud, 113
abdast, 43
Abdelhamid II (Abdülhamit II), 36
Abu Qasim Hamadani, 47
Adana, 79, 97
ad'iyya, 144. See also *du'a; du'anevis*
Afghanistan, 72, 80, 88. *See also* Kabul
Agha, Hadjo, 134
'ahd, 113
Ahl al-Bayt, 10, 22, 30, 58, 153n7, 156n11. *See also* Islam
ajam, 37
akhundha, 115
alcohol, 90
Aleppo, 60–61, 80, 88, 95–96, 104, 124, 126, 132–33, 136–38, 162n6, 165n34. *See also* Syria
'Ali al-Rida, 113
Ali Galip Bey, 115–16
'Ali Shari'ati, 37, 58, 159n19; *Fatima Is Fatima,* 22–23, 32
'Allamih Tabata'i University, 144
Altuğ, Seda, 132
Amman, 16
Anatolia, 92–105, 110, 130, 132, 135; French incursion into, 131, 134; Ottoman, 112, 114–15, 148. *See also* Turkey
Ankara, 16, 96, 131, 142. *See also* Turkey
Antalya, 79, 151. *See also* Turkey
Antep, 16, 27, 79–88, 94–106, 99*map,* 131, 137, 149, 160n22. *See also* Gaziantep
anthropology, 91; of emergence, 17–20; of Islam, 153n4, 156n7; literature on mar-
ketplaces in the Middle East and the cultural form of the bazaar in, 159n2. *See also* ethnography
Appadurai, Arjun: *The Social Life of Things,* 18
Arabia, 114. *See also* Middle East
Arap kağıdı, 135
Armenian genocide, 94–95, 133, 160n22
arms, 123–24, 129
Asad, Talal, 13–14
'Ashura, 9–10, 152. *See also* Shi'a
asker kaçağı, 94
'atabat, 112–13, 117, 119, 148, 162n6. *See also* pilgrimage
Atatürk Pasajı (Atatürk Arcade), 80, 82, 85, 87–88, 91, 100–103, 108
Ateş, Sabri, 117
Atilla, Mehmet Hakan, 164n29
autogestion, 130
ayna-kari, 47, 157n1

Bahbahani, Hazim, 65
Balıklı Göl, 12
Banuvan magazine, 30
baraka, 29, 34, 120
Bassam al-Ghadir, 55
Battle of Karbala, 10
Bayandur incident, 134
Baykan District of Siirt, 12
Beirut, 5–9, 15–16, 27, 54, 67, 70; Iranians in, 65, 145. *See also* Lebanon
Beirut International Airport, 7
bid'a, 119

bohçacı kadınlar, 94, 98, 138, 149, 160n17
Bonyad-e Shadeed voucher program, 32, 85, 117
borders: spatial ecologies of, 110–11, 139; state-employed police officers charged with overseeing customs at the, 123–24, 126–28, 149; trade across, 111–40, 148–49, 163n25; transformations of sovereignty and, 149. *See also* contraband; Iran-Turkey border; merchants; mobility; traffic; Turkey-Syria border
Bourdieu, Pierre, 27, 34, 148–49, 156n7
British American Tobacco Company, 90
buhran, 29
bureaucratization, 87

Çağlayan, Zafer, 164n29
calligraphy, 63
Canada, 57, 65–66
çarşaf, 98
cartels, 5
Çelebizade, Abdulrahman Veli, 92, 94, 102–5, 138, 160n17
charisma, 3, 9, 16
China, 88
Christianity, 26, 37
cigarettes, 1, 5, 79–91, 101–2, 107–8, 122–24, 126–28, 137, 149; Bahman, 80. *See also* tobacco
Cilicia, 132, 134. *See also* Turkey
çırak, 79
citizenship, 91; legal obligations of, 94
Coleman, Simon, 23, 148
contraband, 18, 79–100, 104–5, 107–8, 138, 149; building of compartments into cars and other vehicles to carry, 84, 137; cigarettes as, 89–91, 122–24, 126–28, 149; as duty-free trade, 82; gold as, 122; material conduits of, 119–24, 126–40; medical supplies as, 129, 137; oil as, 123–24, 129–40; sugar as, 123–24, 126–28; tea as, 88–89, 89*fig.*, 123–24, 128, 141, 149, 152; territorialization of national space and the policing of, 139. *See also* borders; *ghachagh; kaçak;* merchants; mobility; *qaçax;* traffic
Convention of Good and Neighborly Relations (1926), 134

corruption, 123, 126–27
crystal meth, 10
Cultural Revolution, 29–30, 38, 117, 159n19. *See also* Iran
Cumhuriyet (Turkish daily), 91, 96–97; "Feryatname," 93*fig.*

Damascus, 1, 6–9, 12, 18, 26–30, 35–38, 40, 44–45, 57–66, 70, 74, 120, 145; bazaar in, 77; Souq al-Hamidiyyeh in, 85, 88, 101; tile-makers of, 69. *See also* Syria
dard, 32–33, 35
darman, 33, 35
de Certeau, Michel, 111
Deeb, Lara, 8, 14
Deguilhem, Randi, 59
Dillon, Sarah, 161n3
Doğan, Celal, 98
donations, 51–60. *See also* patronage
du'a', 144. See also *ad'iyya; du'anevis*
du'anevis, 29, 35. See also *ad'iyya; du'a'*
Dubai, 6, 67

Egypt, 13
electricity, 86
embroidery, 84
ethnography, 2, 13–15, 18, 21, 40; historical, 8; multilingual and multiscalar, 20, 28; road, 16. *See also* anthropology of emergence
Euphrates River, 137–40

factionalism, 15
Faroqhi, Suraiya: *Pilgrims and Sultans: The Hajj under the Ottomans,* 162n6
Fatima, Hazrat-i, 22–24, 144
Fatimiyoun brigade, 15
feminism, 8; progressive "Western" ideals of, 154n11; student group meetings of Islamist, 30. *See also* women
Fernando, Mayanthi: *Republic Unsettled,* 13
feryatname, 91–100, 102, 138
Fischer, Michael, 159n19
France, 65–66, 132, 151
Franco-Turkish frontier, 130–36, 139
Franklin-Bouillon Agreement (1921), 132
Free Syrian Army, 7

Kurds, 1, 124, 126–38; insurgency of the, 123–24, 135; region in Syria controlled by the, 129–36; Turkish anxiety regarding the movement across the border of, 135–36, 163n25

Kurt, Ümit, 160n22

kuzu geçidi, 137

Lacanian psychoanalysis, 24

language: Arabic, 30, 121, 155n1; Azeri, 33; Kurdish, 86; Persian, 26, 33, 42, 78, 80, 84, 86, 90, 111, 155n1; Turkish, 78, 80, 87, 91, 108, 120, 155n1

Lebanon, 5, 7–8, 18, 44, 63, 72, 122; Baqaa Valley of, 63–64; Shi'i Arabs of, 74. *See also* Beirut

Lefebvre, Henri, 110–11, 130, 155n28, 161n2; "Space and the State," 140

Légion Syrienne, 134, 165n42

Levant, 38, 53, 94–96, 105, 110, 130, 132; Iranian pilgrims' mobility across the, 150; post-Ottoman, 136; regional history of Iranian *ziyarat* in the, 139. *See also* Middle East

Lévi-Strauss, Claude, 24

liberalism, 13

lingerie, 27, 77, 83, 85, 100–103, 161n29

livestock, 86, 135–36, 138

Louër, Laurence: *Transnational Shia Politics,* 70

MacIntyre, Alasdair, 38

Mahmood, Saba, 13, 154n11

Mamluk era, 63

maqam, 6, 33, 55, 61

maraji' al-taqlid, 70–71, 158n15

Maraş, 95–96. *See also* Turkey

Mardin, 91–92, 94, 103, 131, 136–37. *See also* Turkey

marriage, 23–24; as socially emergent ritual, 24, 32. *See also* women

Marxian political economy, 24

Mashhad, 7, 32, 69, 72, 117. *See also* Iran

Mashriq, 95; Ottoman, 112, 114. *See also* Middle East

Mawlana (Mevlana Jalaleddin Rumî), 120–21

May Day protests, 3

Mecca, 5, 17, 36–37, 112, 114; Zamzam well in, 155n3. *See also* Islam

medical supplies, 129, 137

Medina, 114. *See also* Islam

merchants, 87–100, 103–5, 145; contraband (*kaçakçı*), 92, 94, 123, 128–30; cross-border, 111, 119–23, 135; jewelry and currency, 120; textile, 91–92. *See also* borders; contraband; Iranian Bazaar; mobility

Middle East, 7–8; histories and geographies of *ziyarat* and *tijarat* across the, 110; Iranian protests of Israeli policies in the, 117; political and socioeconomic precarity in the, 14; territorialization in the post-Ottoman and post-Mandate, 140, 158n9; transnational chaos in the, 7. *See also* Arabia; Levant; Mashriq

Mikdashi, Maya, 8

Milli Mensucat Fabrikasi, 96

mimar, 84, 137–38, 152

Mimar Sinan University, 3, 86, 152

Mitchell, Timothy, 105–6

Moallem, Minoo, 38

mobility: advances in transportation technology and road infrastructure that opened up the possibility of, 63; arrested, 79–106, 128, 134–35, 149, 152; cultivation of techniques of, 18; and diasporic identity, 75; of illegal trade, 98; and immobility, 27–28; pilgrim and merchant, 110–12, 117, 140, 150; poverty of, 16, 17, 28, 35–39, 150; ritual of, 9, 14, 16, 21, 23; shifts in cross-border, 111–40, 150; transnational, 35, 150, 152, 153n7. *See also* borders; contraband; immigrants; merchants; pilgrims; refugees

Mosavi, Mir, 10

Mosul, 104, 132. *See also* Iraq

Moumtaz, Nada, 59

muezzin, 72

Muharram, 9–10, 12, 144, 157n20, 159n19. *See also* Shi'a

muhbir, 124, 127

mujtahids, 115, 158n15

Murtada family: 'Abbas, 61, 64–65, 158n13; Hani, 6–9, 15–16, 32, 43–70, 75, 80, 114, 117, 145; Mahdi, 45, 51, 60, 64–65, 67, 69;

Murtada family *(continued)*
  Muhammad, 64; Muhsin, 65; Musa, 63,
    69, 71; Rida, 64–65, 67, 158n13; Riza, 60;
    Sabil, 64; Salim, 63
Mustafa Emin Effendi, 60
mutawalli, 6, 56, 60–61, 65, 69

Nadi, Yunus, 92, 97, 103
Nahhas, Saib, 44–45, 75
Najaf, 72, 114, 116–17. *See also* Iraq
Nakash, Yitzhak, 113, 162n11
namaz, 13, 37, 44
nationalism, 94, 105, 123; Arab, 132–33;
    Iraqi, 133; Syrian, 132–33; Turkish, 132
NATO Maintenance and Supply Agency
    (NAMSA), 136
neoliberal capitalism, 87, 105
Netherlands, 61
Northern Storm brigade, 7. *See also* Islamic
    Front
Nowruz, 12

oil, 5, 83–84, 86, 95, 123, 137–38; Iraqi, 129;
    Syrian, 124; tapping into the Turkish
    grids of oil distribution to steal, 105
Orientalist scholars, 132
Ottoman era, 60–64, 94–95, 102, 112,
    114–17; Abdülhamit attempted to
    revive the sultan's claim to supreme
    religious leadership enshrined in his
    role as the caliph in the, 115; end of the,
    117. *See also* Turkey
Ottoman-Qajar relations, 113, 115, 157n5

Pahlavi, Reza, 47, 55, 117, 163n24
Pakistan, 55, 72
Palangi, Nasser, 30, 31*fig.,* 144, 156n12
Paliç, Nevzat, 89
palimpsest, 111, 130, 139, 161n3
pan-Arabism, 133
Partiya Karkeren Kurdistan (PKK),
    165n30
patronage: cross-border regimes of, 123;
    notions of patrimony and patriliny in
    regimes of, 51, 56–75, 149; shift of
    organization of political power around
    the shrine toward relations of, 50–51.
    See also donations; genealogy

Persia, 47, 110, 112, 115, 148. *See also* Iran;
    Safavid era
pilgrimage, 6, 9, 24, 130; institutionaliza-
    tion and formalization of visitation in
    Shi'i, 113; in the Islamic world, 112; and
    mobility, markets, and commerce, 15,
    79–106, 119–23, 127–29, 138; as ritual
    traffic, 37, 136; value in the, 18–20. See
    also *'atabat; hajj; hajj-i fuqara';* Islam;
    pilgrims; ritual; Sayyida Zainab shrine;
    tourism; traffic
pilgrims: Iranian, 1–2, 4–7, 12, 26, 36,
    56–57, 70–72, 80–85, 112, 147;
    Lebanese, 7; mobility regimes for,
    139, 150; social praxis of, 23;
    theological and political debates
    about the motives of, 34, 146. *See also*
    mobility; pilgrimage; Sayyida Zainab
    shrine; tourism
pistachio cultivation, 135
Poidebard, Père Antoine, 134
Prophet Muhammad, 10, 12, 22–23, 33, 65,
    70, 153n7. *See also* Islam
Prophet Noah, 63
prostitution, 83, 99, 103

qaçax, 86. *See also* contraband; *kaçak*
qafas, 47, 50*fig.,* 73
Qatar, 7
Qazvin, 29
Qom, 7, 69, 72–73, 107, 117. *See also* Iran
quatrain. See *ruba'iyat*
Qur'an, 34, 121, 146

Rah-i Zainab magazine, 25, 30–31; "Zainab,
    the Hero of Karbala," 31*fig.*
rak'ah namaz, 43
rakı and wine production, 135
Ramadan, 146. *See also* Islam
Rawiya, 51, 60; spatial transformation of,
    57, 66–74. *See also* Sitt Zainab
refugees: Armenian, 133; Christian, 132–33;
    Iraqi, 72; Kurdish, 132–34; Palestinian,
    58, 66, 72; Syrian, 83, 103, 127, 129–30.
    See also mobility
religion: religious ritual in the context of its
    political economy and ecology, 87, 146;
    sexuality and, 32; sites of religious

veneration, 15, 148. *See also* Islam; ritual; Sayyida Zainab shrine; sectarianism; *ziyarat*

resan, 129

rice, 84

Rida, Muhammad Rashid, 113

ritual, 8–10; extrareligious sociality of, 38; feminist anthropological scholarship on Islamic, 28; as generative sphere of political and socioeconomic negotiation, 148; and mobility, 9, 14, 16, 21, 23, 148; of pilgrimage, 12, 18, 21, 26–39; Shi'a, 15, 18, 144, 153n7; sociality of, 28–32. *See also* Islam; pilgrimage; religion

Rohani, Hassan, 10

Roitman, Janet, 17

rowzah, 33, 156n17

ruba'iyat, 120–21, 143, 146

Rubin, Gayle: "The Traffic in Women," 23–24, 39

Ruqayya, Hazrat-i, 35, 37, 122, 145, 155n6

sadaqa, 34

Safavid era, 112, 114. *See also* Persia

Salafi school of jurisprudence, 33, 153n7. *See also* Sunni

Salama, Ghassan, 133

Samarra, 37, 119. *See also* Iraq

sanctions, 108–9, 122, 163n28

Şanlıurfa, 136–37. *See also* Turkey

sarraf, 120–21

Saudi Arabia, 117

Saussure, Ferdinand, 19

Sayyida Zainab shrine, 1–20, 26–39, 44, 46*fig.,* 47, 50*fig.,* 52*fig.,* 53*fig.,* 83, 118, 142, 145; car bomb detonation in the town of the, 15, 114, 152; cemetery of the, 58–59, 151; Damascene heirs (the Murtadas) of the, 60–66; endowment of the, 69, 73–74; expansion plans (circa 1993) of the, 54*fig.;* funding by the Iranian state pledged to the *waqf* associated with the, 50–51, 55; as gate (*bab/dar*), 34; golden dome of the, 53–54; library of the, 54; minarets of the, 55, 56*fig.,* 69; Murtada inheritance case that established the inheritance of the, 158n14; as

Persianate in style, 157n3; religious seminaries around the, 70–74; saint visitation of, 17, 21, 28–33, 36, 75, 120–22, 139, 150; spatial transformation of the, 68–69, 75; as threshold (*astaneh*), 34; tiles of the façade of the, 69; transnational career of the, 57, 74–75. *See also* hotels; pilgrimage; pilgrims; Zainab, Hazrat-I; religion; Shi'a; *waqf dhurri*

Schielke, Samuli, 13

sectarianism, 7–8, 18, 153n1. *See also* religion

secularization, 12–13; of Iran's middle class, 32

şehbender, 116

Selim, Samah, 154n11

Senegal, 54

sex workers. *See* prostitution

seyyar satıcı, 79

shafa'a, 114, 119

Shi'a, 10, 36–37, 54–55, 113–14, 145, 153n7; branches of Prophetic descent to draw *sayyid* genealogies for the, 63; doctrinal debate between rationalists (*al-usuliyun*) and traditionalists (*al-akhbariyun*) in the eighteenth and nineteenth centuries of the, 158n15; Iranian, 58; Iraqi, 65; Lebanese, 58; mass conversions of Sunni Arab tribes in Iraq to, 115–16, 148; as state religion of Persia, 112; Syrian, 65, 71; tombs in Medina and Mecca of the, 114; Twelver, 8, 58, 155n2; Wahhabi challenge to the visitation practices of the, 114. *See also* 'Ashura; Islam; Muharram; Sayyida Zainab shrine

shifa, 32

Shirazi, Hassan, 70

Shirazi, Muhammad, 70

Simpsons, The, 3

Sitt Zainab, 57; seminaries in, 70–73; spatial transformation of, 66–74. *See also* Rawiya

siyasat, 9, 12

smuggling. *See* contraband; *ghachagh; kaçak; qaçax*

sohan, 107

Southeast Asia, 75

Southwest Asia, 8, 153n7
sovereignty: exercise of imperial, 148; and market integrity, 94; political, 20; states of, 130–36, 161n5; as "surplus" of state formation, 136; transformations of borders and, 149
Söylemezoğlu, Kemal, 97
Sri Lanka, 80, 83, 88
state space (*l'espace étatique*), 140, 148; territory as, 155n28
Sublime Porte (*Bab-i Ali*) archives, 115
sugar, 79, 82–84, 95, 99, 102, 104, 123–24, 126–28
Sunni, 10, 29, 36, 112–14, 153n7; Hanafi, 8, 72, 155n2; Salafi, 155n2; Wahhabi, 114, 155n2. *See also* Hanbali school of jurisprudence; Islam; Salafi school of jurisprudence
Sunni extremists, 6, 67, 69. *See also* Islamic Front
Sunni-Shi'i divide, 8, 153n7, 162n13. *See also* Islam
supplications. See *ad'iyya*
Switzerland, 54, 65
Sykes-Picot Agreement, 131, 131*map,* 134, 165n34
Syria, 1, 5–20, 30, 37, 51, 57, 70–72, 79, 83–91, 95, 102–4, 111, 114, 117–24, 128–40, 149; al-Asad regime of, 66–67, 73; Assad regime of, 7; authority over the Sayyida Zainab shrine of, 65; Ba'th Party of, 67; bureaucratic traffic with the state of, 66; conflict in, 7, 16, 26, 45, 67, 74, 82, 84, 110, 124, 127–29, 139, 157n1; Druze revolt in southern, 134; French Mandate in, 132–35; fuel and electricity shortages in, 129; Iranian travel to, 44–45, 99, 103, 122, 128–29, 145; Jazira region in, 134; massive restructuring of state institutions following independence in, 59; medical shortages in, 129; Ministry of Religious Endowments of, 71; revolution in, 67; shrines targeted by the Islamic State in, 145; state soldiers of, 15. *See also* Aleppo; Damascus; Hizballah; Jarablus; Rawiya; Turkey-Syria border
Syria-Turkey border. *See* Turkey-Syria border

Szanto, Edith: "Following Sayyida Zaynab: Twelver Shi'ism in Contemporary Syria," 71

taarof, 43–44
Tabriz, 1, 12, 16, 22, 27, 29, 32–33, 80, 121–22, 151. *See also* Iran
tacirler, 5
tafsir, 13
Tambar, Kabir, 34
tax evasion, 45
ta'ziyeh, 33–34, 144, 147, 156n17
tea, 5, 79–89, 95, 99–102, 123–24, 128, 149, 152; Ceylon, 83; Rize, 83, 89, 141, 159n3
Tehran, 9–12, 16–18, 22, 27–30, 34–36, 40–41, 77, 103, 142–46, 151; Gulistan Mall in, 85; Tajrish bazaar in, 107. *See also* Iran
territorial fragmentation, 18
textiles, 84, 96–97
ticaret, 9, 12, 80; *vergisiz,* 82
tijarat, 80, 87, 105, 108, 110, 117, 123, 147
tobacco, 5, 79, 82–90, 95, 99, 102, 122, 163n27; rolling papers (Arabian papers) for, 135; Turkish, 80. *See also* cigarettes
tourism, 66, 101; burial, 58; mobility regimes for, 139; religious, 73–74, 87; to the Turkish coast, 79. *See also* pilgrimage; pilgrims
traffic, 1–2, 6, 9, 15–17, 28, 35; in arms and medical supplies from Turkey to Syria, 129–30; as bilateral exchange, 23; control across transimperial borders of, 114; of gold smuggling, 119–22; high tariffs introduced to protect domestic textile and consumer goods in Turkish industrial zones fuel the, 97; as illegal trafficking in people, drugs, and arms, 123–24; ritual, 21, 38; urban, 156n8; in value, 19–20, 28, 149; vehicles of, 28–32. *See also* borders; contraband; pilgrimage
Treaty of Lausanne (1923), 132
tüccar, 79, 101
Turkey, 1–9, 12, 18–20, 37, 41, 83–106, 111, 118–24, 130–32, 149; Alevi ritual practices in, 34; antismuggling special forces of, 119; Black Sea region of, 88; cartography of the economy of, 105–6; contra-

dictory regional economic policies and tax regimes in, 82, 90–91, 94–95; Courts of Independence (*İstiklal Mahkemeleri*) of, 94, 104; domestic consumption of tobacco in, 90, 159n11; Erdoğan administration in, 89, 129; French involvement in, 131–36; Grand Assembly of, 95; Kurdistan in, 82, 94, 96, 119; Ministry of Culture and Tourism of, 120. *See also* Anatolia; Ankara; Antalya; Antep; Cilicia; Gaziantep; Hatay; Istanbul; Karkamış; Kars; Kilis; Konya; Maraş; Mardin; Ottoman era; Şanlıurfa; Turkey-Syria border; Urfa

Turkey-Syria border, 7, 12, 84, 92–94, 108–11, 123–24, 125*map*, 126–40; creation of the, 129, 136, 139; mining of the, 136; social history of the, 136; sugar, tea, fuel oil, and cigarette trade across the, 123–24, 126; the Syrian conflict and the pathways of mobility across the, 129. *See also* borders; Syria; Turkey

Turkish nationalist historiography, 95

Turkish War of Independence, 95

ʿulama, 116, 158n15, 159n19
umid, 42
United Nations High Commissioner for Refugees, 151
United Nations Industrial Development Organization (UNIDO), 96
United States, 10, 163n28
University of Damascus, 66–67
Urfa, 80, 94–96, 103, 131. *See also* Turkey
Urumiyeh, 80, 85–86

violence: sectarian, 18, 129, 136; terrorist, 8, 15, 69
visitation. *See* pilgrimage
Visitors of Imam Reza, 7

Wahhabism, 113–14, 147–48, 153n7. *See also* Islam
wali, 60
waqf, 6, 32, 45, 50, 56–59, 65–69, 72–75
waqf dhurri, 51–60, 63, 68, 75, 149, 158n13. *See also* Sayyida Zainab shrine
waqfiyyah, 16; documents of, 61, 63, 158n12

Weber, Max, 3, 9
West Africa, 51
Weston, Kath, 16
Wizarat al-Awqaf, 59–60
women, 10, 12, 18, 156n10; exchange of, 24; Iranian pilgrims as, 38; and Islam, 22, 24; participation in the revolution by young, 30; as peddlers, 94, 98, 138, 149, 160n17; piety movements of, 154n11; political mobilization of, 38–39; in the Prophetic lineage, 24; *Rah-i Zainab* as the venue for an Islamic and anti-imperialist stance for the empowerment of, 30; as saint visitors, 24, 30–32; *ziyarat* and sexuality of, 32. *See also* feminism; marriage
World Health Organization, 89, 159n11
World War I, 95, 130

Yazid I, 10
Yemen, 75
yoldaş, 4
yükçü juveniles, 127, 129, 138
Yüksekova Haber, 119–21

zabıta, 98
Zainab, Hazrat-i, 10, 22–24, 44, 47, 65, 122, 144–45, 152, 153n7; genealogy of, 68; hardships endured by, 34; intercession of, 108, 122, 143, 151; miraculous encounters with, 60; saint visitation to, 23–24, 29–41, 76, 108, 121; as source of inspiration for all Muslims, 29. *See also* Sayyida Zainab shrine
Zainabiyoun brigade, 15
Zainab's Way magazine, 156n12
zakat, 55, 157n4, 158n17
zarih, 34
Zarrab, Reza, 122, 164n29
ziyarat, 2, 5–22, 26–44, 64, 68, 73–79, 84–87, 105, 108–40, 145–52, 153n7; examination by classical jurists of, 162n11; hagiographical map of saint visitation sites (1985–95), 118*map;* Iranian genealogies of, 162n13; as jurisprudentially endorsed in Twelver Shi'ism, 155n2; manuals of, 113. *See also* religion
zuwwar, 7, 36, 116; Iranian, 115, 119

Founded in 1893,
UNIVERSITY OF CALIFORNIA PRESS
publishes bold, progressive books and journals
on topics in the arts, humanities, social sciences,
and natural sciences—with a focus on social
justice issues—that inspire thought and action
among readers worldwide.

The UC PRESS FOUNDATION
raises funds to uphold the press's vital role
as an independent, nonprofit publisher, and
receives philanthropic support from a wide
range of individuals and institutions—and from
committed readers like you. To learn more, visit
ucpress.edu/supportus.

www.ingramcontent.com/pod-product-compliance
Lightning Source LLC
Chambersburg PA
CBHW030830270326
41928CB00007B/974